CULTURE IN CRISIS

CULTURE IN CRISIS

The Future of the Welsh Language

CLIVE BETTS

THE FFYNNON PRESS

ISBN 0 902158 15 5 (Hardback)
ISBN 0 902158 16 3 (Paperback)

Set in 10 on 12 point Baskerville and printed in 1976
by Gee & Son, Denbigh, for the publishers,
THE FFYNNON PRESS
PO Box 2, Upton, Wirral, Merseyside, L49 1SY.

I Eleri, Aled

a Catrin

Wedyn wedi codi ohonom gaer yn y Gorllewin fe awn allan i adfer yr iaith i'r tir y dietifeddwyd ni ohono.

(EMYR LLYWELYN, *Areithiau,* Cymdeithas yr Iaith ac Y Lolfa, 1970, t. 25.)

(After we have built a fortress in the West, we will go out to restore the language to the land from which it has been disinherited.)

CONTENTS

ILLUSTRATIONS

1. Reaction to the Blue Books.

2. Sir George Osborne Morgan, M.P.

3. Robert Ambrose Jones (Emrys ap Iwan).

4. Trefechan Bridge sit-down.

5. Pasting posters on Aberystwyth post office.

6. Start of the road signs campaign.

7. Protest outside Swansea Prison.

8. Occupation of cottage used as a holiday home.

9. Invasion of BBC newsroom, Cardiff.

10. Protestor's departure from a demonstration.

11. Police photographer at a demonstration.

12. Carmarthen ministers erect bilingual signs.

13. March by members of Cyfeillion yr Iaith.

14. The family of Trefor Beasley.

15. Dafydd Iwan at the launching of *Sain*.

16. Demonstration against factory owner Mr. Brewer Spinks.

17. The first Welsh-medium Primary School.

18. Llysfaen Welsh Nursery School.

19. Urdd Gobaith Cymru's first camp.

20. The headquarters of Radio na Gaeltachta in Connemara.

PREFACE

This book is the direct fruit of a suggestion of mine to the Editor of the *Western Mail* that the paper undertakes a major investigation into the present state of the Welsh language, looking at its prospects for survival, and perhaps hinting at the policies most likely to ensure a future for one of the oldest languages of Europe. The resultant 10 articles eventually appeared in the *Mail,* under the general bilingual title *The Welsh Language — Is There a Future?* and *Y Gymraeg — A Oes Dyfodol?* from 14 to 18 April 1975.

I was given a completely free hand to research as I wished, and the conclusions were all my own. It soon became evident that only the tip of the iceberg of research would grace the columns of Wales's national daily, hence the idea of a book, executed, again, with the help of the *Western Mail,* who allowed me a month's sabbatical leave to do much of the necessary work.

As well as grateful thanks to Mr. Duncan Gardiner, Editor, and Mr. Denis Gane, News Editor, for allowing me that most precious of commodities, time, as well as free use of copyright photographs (as did *Y Cymro*), I also owe an immense debt to people throughout Wales who gave me of their time, knowledge and opinions. The names of some appeared in the *Mail* series; the names of others even a High Court judge would not drag from my lips.

For almost all are men and women of stature in society; many of them are public officials who freely imparted of information and opinions as to causes behind decisions bearing on the language that their employers would never allow them to make publicly.

So, better no names than a very incomplete list. To those who helped, thank you.

Some problems have arisen regarding place-names. Firstly, over spelling. Here I have generally used the form in correct Anglo-Welsh usage : nothing annoys me more than to see in English text words or even phrases taken direct from Welsh or Irish. People may speak in such a fashion in Irish and Welsh (and in many other

9

languages around the globe), but that is no reason to corrupt a second language.

So, the capital of Wales is Cardiff, and the capital of Gwynedd, Caernarfon. I'm not so sure, though, about Wrexham (Wrecsam?).

As a good deal of the material incorporated in this volume has its origin in the 1971 census statistics, the old county names therefore make a showing.

I make no particular claim for originality in my proposals. The ideas I put forward must, however, not be seen as the creatures of any particular political party or linguistic group.

CLIVE BETTS.

Caerffili.
Chwefror/February 1976.

1

The Theory of Bilingualism

THE COMMUNITY HOLDS THE KEY

But there I go, lapsing into figures again — an English habit, no doubt, cold and unstimulating.[1]

Is Welsh in the midst of the great transition which will see its death as soon as July follows June? The transition, of course, is from a Welsh-only Wales to a land covered by the invaders' tongue. There is no doubt that in the Anglo-Saxon world the idea of monolingualism is very strongly entrenched. As one of the world's foremost experts in sociolinguistics — the study of language as a social phenomenon — Dr. Joshua Fishman, professor of linguistics and sociology at Yeshiva University, New York, was driven to comment recently :

> American students are so accustomed to bilingualism as a " vanishing phenomenon ", as a temporary dislocation from a presumably more normal state of affairs characterised by " one man, one language . . . "[2]

But it's not only students who take this line. Listen to England's foremost expert on Indo-European languages, Prof. W. B. Lockwood, of Reading University, an old friend of Welsh :

---

[1] Dyfnallt Morgan, " Welsh — A Language in Retreat? ", *The Welsh Anvil*, July 1952, p. 64.
[2] J. Fishman, " Domains Between Micro- and Macro-Sociolinguistics ", in J. Gumpertz and D. Hymes (eds.), *Directions in Sociolinguistics* (New York, 1972), p. 437.

" I'm sorry, but I can see no long-term future for Welsh. In modern conditions, if a language is to survive it must be exclusive and without competitors in part of its area. Everywhere small languages are being swamped because they cannot compete. The advantages of their major competitors are so much greater. No small language has the secret of survival. Certainly not Irish, which is now confined to too small an area in which English is valid as well."[3]

But in the eastern world, according to Fishman, it seems things may be a little different:

Why is it that in some societies, such as south and south-east Asia, major distinctions of language maintain themselves in spite of several centuries of intensive contact, while elsewhere, as in Europe, North and South America, groups tend to give up their native tongues after only a couple of generations?[4]

Unfortunately, there is as yet no cut-and-dried answer: the science of sociolinguistics is too young, facts about the languages of today are still too scarce, never mind facts about the linguistic world of the past. In any case, we want to know if Welsh can survive for centuries, not just for a generation or two — and it's only the latter sort of problem to which we are near finding an acceptable answer.

Plenty of work has been done on the death of languages in a position somewhat similar to that of Welsh. The vanishing of the immigrant languages in the United States has been studied at length.

Usually with the third generation the old European tongue was dead, although some groups managed the switch in two: newly-arrived parents on occasion were so keen that the old tongue would not hold back their offspring from success in the world's greatest melting pot that they made the youngsters use only English, a language the parents could scarce understand.

The similarity with Welsh was the ability of all the second generation to understand English; the dissimilarity was that some forms of ties existed with a monolingual Old Country. What has

[3] Clive Betts, " The Welsh Language, Is There a Future? " *Western Mail*, 14.4.75.
[4] *Directions in Sociolinguistics*, p. 13.

kept the language going longest has not been the number of immigrants or the recentness of their arrival, but the existence in some districts of a solid neighbourhood core of users of the language, in other words, a community where the language could be used in the widest variety of situations.[5]

And in these small districts it has not been some great theory about survival of small nations which has done the trick :

> In these areas, people speak Norwegian simply because everybody else does without reflecting much about it. For them it is not a cultural duty or a programme of behaviour. If you ask them why they do so, it is difficult for them to answer.[6]

Although there is now a greater pride in maintaining the old ways and Welsh English does not have the tremendous prestige accorded American English in the first half of this century, there are lessons to be learned :

> Immigrants whose English was better progressed more rapidly on the American scene and became models *within* the immigrant home and *within* the immigrant organisation and neighbourhood. Thus the home and immigrant life itself became domains of English . . . Since English was the only language of value outside the home and immigrant organisation, only the latter might have been capable of preserving the non-English mother tongue if they had been able to maintain themselves as separate, self-contained domains . . .
>
> Almost everywhere . . . there was no domain where the non-English ethnic language alone was required for " membership ", and as a result there was no domain in which it was retained.[7]

The secret of a language's ability to survive is the number of areas of life where it is, to bilingual speakers, the only accepted medium of communication. Or, in current jargon, a language in a *diglossia* situation depends on the *domains* it controls.

---

[5] J. Hofman, "The Language Transition in Some Lutheran Denominations ", in J. Fishman (ed.), *Readings in the Sociology of Language* (The Hague, 1968), p. 629.
[6] E. Haugen, "The Struggle over Norwegian ", *Norwegian-American Studies* XVII, 1952, quoted in Hofman.
[7] J. Fishman, "The Sociology of Language ", in P. Giglioli (ed.), *Language and Social Context* (Harmondsworth, 1972), p. 52.

The concept of *diglossia* was first put forward by C. A. Ferguson with reference to two varieties of the same language being used by the same community.[8] One of his main examples was Arabic where the classical and regional varieties are so far apart as to almost justify description as separate languages. To the high (classical) form would be reserved a sermon in church or mosque, a personal letter, speech in parliament, political speech, university lecture, news broadcast, newspapers, poetry. To the low (regional) form would be reserved instructions to workmen, etc., conversation with family, friends, colleagues, a radio soap opera, caption on a political cartoon, and folk literature.

Ferguson says this *diglossia* exists as far back as Arabic is known. While he was talking at that time only in terms of varieties of the same language, his system of domains has since been shown to apply in many bilingual situations. Most work has been done on that of Paraguay, but the early assumption that the country was almost entirely bilingual in Spanish (the official language) and Guarani (an Indian language) has been shown to be untrue : whereas 94 per cent. speak Guarani, only 58.5 per cent. speak Spanish, which is almost unknown in the rural areas. And speakers of only Spanish " just don't count on the social scale ".[9]

Despite evidence of increasing use of Spanish, it is said the basic situation has not changed for several centuries. The school, which worked entirely through Spanish, was the most powerful instrument of Hispanicisation; only in 1975 was it decided to teach in the rural areas through the medium of Guarani rather than Spanish.[10] Spanish still is the language of business, the law and government, and thus a split in language use similar to that found in Welsh has developed : Guarani bosses the domains of intimacy, and Spanish those of officialdom. The following table gives the replies from 40 people in a rural area as to which language they use; a double asterisk indicates an overall majority, and thus the dominance of each tongue can clearly be seen.

---

[8] C. A. Ferguson, " Diglossia ", *Language and Social Context*, pp. 232-51.
[9] J. P. Rona, " The Social and Cultural Status of the Guarani in Paraguay ", in W. Bright (ed.), *Sociology, Proceedings of the UCLA Linguistics Conference* (The Hague, 1966).
[10] *New Society*, 10.4.75.

THE USE OF GUARANI IN PARAGUAY

	Guarani	Spanish	Both
With your spouse daily	28**	0	1
With your parents	34**	6	0
With your children	19**	11	4
With your friends drinking tea	28**	0	7
With your boss	9	4	7
With your doctor	7	25**	7
With your *curandero* (quack)	32**	2	2
With your grandparents	32**	0	1
With the police chief or mayor	13	19	8
To confess	15	15	4
With the schoolteacher	0	37**	3
With the authorities in the capital	4	33**	2
In the " country "	40**	0	0
With your neighbours	38**	0	2
With the bus conductor	13	22**	5

From J. Rubin, " Bilingual Usage in Paraguay ", in J. Fishman, *Readings in the Sociology of Language* (The Hague, 1968), p. 518.

With a societal pattern of this type, widespread bilingualism may remain stable for long periods.

> This is because as long as members of the community cannot feel that one code is appropriate to some situations it cannot, as long as the existing social and value systems persist, replace the code conventionally used in those situations.[11]

Similar long-term diglossia situations exist in New York with Puerto-Ricans, in Belgium between Dutch and French, and in many parts of India.[12] In Sauris, in north-east Italy, many of the inhabitants are, and have been for generations, trilingual in Italian, the national language, Friulian (a dialect of Rhaetian, which includes Romansch of Switzerland), which is the regional language, and German, their ancestral language.[13] Italian occupies the high end of the scale, German the lowest, and Friulian the middle.

[11] M. Ó Murchú, *Language and Community* (Dublin, 1970), p. 19.
[12] ibid, p. 38.
[13] N. Denison, " Some Observations on Language Variety and Plurilingualism " in J. Pride and J. Holmes (eds.), *Sociolinguistics* (Harmondsworth, 1972), pp. 65-77.

But bilingualism can exist without diglossia, although it won't be long before one of the languages gives up the ghost. This situation is common in areas of rapid social change, with the abandonment of old norms before the consolidations of new ones :

> Children typically become bilingual at a very early age, when they are still largely confined to home and neighbourhood, since their elders (both adult and school age) carry into the domains of intimacy a language learned outside its confines. Formal institutions tend to render individuals increasingly monolingual in a language other than that of hearth and home. Ultimately, the language of school and government replaces the language of home and neighbourhood precisely because it provides status in the latter domains as well.[14]

The abandonment of old cultural patterns has also sometimes meant the abandonment of bilingualism with diglossia. In situations of rapid industrialisation and urbanisation

> no well-established, socially recognised and protected functional differentiation of languages obtains in many of the speech communities of the lower and lower middle classes . . . [The two languages may be used for communication in a seemingly random fashion.] Since the formerly separate roles of the home domain, the school domain and the work domain are all disturbed by the massive dislocation of values and norms that result from simultaneous immigration and industrialisation, the language of work (and of the school) comes to be used in the home . . . Instead of two carefully separated languages each under the eye of caretaker groups of teachers, preachers and writers, several intervening varieties may obtain differing in degree of interpretation . . . Thus bilingualism without diglossia tends to be transitional . . . Without separate and complementary norms and values to establish and maintain functional separation of the speech varieties, that language or variety which is fortunate enough to be associated with the predominate drift of social forces tends to displace the other.[15]

But where stands Wales? In the heartland areas there probably still exists bilingualism with diglossia, with Welsh for more intimate relationships and English for the more official. In the rest of the country, there are very disturbing signs that diglossia has just about

[14] J. Fishman, *Sociolinguistics* (Rowley, Mass., 1970), p. 83.
[15] ibid, p. 27.

16

vanished. While Welsh speakers may not have switched to English, there will be disturbing incidence of the use of both languages in situations where Welsh should predominate.

Thus, under the misguided impression that it helps to make them truly bilingual, parents will use both languages with children when young. The result after only a few years is that, in an overwhelmingly English environment, the children will turn to using English between themselves, reserving Welsh for times when they are socially obliged to use that language. The chapel is solidly Welsh only as far as the formal service is concerned, and even here, to accommodate monoglot English speakers who sometimes go to Welsh chapels out of ancestral solidarity, translations are sometimes given of the sermon and announcements. Outside the formal bounds of the service, it is almost like the Tower of Babel, with a horrid mix of Welsh, English and Wenglish.

The breakdown of diglossia is most obviously in the domain of " friends drinking tea ", one of the strongly Guarani areas of rural Paraguay. As I point out elsewhere in this book, other factors confirm that the Welsh language has no real future in these anglicised parts of Wales.

But what are the factors which go towards language choice and which, ultimately, decide whether diglossia can exist?

Three main factors have been isolated by one expert: topic being discussed (certain socioculturally recognised spheres of activity are, at least temporarily, under the sway of one language), role relations (particular behaviours are expected of particular individuals vis-a-vis each other), and locales (where the conversation is taking place).[16]

Another expert looks at things only slightly differently and comes up with personal needs (i.e., ability), the background, and the immediate situation.[17]

The *background* factor may be highly potent when the speech setting is public rather than private. For instance, in Israel Jews will speak their first language at home, but Hebrew when on a bus,

[16] J. Fishman, " Domains between Micro- and Macro-Sociolinguistics ', pp. 439-44.
[17] S. R. Herman, " Explorations in the Social Psychology of Language Choice ", *Readings in the Sociology of Language,* p. 493.

while Germans used, in the years immediately after World War II, to feel ashamed to be spoken to on the street in German.

Background is also important when the language spoken may give a clue to group identification and social status. This occurs particularly where the relative prestige of the languages varies widely, where there is public derogation of a certain language, and where language tolerance is low (in Israel, for instance, it is high, with fluent Hebrew speakers going out of their way to help learners).

Background is again important when the speaker wants to identify or dissociate himself from a particular group. This happens when a person is only marginal to a particular society, as an Arab immigrant to Israel who will eschew Arabic more often than an old Israeli.

It also happens when there is a strong loyalty to a particular language :

> Language loyalty will cause a person to use that particular language in a wide variety of situations and he will be impervious to the requirements of the particular situation or to his personal needs. Thus, when Hebrew was battling to establish itself as the language of the Jews of Palestine before the establishment of the state of Israel, protagonists of the slogan " Hebrew, speak Hebrew " insisted on extending the use of the language to all situations.[18]

Personal needs may have high potency in a private rather than a public setting, and in situations of tensions, fatigue, etc.

The *immediate situation* may be highly potent when group identification is unimportant, in a work situation, and where well-established patterns of behaviour characterise a relationship :

> Where an element in the on-going situation changes, it may affect the balance of languages and be reflected in a change in the language used . . . It was observed that South African settlers at Tsora (an Israeli village) would converse in English among themselves, but as soon as a local-born Israeli joined the group they switched to Hebrew.[19]

Thus the choice of language, of Welsh or English, is seen clearly as a matter which can be decided, or at least very strongly influenced, by the speakers of that language as a group. But in the Welsh

---

[18] ibid, p. 500.
[19] ibid, p. 504.

"A dechreuasant lefaru â thafodau dieithr . . ." (Actau 2:4).   (" And they began to speak with other tongues . . . " (Acts 2:4).)

The breakdown of diglossia — outside Welsh-language chapels in Cardiff, the language of worship so often gives way so quickly to the language of the wider community. (Cartoon from *Y Dinesydd*.)

situation, with English so powerful, only a very powerful will can make sufficient difference. In other words, a touch of the old fanaticism, a desire to make only Welsh acceptable in certain situations and domains. Let us be blunt, it means also the exclusion of those unable to speak Welsh. I can hear the cries of horror already, but in a country where scarce a single area is 100 per cent. Welsh speaking, how else can domains be built up giving priority to Welsh? It is, of course, the immigrants rather than the visitors who will suffer, but I don't think it is impossible to learn the language.

It is, however, not much use building up only one or two minor domains in which Welsh is king, for the "contact balance" is important in determining assimilation or not to the other language. By this is meant

> the balance of the frequency and range of communications of the average individual across linguistic or cultural barriers, as against the frequency and range of the same person's communications within the confines of his own group . . . To the extent that contacts [between the newcomer and some members of the assimilated group where he is expected or required to use the predominant language] multiply, the newcomer will experience the need to assimilate. To the extent that his time and energy are taken up by communications in his old language, and with members of his own cultural group, assimilation may be retarded.[20]

This quote applies, of course, to immigrants, but its relationship to Welsh speakers and the "immigrant" English language is obvious. For there is always a nagging fear that in a society in which everyone speaks language A, and a few speak in addition language B (which is spoken nowhere else), the mere fact that individuals will become more proficient in language A will lead it to prevail. William Mackey commented in 1962 :

> An individual's use of two languages supposes the existence of two different language communities; it does not suppose the existence of a bilingual community . . . A self-sufficient bilingual community has no reason to remain bilingual, since

[20] K. W. Deutsch, *Nationalism and Social Communication* (Cambridge, Mass., 1953), p. 121.

a closed community in which everyone is fluent in two languages could get along just as well with one language.[21]

He goes on to pinpoint the supreme importance of the neighbourhood :

A child is surrounded by the language of the neighbourhood into which he is born, and this often takes the place of the home as the most important influence on his speech,[22]

a sentence sufficient to reduce hopes of maintaining Welsh in the English areas.

Recent Irish research emphasises the crucial importance of the community in maintaining the language. Pioneering in many ways, this work came to the conclusion that the only areas where the Irish language was not in retreat were communities where 80 per cent. of the population had the ability to speak Irish in at least most conversations and, at the same time, where 75 per cent. of the local people said they could speak the language all the time in the community if they wanted to. Only eight of 23 Gaeltacht district electoral divisions which were sampled reached this level.

These communities, says the report, approach being unilingual. " Because of changing circumstances, the number of these areas will not grow ".[23]

The biggest changing circumstance is the introduction of " neo events ", non-traditional contexts and persons for which no established associations exist within the local community and, by extension, in the local language. Being non-local in origin, in fact, they are most likely to be positively associated with the non-local language, English.

Only in the Gaeltacht heartland are these roles supplied through Irish. As in Wales, it is the government, local and central, introducing most, and in English.

The report states that " slippage " in use of Irish is more profound when it occurs in existing Irish domains. Most crucial for maintaining the language is its use by children between themselves. Only

[21] W. Mackey, " The Description of Bilingualism ", *Readings in the Sociology of Language*, p. 554.
[22] ibid, p. 557.
[23] Committee on Irish Language Attitudes Research, *Report* (Dublin, 1975), p. 244.

in the plus-80 per cent. communities do 75 per cent. of respondents to a survey agree that this usually happens.[24]

In the Breac-Ghaeltacht (the weaker Irish areas in the Gaeltachtai), the level of competence in the language is high (perhaps because of schooling), but few people with less than the highest level of competence will use the language at all.[25]

In the anglicised areas, the position is far worse from every point of view. Firstly, that dubious census figure of 25 per cent. speaking the language plummets to only 2.5 per cent. with native speaker ability, and a further 9.5 per cent. able to use the language for most conversations.

But even these figures are a considerable overestimation of use. Of those with native-speaker ability, only 59.7 per cent. use the language regularly, while 16.1 per cent. never use it, or have used it only once since leaving school.[26] Of those with " most of conversation " ability, only 24.6 per cent. often use Irish, and 34.9 per cent. never.

More important are the figures for use at home, where the next generation is being brought up. Only 11.3 per cent. of those with native-speaker ability always used the language at home, and 29 per cent. often. The almost complete abdication from Irish use is revealed even more so among people with most conversations ability : only 1.7 per cent. always use the old tongue at home, and 9.5 per cent. often.

It is a shock to discover that in the special Irish-using sections recently set up in the Civil Service, most of the staff rarely, if ever, spoke Irish with their colleagues, or anyone else.

The overall picture is of an overwhelming predominance of English outside the heartland districts of the Gaeltacht. Very often there are just not enough Irish speakers around to be spoken to. The learning process at school — which has given most of them their Irish — has been insufficient to turn them into Irish users in those districts where there is no existing Irish-speaking community to support them.

[24] ibid., p. 271.
[25] ibid., p. 265.
[26] ibid., p. 183.

22

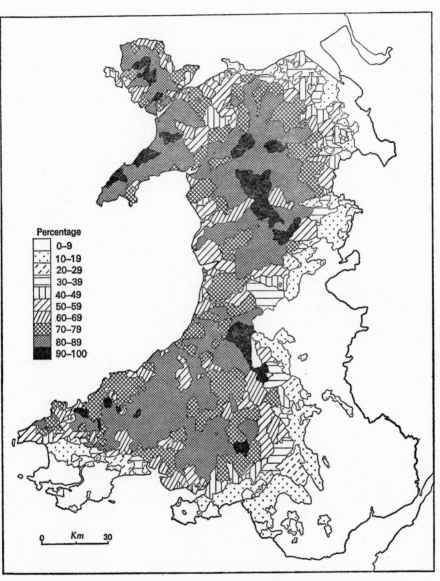

Percentage of the population over the age of three able to speak Welsh by urban areas and parishes. (From *Geographical Journal*, October 1974, p. 433)

To make the situation worse, there has been a clear decline in usage over generations. Of those who heard Irish from someone at home during childhood, only 25 per cent. now hear as much at home. The same figure for the Gaeltacht is 80 per cent.[27]

The future of Irish, and Welsh, thus rests on maintaining an area in which that language has considerable numerical predominance, and allying this to the construction or encouragement of the maximum number of domains belonging to that language.

This brings us to the position of government, both central and local, which, despite party political calls for retrenchment, is bound to expand and fill ever-larger portions of our lives. Even where government does not enforce certain actions, its influence can lead to them happening.

> In the end, we are not able to ignore the central place of the government as an influence for better or worse. The political factor is the most important factor in the development or recession of every language. The reason the English language exists in Wales is because English government covers Wales. It is not through an accident that English grew here. The patronage of government is essential to Welsh.[28]

And :

> One can hardly overestimate the importance of some official status in maintaining a language. It gives it social status among its native users, and serves in part as a barrier against self-depreciation and embarrassment. A little of state support in the form of official printing presses, court proceedings and school use can, at times, do more to establish a language than a vast amount of activity by language activists.[29]

At the same time, Wales being a democracy, government will not act unless the climate is right. It is public demand which will produce government action, not vice-versa. That is what happened in Ireland, where even the British administration had been forced

---

[27] ibid., p. 200. N.B. This does not necessarily refer to passing the language from one generation to another.
[28] C. Rees, *Iaith ein Dyfodol* (Caerdydd, n.d.), t. 22.
[29] N. Glazier, " The Process and Problems of Language Maintenance ", in J. A. Fisher (ed.), *Language Loyalty in the U.S.* (The Hague, 1966), quoted in *Iaith Ein Dyfodol*.

to make concessions in the golden days of the Gaelic League.[30] But with the arrival of independence in 1922, the league, the main driving force behind the revival, felt that this was now the job of the new government, and they bowed out.

However, while the army, full of, needless to say, free state enthusiasts, turned quite a bit to Irish, the civil servants, who had to administer the new pro-language policies, were the same men who had worked for the British. But once a civil servant is stuck in a mould, it is difficult to prise him out of it, especially as the Gaelic League had decided it was scarcely their job any more.

Thus the role of government must never be over-emphasised, and its activities must never be substituted for the popular will.

Yet, for a language to be declared official can have far-reaching effects, provided the extent of its influence and activity is not pushed beyond the bounds of practicability at a particular point of time, for that way lies Irish-style disappointment and evasions.

In Quebec, the concept has been elaborated in some detail :

> The official language or languages must apply wherever the public authority reaches. Here we would look not merely to proceedings in legislatures and courts, but also to all other activities dependent, for their legal existence, upon state authority; or else financed by the state authority . . . Municipal authorities, since deriving their legal status from state power . . . would necessarily be bound by any Official Language stipulations . . . Labour arbitrations, if dependent on state power for their ultimate legal enforcement, would necessarily be covered by the Official Language requirements unless given a special dispensation. So, too, would schools and universities . . . if they accepted financial subventions . . . This consequence of obligatory adherence, by state-sponsored or state-supported, institutions to any comprehensive or unqualified legal requirements as to Official Language or Languages, would seem to flow from those institutions being " affected with the public interest ".[31]

[30] J. Macnamara, " Successes and Failures of the Movement for the Restoration of Irish ", in J. Rubin and B. Jernudd (eds.), *Can Language be Planned?* (Hawaii, 1971), p. 70.
[31] Government of Quebec, *Report of the Commission of Inquiry into the Position of the French Language in Quebec,* Book 2 (Montreal, 1972), p. 24.

Very important is the influence exercised by an official language which really acts as such :

> Quebecers of other language groups can quite legitimately cast doubt on the pre-eminence of French over all other languages as long as the government has not declared its official support for any one in particular; it is also for Canadians and immigrants, who will never learn to make the required language distinctions between Quebec and the rest of Canada until Quebec is officially designated as a " French " province; finally, it is for those on the outside, especially investors, who will continue to ignore the French fact in Quebec as long as their legal advisors are unable to point out that Quebec has legal provisions which makes French the province's only official language, with all that this implies for official exchanges and for the legal and financial administration of business.[32]

Yet this self-same report also emphasises the limits of a government's powers :

> Though the area of application of any " official " or " national " language policy, of whatever nature, is far more limited than the legal layman or man-in-the-street may suspect, having regard to the still quite limited effective reach of the state into the erstwhile " private " domain, nevertheless it may reasonably be argued here that a recording of the " French " fact as a public law, " official " or " national " language norm, would be of more than purely symbolic signifiance. For such a community initiative on behalf of the " French " fact could serve to provide a lead and example for substantial " French "-oriented private initiatives on the part of commerce and industry.[33]

Looking at the context of Wales, a native divided in two by a language " fact ", the Quebec differentiation between an official and a national language is of considerable significance. The latter is in a lesser legal category : it serves to indicate the presence of a secondary, minority language which has historic rights in an area. The concept could be used to apply to Welsh in the anglicised areas : in Quebec it is used to describe the position of English throughout the province.

[32] ibid., Book 1, p. 148.
[33] ibid., Book 2, p. 75.

To designate a language or languages, in either constitutional or statutory form, as national languages is simply to confer on them certain legal privileges as to user. They receive the *imprimatur* of the state in a purely facultative way, without necessarily having the general resources of the state or its treasury brought to their aid. For example, to designate certain languages as national languages, for a particular region or regions, would mean that there is a constitutional privilege to use those languages as the primary or even the exclusive language of instruction in schools in that region or regions . . . There would, however, be no concomitant obligation on the part of the state . . . to aid such national languages, either directly in the form of financial subventions, or indirectly in the form of the interposition of the state administrative apparatus.[34]

It is no coincidence that in this book I quote quite extensively from Canadian experience, for what is happening in Quebec is just another facet of a world-wide awakening of the minorities, of the little people who are no longer content to be trampled underfoot by powerful neighbours. Much of this awakening can be accounted for by the breaking down of isolation : modern communications, media and methods bring the world to everyone's doorstep, for better and for worse.

No longer can a minority cushion itself from the outside by living in semi-torpor, knowing that while the rest of the world may be aflame, no one would bother with them. As these barriers collapse, many minorities will disappear in the wreckage. But what is sauce for the goose can be sauce for the gander too, and there are plenty of examples of previously-submerged languages which have eventually come out top of the pile.[35]

Whether Welsh can emulate Czech, Latvian, Danish (and, indeed, English in the 13th and 14th centuries !) depends, however, to some extent on the size of population reservoir available to that language compared to the reservoir available to English in and around the heartland areas.[36] The Welsh reservoir is small, and in areas where Welsh speakers are half or less of the population,

---

[34] ibid., pp. 24-5.
[35] P. B. Ellis and S. mac a'Ghobhainn, *The Problem of Language Revival* (Inverness, 1971), lists 20, including English, all but three in Europe.
[36] This is fully explained in *Nationalism and Social Communication*.

only a birth rate far in excess of that of English speakers could tilt the balance back.

Were the Welsh Catholic and the English Protestant, there might be hope. But Wales is Nonconformist and large families are now very much the exception : in this respect it is a pity that ideas of world food conservation have considerable currency in Welsh Wales. What that area needs is a population explosion : it would turn the balance in the schools, and help ensure that there were in the heartland far fewer economic opportunities available to outsiders.

With the example before us of India — formed with the intention that linguistic differences would have no major signifiance, but split by 1965 into states delineated almost entirely on language lines — no one can doubt the power of language in politics. The main basis of a modern state's power is the consent of the governed, a factor now more important than ever, which thus increases the potential of language conflicts.

In Wales, connected with the language question, is the straight nationalist argument, again a reflection of an international mood. As the ideas of internal colonialism in the First World gain increasing currency,[37] so the link is likely to intensify, causing concomitant problems for the Government.

The advanced Western world is also experiencing a search for roots. As life increases in tempo, the quest for a place of eternal values is stepping up, just as the old folkways vanish. The roots being sought are social or historical, sometimes both.

In what the English call the Celtic Fringe, the most obvious symbol of the past is the old language. There are some who consider feasible the revival of tongues now dead, such as Manx or Cornish. Well, the Cornish revival has been going 50 years and has produced just three people willing to initiate a conversation in that language.[38]

Their efforts are admirable, as are those of Scots in the Lowlands who have taken to learning Gaelic. But theirs is a romantic movement, a product of our times which could fade as fashions change. It has little to do with the fight to save Welsh, a living language, to prepare it for life in the 21st and 22nd centuries.

[37] See M. Hechter, *Internal Colonialism, The Celtic Fringe in British National Development, 1536-1966* (London, 1975).
[38] *Western Mail*, 23.9.74.

2

A Century of Struggle

HAS LONDON REALLY LEARNED?

" You Welsh deserve all the kicks you get because you do not assert your rights ".[1]

One hundred and thirty years ago three young barristers got their briefs really in a twist while on a trip to Wales. Whether they ever unknotted them sufficiently to make a success of the bar is really irrelevant. For these non-Welsh-speaking Anglicans penned their way into history with three Blue Books that helped launch the Welsh language into its most turbulent period.

The dragon's teeth they sowed in their ignorance are now being reaped. The fruit bears two forms : the Welshman deprived of the language which should be his birthright, and the young Cymdeithas yr Iaith (Welsh Language Society) activist fighting to right the wrongs of centuries.

But in one way things have changed but little. The Whitehall mandarins who control so much of our lives are still as much as ever in ignorance of the wishes, feelings and desires of that Celtic nation which lies not far to their west. One hopes that no one of significance in those powerhouses straddling London SW1 is as ignorant as the Yorkshireman who only a few years ago asked me in all seriousness : " But surely people don't *still* speak Welsh? "

The strongly-centralist ethos of the London-based media (the BBC London news seldom runs a language story, and even the

<hr>

[1] Quoted in E. L. Ellis, *The University College of Wales* (Cardiff, 1972), p. 54.

serious papers often drop them for their later editions) does, however, ensure that little of the fervour at present shaking Wales gets across the Dyke. While a civil servant in London would never, in public, go as far as the Blue Books in deprecating the very existence of Welsh, he is still today as far in retard of Welsh opinion as were those commissioners in 1847.

A number of Welsh forms have, indeed, been issued by London-based departments, but after what battles . . . ! It seems sometimes that the battles have been bitterest not on the streets and in the courts with Cymdeithas yr Iaith, but between Civil Service sections in Cardiff and London.

As one Welsh civil servant told me with considerable feeling : " In London, they have not the slightest idea of the situation here, either about the extent to which Welsh is spoken or where the demand for forms lies. They think they are providing forms for only a few crackpots. They are completely out of touch."

Hence the very restricted availability of many forms. Many have been the rows about publicity for newly-available forms. In nearly every case the people who know (in Cardiff) have lost out to the monoglot mandarins who don't.

How often have I rung up a Government department asking for information about Welsh forms, only to be told : " I don't know about them and I don't know how to find out." If readers wonder why the concentration on what some people call the Imperial Parliament and its doings, it is because the history of the language battle over the last century or so has been mainly focussed around skirmishes with Government.

Not that private enterprise has been covered in glory on the issue. Far from it. But a government has (or should have) an obligation to serve fully all its citizens. Especially this century, the role of government (which includes the local variety which has rarely enough guts or gumption to say boo to the man from the ministry) has expanded so enormously that its clutches can rarely be escaped for more than a few hours at a time. It may be, of course, that history will show that concentration on these targets was wrong, but the keen feeling for individual rights in the language movement has made it very difficult for campaigns to be launched against individuals or private businesses.

It is perhaps fortunate for the Government (of whatever com-
plexion) that the activist who may use the twice daily bus from
Dinas Mawddwy to Machynlleth so seldom comes up against the
true English central government officer on the 8.39 from Surbiton
to Waterloo.

If he did, Wales might be a good deal closer to the state of
revolution Saunders Lewis considers is essential to salvation. Quite
typical is the London Government public relations officer who had
to be almost forced to find details of Welsh forms being produced.
He eventually told me of seven, but forgot to say anything about
the other 40. He was far happier telling me about the bilingual
compliment slips and notepaper being prepared, and that his
department did everything it could to encourage the language : he
had even seen letters which began " Annwyl Syr . . . "

Big deal.

Although the Blue Books were a watershed, sparking a furious
defence of the language, their attitudes to Welsh were merely an
exaggeration of the feelings of many of the language's speakers.
How otherwise could every one but a couple of the schools they
were reporting on, fee-paying all, have been in English, with
farmers, all but monoglot Welsh, willing to pay extra if the teachers
were pure Englishmen? Welsh, to them, had a place : it was the
language of salvation on Sunday, but for their sons English was
going to be the language of business on Monday.

A few voices spoke out against this idolising of English, but
there was little opposition to the 1870 Education Act which set up
a system of compulsory elementary education which ignored Welsh.

It was in the field of university education that this period holds
the real interest for today. In 1864 was issued an address to the
Welsh public which led within eight years to the founding of the
University College of Wales at Aberystwyth. The language question
here was of little importance.

What was significant was successive Governments' refusal of any
assistance, although money was being poured into Scottish and
(particularly) Irish foundations. Aber was founded as a private-
venture college and several times nearly foundered for lack of cash.

But then the Welsh were not the Irish. To argue, as was often
done to try and get a Government grant, that as Wales was much

more law-abiding less had to be spent on police and prisons was to hit the nail right on the head.

He who causes no fuss gets nothing. As Dr. E. L. Ellis comments in his centenary history : " No doubt there were plenty of recent examples of Irishmen forcing ministers to recant, but governments were accustomed to brushing off the habitual cap-in-hand supplications of the Welsh with patronising indifference."[2]

How often has it been said, Wales is a peaceful country. How often it has been said, he who is prepared to fight gets justice.

But let it not be thought that the foundation of this college was a breakthrough for Welsh. The college opened with teaching in chemistry, philology, English, French, geography, German, Greek, Hebrew, history, Italian, Latin, philosophy and mathematics. The language of heaven did not appear until 1875.[3]

This was in character, not only as regards the founders of the college, but the general feelings in Wales. " Without depreciating or wishing to extinguish the vernacular language," the founders had said in a money-raising circular, it was " the diffusion of English " that was needed.[4] Welsh, they added, could look after itself.

The rush to embrace English in this 1864 circular could hardly be blamed on the 1870 Education Act. When there was an industrial revolution careering forward less than 100 miles away in England, and a planet rapidly being painted the red of empire, is it not surprising that the old tongue was not seen as synonymous with progress?

Pro-Welsh activities were few. In 1872, Osborne Morgan, M.P., presented 89 petitions to the House of Commons in protest at the appointment of a monoglot County Court judge to the mid-Wales circuit. In 1884, the Honourable Society of Cymmrodorion circulated a questionnaire to head teachers asking their opinions on the advisability of teaching Welsh. In favour were 339, against 257 and on the fence 32.

The upshot was the Society for the Utilization of the Welsh Language in Education for the Purpose of Serving a Better and

[2] ibid., p. 78.
[3] ibid., pp. 331-5.
[4] ibid., p. 15.

More Intelligent Knowledge of English (1885). In their case, triumph was swift, and by 1888 Welsh was recognised as an exam subject.

Not so successful was the agitation over control of education. Lloyd George had promised a Welsh National Council for Education which would take over all the Board of Education's powers. All Wales got was a bit of devolution with its own department of the board (1907). While politically this was not much, in effect control of language policies was passed just about entirely to Cardiff.

The department has been fortunate in its chief inspectors, but it is a measure of the battle necessary in the field to put official policies into effect that when Sir O. M. Edwards, the first chief inspector, died in 1920 after 13 years, the position of the language in the schools had changed little.

In 1923 the BBC began transmitting, with Wales firmly wedded to the West of England. How sad and significant it was to hear during the jubilee celebrations aged broadcasters proudly remembering the first words of Welsh put out over the new wavelengths, just a couple of words, mark you, surrepticiously slipped into an English programme. But, then, did not Sir John Reith, the BBC's first general manager, say of the rigid centralisation he pursued : " The local cultural loss should be to a considerable extent offset by the quality of the London programmes "?

1927 saw the appearance of the report that has ever since set the tone for Welsh teaching in schools, *The Welsh Language in Education and Life*. The joker in the pack lay in its timing. Education is a county responsibility, and this was the time of the slump and cuts in spending. On cost grounds alone many recommendations were slow to get off the ground.

But this was also the time of the decline of the Liberals, who were firmly wedded to rural, Welsh-speaking Wales, and the growth of the Labour Party, entrenched in the often mixed populations of the southern valleys where the language was dying and where, in any case, the cry was for work.

Once again, the language had far too few friends, and the pass was sold.

Now and again the question crops up in the Commons. In 1932 it was a demand for income tax forms in Welsh, rejected because there was no substantial number unable to read the English or get help from the local taxation office.

In 1936 came the burning of Llŷn bombing school, which raised emotions to fever pitch. Then, in 1938, came the petition for legal recognition. It meant different things to different people, and it was the boys in power who thought it meant least (see below, p. 120). The might of 394,860 signatures produced a pup in the Welsh Courts Act of 1942. Comments J. E. Jones : " Do, fe fradychwyd y Ddeiseb fawr honno."[5] Yes, treachery it might have been, but J.E.'s demands were also before their time.

From 1942, Welsh could be used in court by any person who thought he would otherwise be at a disadvantage, Welsh being his normal language. But by now Wales was in the midst of a war, and Herr Adolf's call meant no time to follow up this " victory ". The world was, however, changing, and Welshmen were beginning to realise at last that the language needed succour and protection.

In 1939, with Hitler's invasion of Poland, opened the chapter of the history of Welsh we are still living through. Almost immediately after the outbreak was formed the National Conference for Safeguarding Welsh Culture (Pwyllgor Diogelu Diwylliant Cymru), soon to grow into Undeb Cymru Fydd.* It might have grown into nothing more than another Hiraeth† group, had not the War Office decided that might was right and ejected 400 Welsh-speakers from Mynydd Epynt for a gun range. In doing so, they moved the language border back 10 miles,[6] so arousing the wrath of the union and the secretary who kept the movement going for over 25 years, T. I. Ellis.

The catastrophe of war also set in motion one of the most potent factors succouring the language today. As Liverpool evacuees flooded the town, Aberystwyth Primary School was forced to close its Welsh-medium classes soon after Owen, the five-year-old son of Ifan ab Owen Edwards, founder of Urdd Gobaith Cymru (Welsh League of Youth), started his schooling.

But Sir Ifan was going to let no war scuttle his son's education, and at the end of September he opened a private school at the

* In English, New Wales Union.   † Hiraeth — longing for homeland.
[5] J. E. Jones, *Tros Gymru* (Aberteifi, 1970), t. 210.
[6] G. Evans, *Wales Can Win* (Llandybie, 1973), p. 69.

town's Urdd centre for Owen and four other nippers. Thus started the great *Ysgolion Cymraeg* movement, and even Sir Ifan did not realise the revolution he had set in train.[7]

In 1947 followed the first Welsh primary school run by a local authority, at Llanelli.

But not everyone realised the world was changing. In 1951 the University set up a committee to examine the possibility of founding a Welsh-medium college. As I write, the University is still looking at the problem.

The next year, Income Tax forms in Welsh were refused yet again, but the BBC started broadcasting television in Welsh with the opening of the Wenvoe transmitter (by 1963, four hours were going out weekly).

1953 saw *The Place of Welsh and English in the Schools of Wales* from the Central Advisory Council for Education (Wales). Unlike its great predecessor of 1927, *The Welsh Language in Education and Life,* it was in English only. It suffered also from appearing before the great research battle into whether two languages helped or hindered a child — and, if the former, when was it best to learn — had really got going in Wales.

This was still the period of Welsh inferiority : when the University rejected the advisory council's plea for a Welsh-medium training college, it was partly because " the consequences might be disappointing and discouraging ".[8]

But the whirlwind was about to break. In March 1955, Trefor Beasley, a coalminer from Llangennech, near Llanelli, appeared in court for not paying rates on an English-language demand. He and his family suffered, as six times the bailiffs raided their home of furniture. Eventually, the family won. At the time it seemed an isolated, and dear, victory. But their courage in the face of the massed forces of Authority shamed others.

It sparked Saunders Lewis into his call in that historic radio broadcast of February 1962 *(Tynged yr Iaith*)* for a movement using direct action. Plaid Cymru, the organisation at which he aimed his call, felt unable to answer, fettered as they were by

[7] Gwennant Davies, *The Story of the Urdd* (Aberystwyth, 1973), p. 77.
[8] *Western Mail,* 15.12.54.
* Fate of the Language.

constitutionalism. Individual members were not so inhibited, and that summer saw the foundation of Cymdeithas yr Iaith Gymraeg.

With their first campaign aimed at obtaining bilingual summonses, early in 1963 members took to wobbling around Aberystwyth two to a bike made for one. But principles aren't much use without publicity and pushbike offences don't usually make page one of the *Western Mail*. Perhaps if they plastered the town's post office and police station with posters they might get both summonses and publicity?

The sit-down blocking Trefechan Bridge, on the main road south, which followed the decoration of the post office and police station, is now a part of the mythology of the language.[9] It set the die in several ways. Firstly, members had to remain non-violent, no matter what local yobs did to them. Secondly, it sanctified the mass demonstration which clearly broke the law. And, thirdly, care had to be taken not to antagonise too much. On that day, the police had orders to make no arrests : the demonstrators knew, however, that they had started along the road to jail.

They would not, of course, be the first nationalists to be involuntary guests of Her Majesty. Saunders Lewis, Lewis Valentine and D. J. Williams had served time in 1937 for the Penyberth aerodrome blaze. But this trail fizzled out with the war. It was Liverpool Corporation's almost jackbooted treatment of Capel Celyn and the construction of the Tryweryn dam that again saw Welshmen in jail again, with Emyr Llywelyn, Owen Williams and John Albert Jones sentenced in March and April 1963 to a year each for blowing up a transformer.

But with Mr. Llywelyn on his release renouncing violence,[10] Wales once more refused to follow Ireland. At the same time as the Tryweryn rumpus, a Carmarthenshire farmer was showing how skilful use of the law, a method used too little both before then and since, can pay dividends.

This was the case of Gwynfor S. Evans (not to be confused with the president of Plaid Cymru) *v*. W. S. Thomas. Evans, a Plaid candidate for a county council seat, had had his self-translated

---

[9] See *Cambrian News*, 8.2.63, for a very full and humorous account.
[10] *Courier* (Aberystwyth), 6.12.63.

nomination papers refused. In May 1962 the High Court pronounced the election of his Labour opponent void.

This great victory was soured by the Labour win in the subsequent by-election. Not until July 1966 did Plaid Cymru really taste electoral success with Gwynfor Evans's astonishing win in the Carmarthen by-election. But while Plaid was failing, the scene was very different just across the road, as it were, with Cymdeithas. Here there was a whiff of grapeshot, and the blood on the deck was not their own but that of the Establishment. Cymdeithas yr Iaith had four years to establish itself, before Plaid hit its winning streak, and the language men succeeded in making a mark and attracting the young idealists who had so much to give and, for those few years of college life, not much to lose.

For ammunition, the Council for Wales kindly provided, in November 1963, their *Report on the Welsh Language Today*. Soon the fortresses started falling, and they have never stopped since. Politicians from the three London parties may vigorously deny it if they wish, but why, but for Cymdeithas yr Iaith pressure and the election court case, was Sir David Hughes-Parry set to work?

His committee's job was to clarify the legal status of Welsh. In their report (October 1965), they called for equal validity. The Government gave the Welsh Language Act, 1967, which did no more than sanctify the use of Welsh in courts and on official forms. The committee had, in any case, been spared the need to recommend over election forms by the passage in 1964 of the Elections (Welsh Forms) Act.

Since then the battles have been many, often bloody, and the victories not always total. By this year (1976) a nicely-worded letter can be enough to get the administrators running for their translators : thus fell British Rail and the National Bus Company. Welsh is now becoming respectable. Cymdeithas yr Iaith have showed that they are capable of making so much trouble that it is easier to go bilingual (at least, symbolically). More than that, since 1974 there have been three Plaid M.P.s in Parliament. It is a brave head of an organisation who will risk incurring the wrath of these three, plus, on occasion, Geraint Howells, the Liberal M.P. for Ceredigion, and Tom Ellis, Labour Member for Wrexham, to

37

give a non-partisan look to the affair. Faced with such pressure, even the Post Office has had to start to crack.

In the midst of all this, I almost forgot the organised backlash, the men who would be on the other side of the barricades, when Northern Ireland civil strife comes to Wales. It seems, though, that it will be a rather one-sided contest. The only real effort to organise the " antis ", whose livelihoods and future are supposed to be under threat, was by Mr. Daniel Rees, an ex-BBC engineer from Swansea, with a group called variously the United Wales Society and the Real Voice of Wales.

Formed in January 1969, it lasted only months. Even the opponents of Welsh on TV never really got organised. I can only assume that in their heart of hearts they realised that the language fighters have justice on their side. Or perhaps they found they were, in truth, well served by the old established institutions of Wales, the courts, the councils and the Government.

3

The Pattern of Decline

THE RETREATING HEARTLAND

The decline and eventual disappearance of the language can be compared to the drying up of a lake. The continuous expanse of water has disappeared and there remains a series of separate pools, patchy and uneven, slowly drying out.[1]

Every language needs a heartland if it is to survive. Usually this is a territory; sometimes a sphere of life will suffice. For centuries the heartlands which have kept both Latin and Hebrew in states of semi-animation have been religion. Welsh, though, can rest on no such base : derided for centuries, no single sphere has developed in which Welsh is the pre-eminent milieu.

Religion is certainly one of the language's fortes and it has been said — in one of these exaggerations which conceal so much truth — that when the Welsh language disappears from an area, religious observance vanishes too.

The Welsh heartland has always been territorial, and if the language is to continue it is on that basis that it will. There are too few years left for language activists to change the entire social basis of the language. It would be narrow-minded to deny the value of such efforts in Anglicised areas, but an objective look at the strengths of these efforts, compared with the massive all-pervading strength of English, reveals them as a useful adjunct to the main effort, but no more.

Their main purpose at present is to help maintain the Welsh of emigrants from the heartlands : a valuable adjunct is to assist

[1] Prof. Emeritus E. G. Bowen and Prof. H. Carter, "Preliminary Observations on the Distribution of the Welsh Language at the 1971 Census", *The Geographical Journal*, October 1974, p. 439.

learners. But the fact that so much of this work is done by native-speakers points the inquirer to the area of greatest concern, the west and north.

The 10 years to the 1971 census showed no slackening in the rate of decline, either numerically or territorially. It did indeed reveal the growth of two factors which pose perhaps the greatest dangers ever to the language. One of them is well-known, the purchase of rural cottages and farms by English speakers. The second factor is within an ace of splitting the heartland into north and south with a wedge of Englishness.

This is suburbanisation. The term has connotations of London and Birmingham, and so have so many of the people who occupy these highly des., semi-det., three beds., secl. gdn. The towns which seem to be providing a fat living for estate agents are Aberystwyth and Bangor, and their clients will be so often English staffs at the towns' university colleges, part of the University of Wales, "the creation not of sovereigns and statesmen, but of the people themselves ".[2]

The basic figures for the decline in Welsh speaking are quite well known in outline, but will bear repeating :

PERCENTAGE SPEAKING WELSH

	1911	1921	1931	1951	1961	1971
Wales	43.5	37.1	36.8	28.9	26.0	20.9
Anglesey	88.7	84.9	87.4	79.8	75.5	65.7
Breconshire	40.5	37.2	37.3	30.3	28.1	22.9
Caernarfonshire	85.6	75.0	79.2	71.7	68.3	61.9
Cardiganshire	89.6	82.1	87.1	79.5	74.9	67.6
Carmarthenshire	84.9	82.4	82.3	77.3	75.1	66.5
Denbighshire	56.7	48.4	48.5	38.5	34.8	28.1
Flintshire	42.2	32.7	31.7	21.1	19.1	14.6
Glamorgan	38.1	31.6	30.5	20.3	17.2	11.7
Meirionnydd	90.3	82.1	86.1	75.4	75.9	73.5
Monmouthshire	9.6	6.4	6.0	3.5	3.4	2.1
Montgomeryshire	44.8	42.3	40.7	35.1	32.3	28.1
Pembrokeshire	32.4	30.3	30.6	26.9	24.4	20.7
Radnorshire	5.4	6.3	4.7	4.5	4.5	3.8

[2] W. Cadwaladr Davies and W. Lewis Jones, *The University of Wales* (London, 1905), quoted by Kenneth O. Morgan, " The People's University in Retrospect ", *University of Wales Review*, Summer 1964, p. 7.

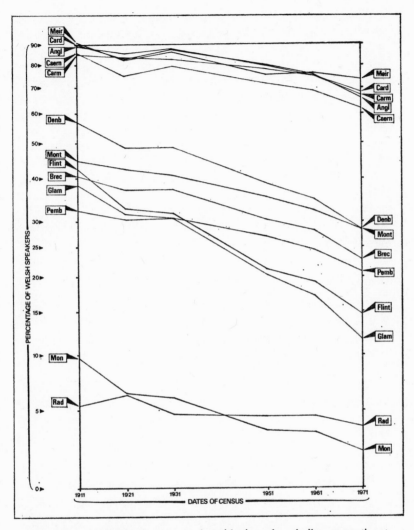

The decline of Welsh, shown on a logarithmic scale: similar proportionate declines appear as lines of similar gradient. Thus the least decline is among the heartland counties, and the greatest in Flintshire and Glamorgan. (Drawn by Roger Jones.)

41

What is not noticeable about these figures — and very relevant to whether or not it is possible to delimit a heartland — is the stability of ranking which each county has enjoyed throughout the last 60 years.[3] In 1971, the heartland counties were Anglesey, Caernarfon, Meirionnydd, Ceredigion and Carmarthen, all with percentages of between 61.9 and 73.5.

Clearly separate, and in second rank, were Montgomery, Denbigh, Brecon and Pembroke at between 28.1 and 20.7. Whereas the heartland counties were overwhelmingly Welsh-speaking, with only small incursions of English speakers, this second rank is characterised by wide expanses where Welsh is scarcely heard, contrasted with smaller areas where it is still the lingua franca.

In third rank are the counties where an outsider would not expect to find Welsh at all, except perhaps in small pockets. These are areas where Welsh is a language for use between consenting adults — as with homosexuals, they are in a small minority. The percentage of Welsh speakers varies from 11.7 per cent in Glamorgan to 14.6 in Flint. Typically, the highest percentage in any district council area will be around 25, and in many areas the language will be all but dead.

The less said about the fourth rank the better. It comprises Radnor and Gwent. Radnor lost the language in the 18th century,[4] Monmouthshire mainly in the last century.[5]

Comparison with the figures for 1911 reveal the amazing solidarity of these groups. The gap between the heartland counties and the second rankers 60 years ago is just as wide as today. The gap between the best and worst of the heartland counties has scarcely changed. All that has happened is that every one has moved quite some way down the scale.

The second and third rankers show a similar drop, with one most significant difference. Today's third rankers have scarcely

---

[3] The first language census was in 1891, but it is not regarded as being very accurate.
[4] J. Gareth Thomas, "The Geographical Distribution of the Welsh Language" in *Geographical Journal*, March 1956, p. 76.
[5] George Borrow, *Wild Wales* (London, 1920), pp. 601-4. Borrow reports that children in Bassaleg could still speak Welsh, although their main language was English. At the time of his tour (1854), he found that the language boundary was seven or eight miles to the east of Newport.

any districts which are mainly Welsh-speaking. Whereas all counties have dropped in their percentage of Welsh speakers, the fall in Flint and Glamorgan has been considerably in excess of the average : they are the only counties to produce serious anomalies on the graph. It seems that the disappearance of heartland districts with built-in social pressures to maintain the language is to blame. The Welsh speakers in these counties characteristically would be rather isolated from their fellows and thus far more likely to give up the linguistic ghost.

There are no mainly-Welsh areas in Gwent and Radnor either. Most Welsh-speakers here are immigrants and the counties are thus better ably to defy demographic trends. In areas such as these, where there are so few Welsh-speakers around to set a linguistic standard, a beginner might be more inclined to mark himself down as a Welsh-speaker. In areas such as Ceredigion, despite the secrecy of the census, he might not have the cheek.

The decline in these border areas in the future will be a function of the decline in the heartland which produces the immigrants, subject, of course, to the production of new Welsh-speakers through the Welsh schools, a factor of importance in these two counties. The industrial character of Gwent is enough to ensure continued immigration and continued Welsh speaking — until the final death of the language. The position is thus fundamentally different from Ireland where the censuses of both 1851 and 1891 showed whole counties with less than one per cent. Irish-speaking.[6] But, then, these were rural areas with little population movement : perhaps there is some similarity with parishes in Radnorshire without a single Welsh speaker.

The trouble with many past analyses of the census results is that few people have probed behind the county figures. As the heartland diminishes, it is more important than ever to examine the situation statistically on a parish-by-parish basis. One such effort was by Dr. John Davies and Dr. Phil Williams, of the University College of Wales, Aberystwyth, whose work on Anglesey appeared in *Welsh*

---

[6] Brian Ó Cuív, *Irish Dialects and Irish-Speaking Districts* (Dublin, 1971), pp. 22-7, for a fascinating study, with excellent maps, of the situation.

Nation.[7] The factors at work on the island are present elsewhere as well, so it is worth giving their analysis in some detail.

Between 1961 and 1971, Anglesey, alone among Welsh counties, showed no fall in absolute terms in the numbers of Welsh speakers. It is surmised that efforts to vary the island's economy have succeeded in halting emigration. Yet, in proportionate fall, Anglesey's was the worst at 9.8, with Carmarthenshire next at 8.6.

In the Dyfed county, the blame can be attributed to anglicisation of the younger generation in the south-east corner.[8] Although this factor is present in Anglesey, and perhaps most marked around Menai Bridge, the fall can be blamed mostly on a substantial influx of non-Welsh speakers. It is the coastal parishes which are most affected, with something approaching collapse along the eastern coast and pockets of severe erosion along the northern and eastern seaboard.

Individual parishes are not uniformly affected, even on the coast. Most of the parish of Llanfair Mathafarn Eithaf is as Welsh as it was a generation ago, and it is the building of estates at Benllech and along Traeth Coch, specifically angled at a retired English clientele, which has resulted in a 21 per cent. fall in Welsh speakers and put the old language in a minority position.

The drop of 14.8 per cent. in Llanbadrig is due to Cemaes Bay, and the 11.8 per cent. fall at Llanallgo can be blamed on Moelfre. Rhosneigr has taken its toll in Llanfaelog parish, which now has only 55.3 per cent. Welsh speakers, and Trearddur Bay has cut Holyhead Rural to 46.7 per cent.

Some coastal parishes, such as Llaneilian in the north-eastern corner, and others at the north-west and south-west tips of the island, are holding out at about 80 per cent. If anything can save them from the greedy grasp of the English-based speculator, who knows next to nothing about the language, it is Gwynedd County Council's structure plan.

---

[7] John Davies, " Retired English bring problems to Ynys Môn ", *Welsh Nation,* July 5, 1974. An accompanying table gave for each parish the percentages for 1961 and 1971, the percentage change, and the number of Welsh speakers in 1971.
[8] Phil Williams, " Paham y mae'r iaith yn marw ", *Barn,* Medi 1974.

At its public examination, the county council told of the pressures on the county from outsiders wishing to buy land for holiday or retirement homes, pressures accentuated by the lack of building land elsewhere and its abundance on Anglesey. Rather alarmingly, they said that it was only the size of the island's building industry that had restricted the growth to the present amount.

The structure plan must be one of the first major planning documents to base many of its policies on the existence and maintenance of the Welsh language. Except for a very limited number of dwellings, house building will be allowed only in order to meet local Gwynedd needs. Tourist development will also be restricted, with emphasis very much on serviced accommodation, which means jobs for the locals.

Not that the county has not run into opposition. The Anglesey Residents' Association protested[9] at the house-building restrictions, pointing out that holiday homes were often in time turned into retirement homes. Perhaps they did not realise that that was one of the reasons for the policy. It is the existence of organisations such as these that has obscured the real views of local people.

Formed basically by vocal, middle-class expatriates, they, nevertheless, try and get a few local people as front men, to be produced whenever a journalist asks the inevitable question : " But surely you just represent English immigrants? "

While Gwynedd may be getting to grips with the English rich, another factor putting the language in peril on the island is the armed forces. The parish with the lowest Welsh-speaking percentage is Llanfair-yn-neubwll (16.3). The game is given away by the sex ratio (1,125 males to 715 females), caused by Valley RAF station.

The extent of the fears was revealed at the public inquiry into the plan when the county council said that the modernisation of the A55 coast road, plus the building of the Dee Barrage, would put Anglesey in the Liverpool commuter belt, a factor already playing havoc in Clwyd.

Demand from outsiders for retirement homes was " probably inexhaustible " the inquiry was told by the county. As elsewhere,

[9] *North Wales Chronicle,* May 29, 1975.

too much land had been allocated for building, and too many planning applications granted, with the result that contractors had been attracted from far afield.

Hopes of cymricising the Servicemen are nil : few stay long, and both they and the local community mutually keep their distance. But it is difficult to see how such establishments can be a strong force in favour of the language. The argument is, of course, based on the jobs provided on the bases for local men, jobs which otherwise would not be available.

To the extent they prevent emigration, the bases are a blessing. But the side effects are not so happy. Sophisticated establishments like the Royal Aircraft Establishment at Aberporth in Ceredigion will bring in long-stay staff who will live off the base, taking a part in the local community as much as they can. Their presence has helped push down the percentage of Welsh speakers in Aberporth parish to 50, fully 25 per cent. below that of adjoining parishes. Aberporth is down to the percentage where the entire community drops Welsh, the school having probably already changed.

Jobs are certainly provided for local men, but at what cost? The language of work is hardly likely to be Welsh — but, then, to be fair, there are not many work places where it would be, apart from the farm.

If the Servicemen cannot be cymricised, neither can Anglesey's aged retired, who can sometimes be heard in Bangor cafes exulting in the fact that they have no Welsh neighbours. But there is perhaps more hope with the third factor on the island.

This is the suburbanisation spreading from Bangor across the Menai Straits into southern Anglesey, particularly the strip between Porthaethwy (Menai Bridge) and Beaumaris. Affected parishes include Llandegfan (down 17.3 per cent. to 46.7), Llansadwrn (down 14.2 to 71.4), and Llanddaniel Fab (down 26.1 to 54.8).

In the sheer weight of its sudden impact, suburbanisation can be devastating, particularly as the newcomers are neither short-stay nor inclined to keep out of local community affairs, often playing indeed the very active part played by any new arrival, Welsh or English speaking. Inevitably, some communities will be pushed firmly towards anglicisation.

Interest in the community, however, usually includes an interest in the language. It is certainly not sufficient for the adults to learn it properly, but it is a different matter with the children. Here it is up to the school system.

The map of Welsh speakers, in Anglesey as elsewhere, glosses the true situation in the high percentage areas. At the 1961 census Llandrygarn, between Llangefni and Holyhead, still had every inhabitant a Welsh-speaker. There are still on the island eight parishes with over 90 per cent. of Welsh speakers, but all, except Llannerch-y-medd, are thinly-populated areas with no villages of any size. If these can be taken as the parishes which are wholly Welsh, they encompass less than one in ten of the county's residents.

The towns throughout Wales show a great variety of linguistic complexions, and display points of very serious concern for the fate of the language. Whereas the primary school language survey carried out by Gwynedd County Council in January 1975 revealed that heartland villages like Llannerch-y-medd were maintaining their Welshness (census 93.3 per cent., school survey 91.8 per cent.), in most of Anglesey's towns the fall-off has been alarming.

Holyhead has always been considered an Anglo-Hibernian enclave. The census, which reports 61 per cent. of the population as Welsh-speaking, contradicts this. But the schools survey reveals that of the 971 pupils in primary schools, only 151 were native Welsh speakers and only 25 more had learned the language thoroughly, a total of 18.1 per cent. Reported as " di-Gymraeg " (without Welsh) were 553 pupils.

It is very difficult to compare most of the rural figures, because the census parishes seldom coincide with school catchment areas. It is easier in towns. Beaumaris is little better than Holyhead, with a census proportion of 41.2, to be compared with a schools figure of 13.7 per cent. Porthaethwy's census figure of 58 compares with a schools figure of 43, and Amlwch compares 68.6 with 44.9.

Only in the strongest areas can the percentage be maintained, such as Llangefni, which shows a census proportion of 82.6 and a schools one of 71.9 — which would seem to indicate that the Welsh-speaking population of the future (the retention percentage) will be 87 per cent. of the size of today's Welsh-speaking populace. As the Welsh-speaking proportion gets smaller, so does the retention percentage.

This retention percentage for Porthaethwy is 74.1, Amlwch 65.5, Beaumaris 33.3, and Holyhead 29.7.

Llangefni is also a bit of a showplace in that the drop in Welsh-speakers between the 1961 and 1971 censuses was only 2.8 per cent., the smallest of any urban area on the island. Credit for this can go to industrialisation in the town during that period. Once more, economic development of the right type has given considerable help to the language. But for how many other towns in the west and north, remote from the "golden ribbon" stretching from Dover to Liverpool, can that be said?

On the mainland, the danger of tourism to the language is clearly shown with obvious and long-standing areas of anglicisation around Betws-y-coed and Capel Curig, perhaps due to the presence of climbers on the April enumeration day. Llŷn, despite expectations to the contrary, remains overwhelmingly Welsh-speaking, but with the less accessible north coast considerably more Welsh than the south.[10]

Along the other shores of Cardigan Bay, tourism has really taken its pound of flesh. In Meirionnydd it is only near Llanbedr that a strongly Welsh-speaking area (more than 70 per cent.) reaches the coast. In north Ceredigion, tourism has allied with that other blight, suburbanisation, to drive the Welsh speakers inland. All down the coast, little English patches appear, some associated with towns, but others with all the fun of a fortnight away from work.

Bowen and Carter are blunt about the impact of suburbanisa-tion. Referring to Aberystwyth area, they say :

> A well-developed process of suburbanisation has been in operation for some time. There is very little land suitable for residential development left in the town itself, and, moreover, a house in the surrounding countryside has its own attractions. In addition, private housing estates have been grafted on to many of the immediately surrounding villages, which have become commuter settlements, for the patterns apparent in the large cities are repeated in the small towns. But the impact of urban commuters on the cultural and social patterns of the

---

[10] For much of this material I am indebted to Harold Carter and E. G. Bowen, "The Distribution of the Welsh Language in 1971, An Analysis", *Geography,* January 1975, pp. 1-15, and *The Geographical Journal,* October 1974, pp. 432-40.

villages is immediate, and the anglicisation which traditionally characterised the towns of Wales is by this means extended into, and occasionally far into, the surrounding countryside.[11]

Of course, a planning officer and committee with courage have the remedy in their own hands. They can refuse planning permission for such development except on pre-arranged sites. By guiding development which really cannot be stopped, much of the damage can be avoided. But first planners must get a wider view of life, one which states that it is far more important to save the Welsh language than a beautiful view.[12]

The effect is two-fold. The growth of semis in the satellite villages to Aberystwyth — communities such as Bow Street, Talybont and Capel Bangor — allied to the age-old advance of English up the Severn valley into the foothills of Pumlumon, is within an ace of splitting the Welsh-language area of the north from that of the south. It could be a fateful division.

The other effect is more dramatic. For years we have been accustomed to dealing with the frontier moving against Welsh from England and the east. Now there is another frontier, moving from the sea and the west. In the words of the two professors :[13]

> Two frontiers, one from the east and one from the west, are moving together, pushing with greater rapidity up the valleyways and surrounding the last isolated fastnesses of the Welsh language.

And these fastnesses are getting smaller. The largest group of parishes of over 90 per cent. Welsh speakers lies near Bala — the parishes of Llanuwchllyn, Llangywair, Llanymawddwy and Garthbeibio. Outliers also over 90 per cent., detached portion of a once greater core, are Llanerfyl in Montgomeryshire, Eidda in Caernarfonshire, and Tir Ifan and Llangwm in Denbighshire.

> It can be argued that these basic linguistic features of the geography of Meirionnydd reflect the fact that the ancient commote of Penllyn . . . represents at the present time the most characteristically " Welsh " area, in the full cultural sense of the term, in the whole of Wales.[14]

[11] *Geographical Journal*, p. 439.
[12] For a discussion of this, see Dafydd Iwan, "What I understand by Conservation ", *Planet* I, pp. 21-6.
[13] ibid, p. 440.
[14] *Geography*, p. 8.

The importance of this core to Welsh literature today is obvious. Significantly, another area over 90 per cent. is Dyffryn Nantlle. But just one parish, albeit an urban one, now forms this Nantlle core.

Another core area appears in industrial Carmarthenshire, in Quarter Bach, better known as Brynaman. The neighbouring township of Cwmaman reaches 89.1 per cent. The influx of English and hippies into many pleasant rural areas, particularly in Carmarthenshire, has almost pushed them out of the heartland category (i.e., parishes over 70 per cent.) : Myddfai, for instance, is only 73 per cent. Welsh speaking, and Talyllychau 72 per cent.

Increasingly it is in towns that English is hardly ever heard, in areas like Caernarfon south ward (90.4 per cent. Welsh) and Blaenau Ffestiniog (four of the nine wards are over 90 per cent.).

Travel east from Brynaman and you reach the area of the " Glamorgan fixation ". This can be attributed to certain Welsh speakers who consider the absolute number speaking the language in an area more important than the percentage. Thus, to them, Glamorgan, with its 141,000 Welsh speakers, is more important than Anglesey with its 37,000. Not much harm is done until they start to formulate policies on this basis. A quick glance at the census details for the industrial county will show that such action is akin to building a house on slurry.

For this is the area of a decline so catastrophic as to be almost unbelievable. Even adjacent parts of Carmarthenshire have been declining for a long time. Thus, at one school in the Aman valley the percentage of Welsh-speaking pupils dropped from 68 per cent. in 1935 to only 32 per cent. in 1950.[15] In the county as a whole, the drop was from 84 per cent. to 70.

Writing of the 1951 census, J. Gareth Thomas of Glamorgan said :[16]

> This is the region where the language, though still in use, is waning; it is fast becoming confined to the older generations.

[15] Ministry of Education, *The Place of Welsh and English in the Schools of Wales*, abridged version (London, 1953), p. 4.
[16] J. Gareth Thomas, p. 77.

By 1971 these older generations were fast dying, but there is not enough time for them to die to allow the Glamorgan fixation a natural death. It is clear that for years many Glamorgan residents have had little intention of passing the language on to their children, which is the crux of whether or not a person cares for the language. A 1950 survey[17] found that whereas in Meirionnydd 96 per cent. of parents who both spoke Welsh would pass it on to their children, only 42 per cent. would in Glamorgan. If only the father spoke the language, the percentage dropped from 20 to 4, and from 39 to 7 for the mother.

The language is now reaping the whirlwind, with the Welsh-speaking population dropping by more than twice and three times the national average over wide areas of west Glamorgan, as well as in the Clwyd coal mining districts. The collapse of the language in these regions is indeed one of the outstanding features of the 1971 census.

However, in a couple of townships the figures are not quite believable. In 1961, Treorchy returned 4,158 and Treherbert 2,942 Welsh speakers. Ten years later these figures were down to 2,295 and 1,515. Similar demographic feats were managed in Ferndale and the Bedlinog and Fochriw wards of Gelligaer. It is unlikely that a plague struck down the Welsh speakers, even one spread by the late Mr. Iorrie Thomas, the Welsh-speaking Rhondda M.P., renowned for his hatred of the language.

The solution could be that the literacy questions introduced in 1971 forced them to examine their Welshness with a little care. The arrival of television programmes in Welsh may also have jolted them into realising how poor in truth was their command of the language.

These anomalies do, however, make little difference to the general Glamorgan collapse. One effect of this collapse has been that the marginal zone which used to exist between the totally anglicised and totally Welsh areas is in danger of disappearing.

Wales is approaching the Irish situation where Irish-speaking settlements abut communities where the language is scarcely

---

[17] Ministry of Education, p. 6.

heard.[18] The Welsh marginal zone could be taken as the areas where between 40 and 70 per cent. speak the language. In many areas this zone no longer exists and rarely is it more than one parish wide. It is being squeezed out of existence by the disappearance of the language in the areas where it has little community value, and the retention of Welsh where it has some real value.

For it is a remarkable feature of the last census that where 80 per cent. or more of the population speak Welsh, there has been little drop over the previous 10 years in the ability to speak the tongue.

Indeed, attitudes has considerably hardened in some areas. In the biggest core area of all — around Penllyn — there has been a big jump in the numbers who refuse to admit they can speak English. In Penllyn rural council's area, almost one-third of the population say they cannot speak English; in Llanuwchllyn, for example, the total has risen from 129 to 225.

In fact, the last true monoglots died about 10 years ago. Although there is no doubt that the English of many of these present-day "monoglots" would not be very good, the answer to the census question is more indicative of an attitude, an attitude which indicates real hope for the language, an attitude which says: "We will not be moved."

The only county in which this attitude is widespread is Meirionnydd, with increases in "monoglots" recorded in Bala (quadrupled), Barmouth, Dolgellau, Ffestiniog, Tywyn, and Edeyrnion and Penllyn rural districts. Whereas in Bangor and Aberystwyth this factor can be put down to students, in Meirionnydd only the local people can be blamed.

Significantly, Meirionnydd is the largest area showing either an increase or a decrease less than the national average in the proportion of Welsh speakers. The only other such extensive area is Llŷn.

One of the few other bright spots in a gloomy national picture is the growth in the numbers of children speaking the language in some anglicised areas. In every case, this can be traced to the existence of a Welsh school. For instance, in Caerffili urban district

---

[18] See school census figures prepared by Conradh na Gaeilge, Dublin.

there were in 1951 306 Welsh-speaking children aged five to 14. In 1961 the number had dropped to 270, but 10 years later it was up to 545.

In 1971, the Welsh-speaking percentages for Caerffili were 4.6 for aged three and four, 8.3 for five to nine, 7.6 for 10 to 14, 4.5 for 15 to 24, 4.3 for 25 to 44, 7.3 for 44 to 64, and 15.3 for 65 and over. Significantly, Senghennydd Welsh School opened in 1963 and Caerffili in 1969.[19]

These gains are, however, insignificant when compared with the losses which are inevitable through death, and through Welsh speakers marrying non-Welsh speakers and then deciding not to teach the language to their children. Dr. Phil Williams and the Plaid Cymru language research group have calculated the deaths to be expected between 1971 and 1981 and, using a formula described in Dr. Williams's article in *Barn* for September 1974, have calculated the number of births of children who will be brought up Welsh-speaking.

In every county there is a net loss of Welsh speakers which can only be made up by teaching as a second language. In Anglesey the figure is 1,260, Caernarfon 5,920, Meirionnydd 1,660, Flint 4,220, Denbigh 8,060, Montgomery 1,780, Radnor 120, Brecon 1,920, Ceredigion 4,090, Pembroke 2,690, Carmarthen 10,280, Glamorgan 30,450, and Gwent 1,710, a grand total of 74,160.

The only evidence of these figures being even remotely approached in the schools is in the heartland areas where the language is strong enough to absorb the English speaker.

But is the heartland really strong enough? One register of the store a person sets by a language is his ability to write in it. If he can only speak it, the tongue is obviously not considered necessary or appropriate for every sphere of life. Indeed, only 73.2 per cent. of the Welsh speakers throughout Wales are literate according to the 1971 census, the first which asked such a question.

What is worrying is that lack of literacy is strongly regionalised. In some of these areas the reason is obvious — these are the areas

[19] Figures based on Council for the Welsh Language, *Report on the Welsh Language in Nursery Education* (Cardiff, 1975), p. 25. Similar figures are given for Wrecsam, Barry and Pontypridd, and the same happens in Maesteg.

of rapid decline in the language's use, where the language's commercial value is falling, where the language is learned at the mother's knee, but the youngsters don't consider it worthwhile learning to write as well.

This lack of literacy is strongly centred on the narrow margin at the edge of the heartland where incidence of Welsh drops suddenly. There is one heartland area, though, which exhibits a similar lack of literacy.[19] That is almost all Carmarthenshire and north Pembrokeshire. Surely this great district cannot be on the verge of collapse?

[20] See map, p. 147.

4

Behind the Decline

THE LAST BASTION

Whether in the country or among the furnaces, the Welsh element is never found at the top of the social scale . . . Equally, in his new as in his old home, his language keeps him under the hatches.[1]

Never has Wales experienced changes as rapid or as far-reaching as those of the last half-century. And almost every one has been to the detriment of the Welsh language. It is not only in the urban districts that a man's life style is now unrecognisable compared with 50 years ago; in the rural areas, too, the heartland of the language, an entire pattern of living, so vividly chronicled in the volumes of the Rev. D. Parry Jones,[2] has now vanished in a puff of motor-car exhaust smoke.

A new mode of living means new institutions to service the community, new societies and new clubs. Sometimes it is the English-speaking newcomer, espying a gap in the social life that has gone unnoticed by the locals, who forms the new organisation. In this case, the official language will naturally be English.

Sometimes it is the tastes and needs of middle-class England which have to be reflected as the life styles of everyone as the British Isles approximates more and more to a mid-Atlantic norm. The new

[1] *Blue Books*, quoted in A. R. Jones and G. Thomas (eds.), *Presenting Saunders Lewis* (Cardiff, 1973), p. 131.
[2] See, for instance, D. Parry Jones, *Welsh Country Upbringing* (London, 1948; Wirral, 1974), who writes of north Carmarthenshire.

organisation may be subconsciously, or even consciously, modelled on an English norm, and that will entail use of the English language.

If the new group is a branch of a "national" concern, use of Welsh by a local branch either for meetings or administration would often be viewed with alarm. To an Englishman in London, this would involve excluding his compatriots, producing a "ghetto" and giving the society a "bad image".

Something approaching this attitude was experienced by the Parc branch of the Women's Institute, near Bala. The branch was entirely Welsh-speaking, as was the village, and in 1966 the members decided to keep their minutes and correspond with the Meirionnydd county federation in Welsh.[3] The uproar which resulted was heard as far away as London, and a couple of top officials were sent down to get the branch to toe the line.

When they arrived, after traversing a goodly selection of Meirionnydd's narrowest roads, they found to their surprise not the group of country bumpkins they had expected and might, indeed, have found in a similar area of England, a country without the rich rural traditions of Wales.

Awaiting them were a cultured group, including several university graduates, led by a Yorkshirewoman. Unfortunately, the W.I., founded in Anglesey and seemingly so proud of its Welsh ancestry, could not bend. Parc branch walked out, and Merched y Wawr has been growing ever since. Perhaps it was too much to expect concessions from an organisation which sings at each of its meetings a hymn which includes the words "And we shall build Jerusalem in England's green and pleasant land".

The crunch was not over the language of the meetings — after all, many W.I. branches meet in Welsh, although they show a shameful propensity to change to English at the approach of the first English speaker — but over the language of record and communication.

Headquarters officials in London of the National Union of Journalists have been known to complain, in vain, about the practice of some Irish members using the Gaelic versions of their

---

[3] Dafydd Glyn Jones, "The Welsh Language Movement", *The Welsh Language Today*, ed. M. Stephens (Llandysul, 1973), p. 292.

names. Goodness knows what their attitude would be if a Welsh branch kept all its correspondence, including with managements, in Welsh, and then struck over the interpretation of some clause or other!

It is a source of considerable weakness to Welsh that such an important and locally-based institution as a football team considers it natural to use English as the official language. Welsh does, of course, have a place — to use between players and baffle English-speaking opponents!

Historically, the most important institution to the language has been the chapel. Indeed, Protestantism and the Bible — translated into Welsh to help drive out Catholicism — have been two of the most important factors in the language's salvation. But Wales has not been shielded from the world-wide trek from religion.

There is no doubt that Welsh speakers are more religious than English. Of the 400,000 acclaimed as members or adherents by the Nonconformist churches in 1961, only 110,000 worshipped in English.[4] But within just six years, 79,000 of all these adherents had gone,[5] and by 1975 the figure had slumped to only 289,000.[6] In areas such as Carmarthenshire, whose linguistic tradition is based not on books and newspapers but on the chapel, the trends can only be viewed as alarming.

Ffred Ffransis, deputy chairman of Cymdeithas yr Iaith, has no doubts about the situation : " In the south (of Wales), the Welsh language has been a completely oral and superficial tradition, except for the influence of the chapels. If the chapel were still the ruling influence in Llangadog (Mr. Ffransis's home village), Welsh would still be very much the language of the community, but the pubs have now taken over."

Time and again people concerned about the fate of the language lament the decline of the chapels. For example, Mr. Gwilym

---

[4] Council for Wales, *Report on the Welsh Language Today* (London, 1963), p. 80.
[5] Alan Butt Philip, *The Welsh Question* (Cardiff, 1975), p. 52.
[6] Figures supplied by the denominations: Presbyterians 100,000, Independents 82,000, Baptists 65,000, Methodists 30,000, United Reformed Church 12,700.

Humphreys, former headmaster of Ysgol Gyfun Rhydfelen, the Pontypridd secondary school, laments that the Welsh chapels no longer exist in the district to support the school's efforts in teaching Welsh.

To some city dwellers, one of the most idyllic existences is as landlord of a little country pub, preferably among the beautiful hills and valleys of Wales. To the Welsh-speaking customer of the public house he takes over, this yearning can be the reason for the Welshman changing the language of many of his leisure hours from Welsh to English.

There is a tradition among Welsh speakers that English is turned to when a monoglot comes into the company, and, unfortunately, most landlords feel they have a divine right to join in or initiate conversations, on the basis of trying to keep a happy house. Mr. Ffransis again: "If the bar in a Llangadog pub is busy, the customers will use their own language — Welsh.

"But if only four people are there with the landlord, they will automatically use English. The previous tenants of one pub even told me of a couple of people rude enough to continue speaking Welsh when they were around."

That the brewers do not seem to care what language their publicans speak is evidenced by the fact that in February 1975 every pub except one in Llangadog had an English-speaking landlord. When free houses come up for sale they will, of course, go to the highest bidder, and there are enough well-heeled Englishmen around to ensure that that won't be a Welsh speaker.

In the Irish Gaeltachtai, on the contrary, the local pub is one of the strongest forces maintaining the language. In strongly Irish-speaking areas, such as around Casla, site of the Radio na Gaeltachta station, it is said that no publican or barman could survive without the language. With few tied houses, ownership is fundamentally different from Britain. There is a tradition of family ownership: the owner will even spend some years working in Britain, leaving an Irish-speaking tenant in charge, before returning in semi-retirement to take over.

This question of the language spoken by the landlord is important outside Wales and Ireland. One of the standard texts on socio-

58

linguistics[7] refers to the use of Friulian (a dialect of Rhaetian, another dialect of which is Romaunsch, one of the official languages of Switzerland) in bars in Sauris, a rural part of north-east Italy.

This is a trilingual area, with German the home language and Italian used in church and at school. But Friulian is used in the bar, probably because of

> the semi-public nature of the primary transaction (ordering drinks, counting change, the frequent presence of outsiders), which is responsible, together, at La Nuova Maina (the bar in question), with the habitual use of Friulian by the landlord's family.

To television is often ascribed much of the blame for the decline of Welsh. To quantify the effect unfortunately seems impossible except in terms of hours broadcast — the BBC alone broadcast 10,532 hours in the financial year 1972-3 (some of this regional and thus not seen in Wales) of which only 493 hours were in Welsh (4.7 per cent.).[8]

Even academics who have probably never heard of Cymdeithas yr Iaith Gymraeg dub this "cultural imperialism". For instance, Prof. Dallas Smythe, of the department of social studies, University of Saskatchewan, told a Finnish conference:

> TV programme content has been developed as an important tool of cultural strategies in the capitalist nations for the expansion and defence of their respective systems.[9]

Prof. Elihu Katz, of the Communications Institute, Hebrew University, Jerusalem, added:

> An inventory of the cultural diets of the world is surely as basic to the human enterprise as a comparative study of nutritional diets.[10]

Behind his comments was the thought that the nation state might vanish quicker if television and other cultural media were

---

[7] N. Denison, "Some Observations on Language Variety and Plurilingualism", *Sociolinguistics* (Harmondsworth, 1972), p. 71.
[8] BBC *Handbook 1974*, p. 126.
[9] K. Nordenstreng and T. Varis, *TV Traffic — A One-way Street?* (Unesco, 1974), p. 50.
[10] Institute of Journalism, University of Tempere, *Proceedings of the Symposium on the International Flow of TV Programmes* (Tampere, 1973), p. 72.

homogenised.[11] He was particularly concerned about American "cultural imperialism"[12] : however, even just outside Uncle Sam's back door, in South America, not one country has to put up with so much material not of its own origination. Even the banana republics and their kin transmit a higher proportion of their own material than does Wales, although Costa Rica, with between 80 and 90 per cent. imported, comes close.[13]

This amount of cultural imperialism must be taken its toll in Wales, particularly as the U.K. is a state peculiar in Western Europe in the amount of broadcasting it allows on the box. The impression that the British spend far more time than other peoples developing square eyes is born out by the number of hours broadcast on the main West German station (2,750); France puts out only 5,400 hours, Italy 4,500 hours, and the Netherlands 3,400 hours.[14]

It was at the Urdd Gobaith Cymru National Eisteddfod at Bala that a number of the adjudicators spoke out : they said the competitive Welsh being presented was declining in standard because of the deterioration of the spoken word, partly due to television. Poet and editor Gwilym R. Jones enlarged on the poor standard of spoken Welsh in his paper, *Y Faner,* on April 9, 1976. The box's influence is two-fold : it presents an almost unbroken diet of English, and cuts down the amount of conversation, which could have been in Welsh.

Ned Thomas, a lecturer in English at the University College of Wales in Aberystwyth, goes as far as to say that all that has been done for Welsh in education has been cancelled out by the impact of television.[15] A community running its entire life through one language could perhaps accept and absorb without damage television in another language, but this can hardly happen when English is almost all-pervasive.

In a bilingual, diglossia situation, one of the domains which should be reserved for the home language is children's play. That

[11] ibid., p. 73.
[12] ibid., p. 74.
[13] Nordenstreng and Varis, p. 12.
[14] ibid., p. 14.
[15] Ned Thomas, the Welsh Extremist (2nd ed. Talybont, 1973), p. 196.

this often is not can be blamed not only on friends who are happier in English, but also on television. Mrs. Eluned Elis Jones, the primary schools organiser in Gwynedd — she refuses to communicate with schools in English, even if none of the staff can speak Welsh — tells of arriving at a rural school to hear the pupils playing in English.

" But don't you speak Welsh? " she inquired. " Oh, yes, Miss, we do, but we are playing Indians " came the innocent reply. The answer to this problem has been the introduction of Welsh playground games, apparently readily accepted by the pupils.

Not that the problem is new. It used to be the cinema which got the blame.

One factor which is praised by some for halting the decline of the language, and cursed by others for accelerating it, is industrial development. It has already been noted how it has helped to preserve Llangefni's Welshness. But its position in the language struggle largely depends on whether the development pulls in workers from outside.

The new town at Newtown was certainly designed and was certainly intended by the Labour Party to prevent " erosion of Welsh culture ".[16] Development has been too recent for the 1971 census figures to indicate success or failure. Local Press reports, however, indicate that the population influx has been from outside the area (mainly the Midlands) and the character of the incomers has been such that they cannot get on even with the anglicised population of Newtown.

With a population growth of 600 in the previous ten years, the last census shows a tiny growth in Welsh speakers to 12.3 per cent. But if the town were drawing on local people, who would otherwise have moved from the area, a much bigger growth of Welsh speakers would have been expected, for Newtown lies only a couple of miles from parishes over 80 per cent Welsh-speaking.

When Mr. James Griffiths, then Secretary of State for Wales, first introduced the plans, all the talk was of drawing back Welshmen who had emigrated to the Midlands. Pious hopes, though, need backing with practical planning, and here the Irish seem to have

[16] Labour Party, *Signposts to the New Wales* (London, 1962), p. 12.

the answer with Gaeltarra Eireann, the development corporation for the Gaeltacht (see chapter 16).

Sometimes a political "success" of one generation comes home to roost in the next. This is precisely what has happened with the break-up of the great rural estates and the widespread abolition of landlordism which happened particularly after World War I. This had been pressed for over decades. But what those new owner-occupiers sowed, the present generation is reaping.

The crop appears in the form of the Englishmen who are buying up such a large proportion of the farms currently coming on to the market, particularly in areas such as Ceredigion and Carmarthenshire. Some estimates put the number of farms sold to Englishmen at 80 per cent.; of the new occupiers, perhaps half are permanent, the rest being driven out by the uneconomic position of the farms or a yearning to return to the town.

The break-up of the estates had two other effects.[17] It destroyed the agricultural ladder for labourers which the reformers had worked so hard to construct. A man had not only to stock a farm, but also find deposits and securities, cash which could be found much easier on an urban wage. Even worse has been the desire of the new freeholder, when selling, to obtain the highest price. Thus an agent will hardly confine his advertising to Wales.

The landlord, having a permanent interest in the land, was concerned to sell to good farmers, and this would usually mean local men already known to him. Some landlords certainly had at least a degree of concern for the character of the community, and would certainly have hesitated at bringing in an Englishman. Today's estate agents have no such compunction and, indeed, argue that they have a legal obligation to obtain the highest price possible, regardless of the effect on the community — or on those poor suckers who end up with a completely non-viable holding on marginal land.

The extent to which immigrants have taken over farms in the heartland is vividly revealed in a survey conducted in spring 1975 in the south Ceredigion parish of Llandysilio Gogo, which includes

[17] See John Davies, " The End of the Great Estates and the Rise of the Freehold Farmer in Wales ", *Welsh History Review*, Vol. 7, No. 2, for a complete treatment.

the villages of Talgarreg, Plwmp, Caerwedros, Llwyndafydd and Nanternis. In 1961, 86.9 per cent. of the residents were Welsh speaking, and the parish had one of the county's largest numbers of monoglots. Ten years later, the rot was setting in and the percentage was down to 82.5.

By 1975, more than one dwelling in four (26.9 per cent.) was occupied on a permanent basis by a monoglot English speaker, and only in a couple of cases are these Anglo-Welsh. Even the farms, long considered the bastion of Welshness, had been penetrated, to almost the same extent.

It seems that little of the settlement is likely to be temporary. Of the 52 dwellings occupied by English speakers, two, both farms, had been taken over as long ago as 1947. Between 1955 and 1960, seven homes had been taken over; 1961-5, six; 1966-70, 17; and since 1971, nine.

A survey by Cymdeithas yr Iaith in the summer of 1975 *(Byw yn y Wlad, Ceredigion)* shows both the extent of penetration of holiday homes and the lack of interest by English immigrants in learning Welsh.

The society surveyed a small village in the shadow of Pumlumon which attracts many thousands of visitors each summer. Of the 88 dwellings in and around the village, 25 are holiday homes. Of permanent residents in the village, 23 per cent. are English monoglot, and of these 15 only two say they are learning Welsh. During the summer, only 56 per cent. of the village speaks the old tongue.

As the frontiers of the Welsh language retreat, it becomes ever more important to safeguard the remaining areas. And yet, some councils insist on pursuing a policy of building large council estates tacked onto the edge of a small village, concentrating their resources often at the expense of the most Welsh areas.

For some years now, the pattern of rural settlement has been changing. In the past the area around a village was a mixture of large and small farms, many of between 5 and 20 acres. These were worked part-time by village tradesmen or by workers in local industry (such as wool or slate).

With the decline of this industry and rural crafts, these cottages became vacant one by one, and there came a great change in the order of society. Over 25 years, these cottages were sold, mostly as holiday homes. The land usually went to surrounding farmers. While this strengthened the agricultural industry, it weakened the fabric of Welsh society.

The real danger developed in the last 10 to 15 years, as cottages in the villages themselves were sold and went to Englishmen, who could most times outbid local people. Sometimes this pattern was due to depopulation; usually, though, the Welsh were forced to move to council houses.

Unfortunately, councils, ever with an eye open for standardisation, commonly build their properties in estates on village outskirts.

Although council officials are reluctant to admit it, they much prefer their estates to have a minimum size. This not only means slightly cheaper building costs, but also easier management and maintenance. Thus, typically, certain villages are earmarked for development (not necessarily publicly), and a new social pattern arises.

This is of farms which are predominantly Welsh, village centres which are predominantly English (or empty), and council housing estates on the peripheries which are almost entirely Welsh. How Welsh varies: Teifiside Rural Council, in its dying days, built a very large number of houses in one village. Unfortunately, there were not enough people on the housing list willing to live there, and the homes had to be advertised in England.

The disturbance involved in moving to one of these new estates has also been considered by some researchers as a possible reason why some people switch to English from Welsh. Perhaps it is a new neighbour who is English-speaking, or perhaps it is just the surroundings.

Very few councils, perhaps only Dwyfor, have tried to turn village-centre dwellings as they become vacant into council homes, thus ensuring that the Welsh continue to occupy the village centres, instead of looking in as outsiders.

To some people it is mechanical factors such as these which are the prime cause of the Welsh's decline. Others, though, put more emphasis on the attitude of the Welsh speakers themselves. An historical and international perspective does indeed give this view much weight. Until the 1850s, Welsh was overwhelmingly the language of Wales, despite the presence of millions of monoglot

English just across the border. The same could not be said of Irish, despite the presence of a sea between them and the bulk of the English. In the Emerald Isle the Irish had lost their language over most of the country and only 23 per cent. of the population spoke the old tongue.[18]

The survival of Welsh has often been dubbed a miracle; but miracles don't happen, they are achieved by the people. Although factors such as Government policy and economic conditions set the scene, it was the Irish themselves who let the language go and clung to their religion. The Welsh, in contrast, who centuries earlier had turned with astounding ease from Catholicism, clung to their tongue. The tremendous increase in Governmental involvement in everyday life, particularly through schooling, in the last quarter of the last century was the weight which broke this determination.

The Scots, of course, had started giving up Gaelic much earlier. Despite their independence, they started switching to English from the middle of the 11th century.[19]

In Wales, the Blue Books of 1847, the report of the Commission of Enquiry into the State of Education in Wales, were reviled, but accepted.

> Although the report created a furore, and was nicknamed Brad y Llyfrau Gleision (the Treason of the Blue Books), and although its Anglican bias and distortion of some facts (e.g., illegitimacy rates) were obvious and were exposed by Welsh writers, yet, as Mr. Saunders Lewis has pointed out, the Welsh people eventually responded to the report in the way that the commissioners had hoped, by an all-out effort to acquire English.[20]

And again :

> Towards the end of the century, when a little village called Cross Inn had become a booming coalmining community, it was rechristened Ammanford — not by the English but by the Welsh. In that same town, when a massive Congregational chapel was built, it was called Christian Temple; the general belief was that the Welsh language would disappear within a few years.[21]

[18] Ó Cuív, p. 23 and map.
[19] Kenneth MacKinnon, *The Lion's Tongue* (Inverness, 1974), p. 19.
[20] Gerald Morgan, *The Dragon's Tongue* (Cardiff, 1966), p. 51.
[21] ibid.

Fortunately, it was not all a one-way traffic, or I might not be writing this book. In the 1880s, the Post Office, never, it seems, a friend of the Welsh language, tried to change the name of Cilfynydd at Pontypridd to Albion Town. But the inhabitants of this village, even today the part of Pontypridd with the highest proportion of Welsh speakers, rebelled and forced them to change it back again.[22]

Out of the inferiority attitude to Welsh arose the snob value in being able to speak only English.

And then comes politeness. It is considered the height of bad manners for a group to continue conversing in Welsh after the arrival of a single monoglot. Such social conventions rapidly lead to destruction of the language once a community contains a substantial number of monoglots : once, for instance, only 50 per cent. of a village speak Welsh, it becomes very difficult ever to hold a conversation in Welsh.

The power of social mores in public or committee meetings is as great, and even translation, unless it be simultaneous, does not overcome convention. In a revealing article in *Impact* (May 1972), the Rev. F. M. Jones, of Llanbedrog, reveals what happens to Welsh at meetings in the supposedly bilingual Church in Wales :

> The general tendency has been to hold the meetings in English, with provision for translating when someone insists on speaking in Welsh. And anyone who insists on doing so is regarded by nearly all the other members of the meeting as a nuisance.[23]

Much can be saved in a situation such as this if a lead is given by our " betters ". Unfortunately, some of the greatest men of Welsh letters failed to teach Welsh to their children, even in the middle of this century. The trend continues . . . a couple of very senior native Welsh-speaking members of Plaid Cymru do not speak Welsh to their children until after they had been taught the language at school. There is today, fortunately, a road to salvation for these younsters — the Welsh schools. Yet this road is not always taken

[22] *South Wales Echo,* 28.3.1975.
[23] Quoted in R. Tudur Jones, " The Welsh Language in Religion ", *The Welsh Language Today* (Llandysul, 1973), p. 76.

by the grandchildren of some of the great names : to them the literary heights of their recent ancestors will remain a closed book. One Plaid executive member is said to speak English to his children, reserving Welsh for the dog.

To many, the great hope for the language is the legion of learners being produced by the Welsh schools. It is still too early to tell whether they will justify these hopes and pass Welsh on to their children. If they don't, the Welsh schools of the anglicised areas will be little more than giant factories, converting English speakers into bilinguals who have no real future in the language struggle, for the same job will have to be done on their children.

The Irish have been following this path for half a century, and they are probably now converting the grandchildren of the first learners. Even mothers who have taken jobs and worked through Irish, using scarcely any English, freely admit that English will be the first language of their children. Col. Eoghan O'Neill, of Comhdail Naisiunta na Gaeilge, the co-ordinating body for the language movements, is blunt : " Only to a certain extent do learners teach Irish to their children. I put this down to three factors. First, the parents must know the language extremely well; secondly, they must be absolutely dedicated, bearing in mind the problems of communicating with their children when they are teenagers; and, thirdly, the parents must be dedicated to each other. I know parents who have given up because they did not have absolute fluency in Irish and could not properly show their love for their children in that language."

In the face of all this, what hope is there? The hope lies in the radical change of attitude in the rural heartland, where there are now said to be no Welsh-speaking parents who are not passing on the language. It's different in some of the towns; in Bangor, the old attitude that Welsh is no good and the children will have to learn English anyway persists. There are problems, too, in Penparcau, the council estate suburb of Aberystwyth, but the fall-off rates is now less and the number of Welsh speakers admitted to the local primary school is increasing.

It is the Welsh-speaking parents who are crucial, for if they cannot be persuaded to keep the language, why should the learners bother?

5

Nursery Schools

A SLENDER GROWTH ?

Language is the amber on which a thousand precious and subtle thoughts have been safely embedded and preserved.[1]

The growth of Mudiad Ysgolion Meithrin, the Welsh nursery schools movement, has been one of the success stories of the language fight. But it is a story with a debit side and, worse, it is a story which, if Government policy is to be believed, may not have many chapters. In theory, the decision to offer state nursery education to all will lift an immense load from the shoulders of those Welsh speakers in each town who have so many other battles to fight and funds to support.

In practice, the way many local authorities are interpreting Welsh Office guidelines could leave Mudiad Ysgolion Meithrin with a tougher fight than ever. They would be trying to provide Welsh-medium education, which has to be paid for by the parents, in direct competition with free state nursery schools with professional staff, lavish equipment and purpose-built premises. In the eyes of certain doctrinaire members of the Labour Party, the parents would be providing private (by inference, middle-class) education for an elite. This looks like a recipe for a repeat of the action taken against the direct grant schools, although I am sure anyone who pushed that line would not get much support.

It was in 1947 that the first precurser to the movement was opened. This was a group which met every Saturday in Cardiff so

[1] Archbishop Trench.

68

that Welsh-speaking children could meet and play with other Welsh-speakers. The first proper school (as far as these groups are schools) opened in 1949 in Glynneath, followed by Cardiff in 1951, and then Port Talbot and Barry. Their purpose was to feed existing Welsh primary schools and it was assumed they would be only for Welsh speakers. Early growth was very low, and by 1965 there were no more than 20.

But then numbers leapt and by 1970 there were 70 such schools, by June 1974 173 and by February 1976 244, with, perhaps, 4,200 pupils. The big push has come with the employment by the movement of its own staff, including full-time development officers, eventually, it is hoped, one to a county. Each county has its own committee to spread the message.

The big growth of the late 1960s coincided with the movement, almost casually, switching to helping resurrect the language in anglicised areas by admitting non-Welsh speakers. The movement now works on the basis that the sooner a child is introduced to a language, from the age of three on, the better and quicker will he gain command of it. Recently, however, with the realisation that there is a language problem throughout Wales, the movement has concerned itself as much with the heartland districts.

It is in these areas in particular that the Welsh schools take on the whole gamut of education, including teaching the home language to youngsters scarcely able to speak, a not uncommon problem in poorer urban areas, and enriching the quality of the Welsh learned at home. With so many complaints about the standard of spoken Welsh, no one would be justified in arguing that the movement's attention to the Welsh areas is an extravagance.

Considering the difficulties, it is amazing that the movement has advanced this far, but the size of the problem still to be tackled is enormous. In schools attached to Mudiad Ysgolion Meithrin there are about 4,200 pupils; this is only 4.9 per cent. of the total three to four age group. An unknown but in total small number will be in local authority Welsh-medium nursery schools, mainly clustered in Flintshire, and another unknown number will have been admitted to Welsh-medium primary schools at the age of three or four.

If it were not that the movement has transformed the situation in only a couple of years, one would doubt the prospects of further advance. But the strains are telling on the staffing side. One school in the southern valleys has only one of its four staff a fluent Welsh speaker. The two English speakers who take the three year olds can, indeed, deal with the simple sentence structures introduced to native English speakers at that age, but it is little surprise that Welsh-speaking parents wonder what advantage their children would gain in the class.

The upper class had the Welsh speaker, a qualified teacher, and an assistant who could speak only English. The pay in these schools could never support a career (most are only four mornings a week) and few teachers stay more than the two years their children are at the school. The staffing knife-edge on which many schools exist can be realised from the fact that 19 of the 20 pupils at Senghennydd were English speakers, and every one at Llanbradach.

A far larger proportion of the teachers at the Welsh schools have teaching certificates than at the English schools or play-groups, and there is a real reluctance to allow a non-teacher to take charge of the larger schools. But often there is only one suitable person available in a town, and sometimes staff have to be " snatched " from other Welsh nursery schools better placed to find replacements.

Mudiad Ysgolion Meithrin admits that the United Kingdom's continuing economic crisis is taking its toll. Said Mrs. Bethan Roberts, the movement's general secretary until September 1975 : " The big problem is certainly the supply of teachers, and we are coming up against it, especially with rising mortgages. Wives with jobs are having to try for full-time posts. It is particularly a problem in areas like Cardiff where there are a lot of vacancies and there is no difficulty getting a supply post."

A partial answer is more pay. At present, teachers get from nothing to over £3 a morning, all paid from local funds, but an application from the movement for Government money to enable £4 a session to be paid has fallen on deaf ears.[2] Money has been paid, but only for central administrative use.

[2] *Meithrin* 8.

In the rural areas, the staffing problem is so acute that new schools have had to delay their opening until a particular person became available as teacher. In farming communities it is, after all, not usual for women to wile away their time doing nothing.

Very few of the teachers are trained for nursery education; the only plus point is that the situation is worse in English-medium schools. The shortage will really bite, though, when local authorities move in with their insistence on properly trained staff. Already the Welsh Joint Education Committee has found a shortage of 59 nursery teachers, a total, presumably, excluding the needs of Mudiad Ysgolion Meithrin.[3]

This report, which is hard-hitting in some of its comments, says in its recommendations:

(1) The present arrangements for training teachers of Welsh for the nursery stage are inadequate. More provision should be made to meet this deficiency both in initial and in-service training, and

(2) The attention of the National Nursery Examination Board and the local education authorities should be drawn to the need for making provision for the training of nursery assistants through the medium of Welsh.

Fine hopes. But a course at Bangor Normal College had to close because of lack of funds. As I write, another course at Bangor Technical College is " under review ". Not that either course lacked students. In Welsh-medium higher education, low numbers, because of the small catchment group, are a problem. In days when colleges are becoming ever more cost-efficiency conscious, to run a course for only a few Welsh speakers each year is unacceptable to administrators. This factor, plus lack of understanding, plus inertia, are powerful reasons for an independent comprehensive college, including university departments, working entirely through Welsh.

It is difficult to gauge the extent to which Welsh, rather than English, nursery education has the lead. The foundation of the English sector is different and indeed goes back many years to the era of child-minders. As there was often an element of financial

---

[3] WJEC, *Report on the Teaching of Welsh in Primary and Secondary Schools* (Cardiff, December 1974).

71

interest in that job (hence stringent local council controls over numbers), so pecuniary advantages are often seen, and sought after, in the present-day nurseries and playgroups. The fact that some have turned themselves into limited companies, establishing branch nurseries and running new, brightly-painted child-carrying vans, seems to indicate that the job is not done just for love.

One can only guess at the extent of their penetration into the English-speaking areas. In anglicised towns like Cardiff, Barry and Rhyl, I would expect them to be far away in the lead. In a valley town, with an active *ysgol feithrin,* perhaps 30 per cent. of children attending nursery school would go Welsh. This percentage may seem high, but most parents are uninterested in nursery schools. If they become compulsory, they can be expected to plump for English.

It is in the heartland areas that the English-medium schools are doing the most damage. To the credit of the Welsh language, local people have been fighting back and teaching the cultural imperialists from the university colleges a lesson in humility. The biggest fight was probably at Waun Fawr, one of the villages near Bangor gradually being suburbanised. The biggest problem came with the University College lecturers, busily climbing the English academic ladder.

Described by a participant as " a rather vociferous group," they set up a nursery school in the image of those existing around Leicester, Reading and other redbrick universities. With the confidence that comes from the Welsh language winning many battles with authority, the people of the village (80.7 per cent. Welsh-speaking in 1971) promptly founded an *ysgol feithrin.* Even an uninvolved council official described the two groups as being " like daggers drawn " for a time.

This battle was not racialist or nationalist; it was linguistic. Children from Welsh-speaking families who had been sent to the English nursery entered primary school with English as their main language. Fortunately, Gwynedd County Council knows where it stands vis-a-vis the language, and an official Welsh-medium nursery department was before long open at the primary school. It is a sign of the tenaciousness of the immigrants that even then the nursery school did not give up the fight.

At Llannon in Ceredigion the same situation threatened. It seems here, though, that persuasion from county council officials was instrumental in securing a take-over by the *ysgol feithrin*.

English schools do, however, continue throughout the heartland. At Llandeilo the pupils were one day heard reciting Little Miss Muffett, a rhyme of real Welsh significance. There is no doubt that local headmasters play a part in the language chosen by groups : in some areas lack of a firm county council policy has enabled them to demur from insisting on Welsh. Local conflict is, however, not reflected at national level where Mudiad Ysgolion Meithrin and the Pre-School Playgroups Association happily co-exist and co-operate.

The problem with English extends, however, into the *ysgolion meithrin* of the south-east. The numbers of learners in the Welsh schools in this area are exerting serious strains. With perhaps only one Welsh-speaking pupil to a class, how much Welsh do the English learn?

More serious from the point of view of the Welsh speakers who keep these schools going, what happens to the Welsh of the native? Because of their voluntary nature, it is no surprise that a linguistic split first came in the nursery sector when parents in the catchment area of Heath *ysgol feithrin* in Cardiff decided to boycott the school and set up their own.

Reasons for the boycott were alleged to be the high proportion of English speakers, and the resultant poor standard of Welsh. The result was Ysgol Feithrin Llysfaen which has a clause in its constitution that at no time will there be more than one-third learners at the school, and even then the school would expect one of the parents to be learning, too.

The moving spirit behind the school was Mrs. Tegwen Evans, who had been a teacher at Ysgol Feithrin Llandaf. She said : " Five of the 20 children there were Welsh speakers, but even with this proportion they did not hear enough Welsh and the standard of their Welsh was declining.

" It was dishonest to the others, indeed, to say we were teaching them Welsh, and some of them knew no more at the end of two years than they did at the beginning. Worse still, some parents who had no particular concern for the language were using it as an area nursery school."

Since then, Llandaf has faced up to the problem. As well as some special arrangements for the Welsh children, the English children during their final period before going to the Welsh primary school at Bryntaf are once a week given a special crash course in Welsh. The difference is noteworthy. Another hope for the future is the use of teachers who have learned Welsh at Ulpan intensive learning classes. They should be well able to do the work which will, at the same time, overcome those dreadful problems of slippage, and acquiring confidence.

The real crunch for the nursery school movement, though, will come with extensive local authority entry into the field. This was really heralded with the announcement by the Secretary of State for Wales, John Morris, that £5m. may be spent from 1975-9 in providing nursery school places.[4] This followed quickly on the call in the Council for the Welsh Language's *Report on the Welsh Language in Nursery Education* for education authorities to make adequate provision for all children who wanted Welsh nursery education.[5]

In his announcement, Mr. Morris said : " With this extra assistance, I am satisfied that LEAs are now receiving the resources and guidance which will enable them to act on the recommendations of the council. . . I urge all education authorities, in planning their nursery education, to pay particular heed to the linguistic needs of their areas."

Within a fortnight the answer came back from the anglicised south-east : Thanks for the money, but there will be no provision. Gwent, hardly surprisingly when the attitudes of the education committee's chairman are considered, said : " We have no plans to provide Welsh language nurseries because we do not believe there is any demand for them."[6] Perhaps the authority could explain, therefore, how groups came to be set up in Newport, Cwmbran,

[4] *Western Mail*, 6.3.75. The economic situation has since caused delays.
[5] Council for the Welsh Language, *A Report on the Welsh Language in Nursery Education* (Cardiff, 1975), p. 30.
[6] *Western Mail*, 14.3.75.

Brynmawr, Tredegar and Risca.[7] There is even one in Caldicot, home village of that education chairman!

Mid-Glamorgan made a similar statement: " Our priority is to place nurseries in socially-deprived areas, and these are not the sort of places where there is any demand from parents for bilingual education."

This statement just does not accord with the facts : Senghennydd, for instance, has had a Welsh primary school since 1963. And yet, when a local authority nursery school was opened there under the Urban Aid Programme, it was entirely in English.[8] The Council for the Welsh Language was driven to comment :

> It has caused us concern to find how little consideration appears to have been given by the authorities to the Welsh language . . . We can understand why it has been thought right to concentrate effort on socially deprived areas; but we feel that more thought could have been given to provision for the two languages in doing so.[9]

The feebleness of the Government's activities in this area was made absolutely clear in a Welsh Office statement :

> A spokesman for the Welsh Office emphasised it was up to the local authorities to decide for themselves how they spent the money, and Mr. Morris's statement that he urged them to consider linguistic needs was all the pressure there would be.[10]

It has been argued by some that a friend as lukewarm as this is in truth no friend, because the reality of the situation is concealed. The language movement would at least know where it stood if it were faced with arguments such as :

> The recommendation that Gaelic-medium nursery schools be set up is a recipe for educational retardation. Teaching very young children through the medium of a language that is not spoken in their homes is an educational malpractice,

---

[7] *Western Mail*, 26.3.75.
[8] Mudiad Ysgolion Meithrin, *Memorandum to the Secretary of State for Wales following publication of the White Paper on Education — Framework for Expansion (12.72) and Circular 39.73 (1.73)* (Cardiff, undated).
[9] Council for the Welsh Language, p. 26.
[10] *Western Mail*, 14.3.75.

and to propose such a practice in the cause of language replacement is utterly irresponsible.[11]

Opposition in Wales is much more subtle. It sometimes hides under the guise of " equality " — everyone should get the same regardless of whether the needs of each group show that they require such equality.

This was shown up in the scandal of Cwmbwrla Welsh nursery school in Swansea.[12] As the result of voluntary efforts, since about 1963 Welsh schooling had been available full-time. Then, in 1972, Swansea Education Committee (now defunct) decided that to enable twice as many children to have nursery education, it should be provided only on a part-time basis.

Despite protests from the local parents' organisation that the social and cultural position of the Welsh language was very different from that of English, and considerable doubts expressed by the Welsh Office about the move, it took place that September. It soon emerged that the Welsh were not even to get the same treatment as the English. While English classes were split into morning and afternoon sessions, the Welsh classes were restricted to the morning and the schools forced to take English pupils in the afternoon. Thus Cwmbwrla Welsh primary school included an English nursery class !

Why the stubbornness on the part of the city education committee? It seems their argument is much the same as that of Labour councillors in Cardiff : the schools cater for the professional classes and are breeding grounds for nationalism.

It does not help, of course, from this point of view that leaders of the campaign include strongly nationalist professors at Swansea University College !

But then it is often said that the most vehement opposition to Welsh comes from those who have recently lost it, which could well be the situation in Swansea.

---

[11] From Language Freedom Movement press statement, Dublin, 14.8.74.
[12] See D. Z. Phillips, " Attacking the Roots of a Language ", *Meithrin*, Pasg 1973.

6

Primary Schools of the East

HEADING FOR FAILURE?

In any community in which there is a serious, widespread desire or need for a bilingual or multilingual citizenry, priority for early schooling should be given to the langugae or languages most likely to be neglected.[1]

" I didn't send my child to a Welsh school to learn English " — this comment from a Welsh-speaking mother living near Cardiff sums up the problem besetting the anglicised valleys. With perhaps just one Welsh-speaking pupil to a class, if that, serious strains appearing in the fabrics of the primary schools are being passed on to Ysgol Gyfun Rhydfelen, the Welsh comprehensive school, at Pontypridd.

As with the nurseries, so with the primaries, their entire basis has changed in recent years. Welsh schools were first urged in 1927.[2] Although the first was set up in 1939, it was not until 1947 that local authorities moved into the field. Their aim was education of children whose first language was Welsh; to this day no special course of instruction has been devised to deal with their changed, and very special, circumstances.

Many people believe that these schools are the salvation of the language, resurrecting it in the valleys to make up for the losses

---

[1] W. Lambert and G. Tucker, *The Benefits of Bilingualism* (Dublin, 1973), p. 11.
[2] Central Advisory Council for Education, Wales, *Primary Education in Wales* (London, 1967), p. 221.

elsewhere. These children are seen as carrying the conscience of a nation : their conversion into bilinguals is atoning for the sins of their parents and grandparents, who wantonly allowed *yr hen iaith* (the old language) to disappear.

But are we asking too much? The figures seem to say so, despite recent great advances. In 1965 there were 34 Welsh primary schools with 3,948 pupils; by 1973 the number had risen to 48 schools with 7,600 pupils; a year later the number of schools was the same, but the total of pupils had risen to 7,992.[3]

Even doubling these figures to allow for two complete groups of children to pass through each school in the inter-censal period produces nothing like the figures demanded by Dr. Phil Williams to maintain the Welsh-speaking percentage (see page 53).

A close look at the Mid-Glamorgan figures is even gloomier. The county has about 2,500 pupils in Welsh primary schools out of a total primary school population of 65,000, a percentage of 3.8 for 1974. The totals are certainly rising impressively. In the Rhydfelen catchment area, there were at Welsh schools in the spring term of 1975 181 pupils in the 10-11 age group; for the 4-5 group there were 271 pupils. In the Mid-Glamorgan section of the Llanhari catchment area, the figures rise from 96 at 10-11 to 170 at 5-6.

In percentage terms, this is 3.09 of the 10-11 group, and 4.93 of the 5-6 group.

Bearing in mind that almost all these valley pupils are Welsh learners, with what standard of Welsh do they emerge from the primary school? Professional Welsh-speaking educators of standing have expressed reservations. Like any school, there are grades of ability to speak Welsh, and certainly teachers at Rhydfelen find a person's rankings in Welsh and English to be similar.

This, however, disguises, among some learners, a poor framework to their Welsh, shown up by, for example, which word to use for " Yes ", a basic grammatical point in Welsh. Errors in mutations are certainly not ironed out in primary schools and can still be seen as high as the sixth form. Although the pupils' vocabulary is good — and better than the average native speaker in that few words

[3] Figures from Welsh Education Office, Cardiff.

Ysgol Gymraeg,
████████████

3/10/75

Dear Mrs. ████████████ ,

There is 45p dinner money owing from week ending 3/10/75 . I would be grateful if you would send it to school as soon as possible.

Yours faithfully,

An official note sent from a Welsh-medium primary school in an anglicised area to a Welsh-speaking parent. Has the language of the school no place in the outside world? Actions such as this, which occur regularly, raise very basic questions about the purpose of these schools, and the success they are expected to achieve in the wider community.

are borrowed from English — the language is not very rich, as expressed by lack of idioms.

Secondary school head teachers place the blame firmly on the primary schools, where a lowering in standard of teaching is alleged. It is said that education authorities are not being careful enough in their appointments with posts going to younsters not having the missionary zeal needed for a very anglicised area.

There have been plenty of allegations in Glamorgan, for instance, that councillors who do not care about the language and, indeed, often see it as a Plaid Cymru weapon, have been appointing party faithful to posts. It has been alleged by a senior official of one of the teaching unions that one such appointment, to a headship, of a teacher whose command of the language is poor, has so demoralised the school, combined with the overwhelming presence of English pupils, that native Welsh-speaking children have been withdrawn.

It is significant that teachers will not come on the record about the situation — they all want advancement without having to move to a non-Labour county. It is sad that good sources indicate that Plaid Cymru may be playing the same game in the parts of the valleys they control. For Welsh-medium education, though, that should mean an improvement.

Even at some of the better primary schools, the overwhelming preponderance of English pupils is worrying the few Welsh-speaking parents. Some education officials, in their gloomier moments, wonder how these English pupils can ever be taught Welsh.

But this is going a bit overboard.

It is in Canada that most of the monitoring of this form of education has been done. Known as " immersion classes " and designed for members of one language group only, they, however, seem little different from Wales. And their experience seems similar, too. The St. Lambert programme in Montreal has been running since 1965, teaching French to English speakers.

Achievement in English has been the same as their grade six (10-year-old) peers educated only through English. In French, a difference showed up compared with native French-speaking pupils :[4]

[4] M. Swain, " More about Primary French Immersion Classes ", *Orbit*, April 1975.

LIFICATION OF WITNESSES .

EVIDENCE GIVEN.

THE UNLUCKY VISIT.

1. The scandal of the Blue Books — a contemporary Welsh nonconformist view. Yet, despite their fury, Welsh speakers accepted many of the strictures and the old tongue was banished from the schools. *(National Library of Wales)*

2. Robert Ambrose Jones (Emrys
ap Iwan) was far ahead of his time.
Before ordination, he clashed with
his church over their establishment
of English chapels in Welsh-
speaking areas. Throughout his life,
he campaigned to restore his
fellow-countrymen's feelings of
self-respect and confidence.
            (National Library of Wales)

3. One of the first men to fight for
the Welsh language in the House
of Commons, Sir George Osborne
Morgan, M.P. for Denbigh West,
who presented in 1872 a host of
petitions protesting at the appointment of a monoglot county court
judge.   *(National Library of Wales)*

They were somewhat behind in vocabulary knowledge; they wrote compositions in French that, although they contained no more grammatical errors, were less rich in content; and they scored at approximately the 60th percentile on a test of French achievement that had been standardised on a group of native French-speaking grade six students.

When asked to tell in English about a film they had been shown, the bilingual students performed similarly to their English-taught peers on all measures, including the number of episodes, details, and inferences recounted, as well as the number of false starts, grammatical self-corrections, and content self-corrections made. When asked to tell in French about the film, the bilingual students made more grammatical and content self-corrections than native French-speaking students, but otherwise performed similarly.

A number of phonological traits not characteristic of native French-speakers were noted in the speech of many of the bilingual children. They included the diphthongization of the mid-vowels, the aspiration of voiceless stops, and inappropriate placing of stress on the first syllable.

For other subjects, such as maths and science, and in general development, the bilingual-taught pupils have suffered in no way, even when the same tests are conducted in working class districts, where the pupils have a lower measured IQ. Indeed, it is possible that the St. Lambert immersion pupils do better than their English peers in these extra tests.[5] For some years it has been argued that two languages are better than one for a student's intellectual development : unfortunately, these figures do not seem conclusive.[6]

Much of the argument in Wales centres around the main role of the Welsh primaries. If they are primarily for second-language teaching, the parents of native Welsh speakers have no right to complain. But Canadian experience has shown that native speakers are unnecessary for success, which puts the " rights " of the native Welsh speaker in a different light. Parents then have rather more right to complain if they feel their children are held back during

[5] W. Lambert and G. R. Tucker, *The Benefits of Bilingualism* (Dublin, ?1973), pp. 9-11.
[6] It is interesting to note that there is no reason why children with learning disabilities should not be included in these classes, contrary to the general view. See M. Bruck, M. S. Rabinovitch and M. Oates, " Effects of French Immersion Programmes on Children with Language Disabilities ", *Working Papers on Bilingualism* 5 (Toronto, 1975).

their first years (although there is no evidence they are held back ultimately).

If, in urban centres such as Swansea and Cardiff, there should be an attempt to revert to the original idea of Welsh schools, to foster Welsh language and culture (immersion schools would presumably run parallel) the question of quotas would need examining. It seems that if a school is to remain truly Welsh, with that language used naturally by the pupils in the classrooms and at play, no more than 40 per cent. of the intake may be monoglot English.

Such a percentage is enforced by the Collège Militaire Royal de Saint-Jean in Canada. This principle was considered of sufficient importance to warrant a specific recommendation from the massive and thorough-going Royal Commission on Bilingualism and Biculturalism of the Canadian federal government.[7]

Of course, a ratio is no use if the local authority forces Welsh-speaking children or those desiring a bilingual education into an English primary school. No standard exists for acceding to demands from parents, and campaigns can continue for years, as at Merthyr and Brynmawr. Often official education department surveys are blatantly ignored or misinterpreted by councillors.

For instance, it is a cardinal point of Gwent, and, before that, of Monmouthshire, education policy that hardly anyone in the county wants Welsh education. " I think the people in this county are more sensible about pressing for Welsh than those in Mid-Glamorgan," said education committee chairman Councillor Graham Powell, a Welshman be it noted.

Yet in 1957 an Abertillery and Ebbw Vale Divisional Executive survey showed half the parents wanted Welsh taught as a subject.[8] After considering a long memorandum from the NUT listing every possible objection and including a number of statements which would now be considered educationally untenable, the executive decided the difficulties were " insurmountable ", and eventually decided to teach some Welsh history.

[7] Royal Commission on Bilingualism and Biculturalism, *Final Report, Book 2, Education* (Ottawa, 1968), pp. 158-9.
[8] Gwent Record Office, Divisional Executive Papers, C.DE.M-12, and subsequent references.

In Radnorshire, in 1967, six out of 10 parents replied they wanted Welsh taught. The authority were so alarmed that they sent out a second questionnaire including French, but still almost 40 per cent. wanted Welsh.

In 1969, Swansea asked parents if they wanted Welsh or French taught. On hearing that 10,000 in the primary schools wanted Welsh and only 5,000 French, a councillor said German should also have been included on the questionnaire.

In 1972 Cardiff found two-thirds wanted Welsh teaching, and one-third called for bilingual education. At schools in the Pembroke Secondary School catchment area, between 70 and 100 per cent. of the parents wanted Welsh teaching. Yet so often the authorities lag. As one HMI said : " It comes down to a matter of the parents making a nuisance of themselves."

Pembrokeshire certainly acted, and there was a response in Swansea. Cardiff maintained its basically Welsh-for-all policy, but fluffed the crucial point of bilingual streams : most parents had their demands ignored and streams were provided at only one middle-class school (Heol Llanishen Fach, Rhiwbeina), whereas some of the highest percentages in favour were in working class and immigrant districts.

Obviously growth in this field, the one which could really transform the picture in the anglicised areas, is going to be very slow in the absence of a law such as the Schools Administration Amendment Act, 1968, of Ontario. This Act forces a local authority to provide a French school or classes on written request from 10 or more Francophone ratepayers, provided there are a minimum of 30 pupils at the primary, junior or intermediate divisions.[9]

In Quebec, overwhelmingly French-speaking, every child has a right to education in his mother tongue throughout his school life, despite the enormous administration difficulties in the rural areas : one English language school board, for instance, functions for just six pupils.[10]

In Wales, the work of the Welsh schools is undermined by allegations that they are middle-class preserves. As the schools, particularly in the southern valleys, have grown and taken in local

[9] Royal Commission, p. 76.
[10] ibid., p. 56.

English speakers, the charge has become impossible to sustain, except in Cardiff, where there has been very little growth among the working classes.[11]

The lack of growth may be due to the attitude of Cardiff's Welsh speakers, or the provision of only one school for the entire city, allied with the refusal of the city, and then South Glamorgan county council, to pay full transport costs, which can be a burden for even a middle-class family.

For a school in a city where the Labour Party still believes in class warfare, this situation is a trap. When a Labour councillor fears loss of the ward nomination merely because he sends his children to a Welsh school instead of the local comprehensive along with the other working-class children of the neighbourhood, the school and the language itself can expect little help.

It is not as if compulsory Welsh lessons for all do much good in Cardiff, or elsewhere in the anglicised districts. Knowing of secondary modern school pupils still trying to learn the same basic Welsh lesson at the end as at the beginning of their career, it is difficult to disagree with the remarks of Mr. John Brace, Mid-Glamorgan Director of Education.

Glamorgan had a policy of making the county bilingual by 2000, utilising six lessons a week of Welsh, and half the primary school staffs were supposed to be able to teach the language. Ask how many pupils learned the language and you get the answer appropriate to a silly question.

Mr. Brace said :[12]

> The policy of compulsory Welsh in the primary schools has not only been, in the main, unsuccessful; in many respects it has been counter-productive. In many primary schools, Welsh is taught with a distinct lack of enthusiasm and there are some schools where it is hardly taught at all.
>
> On the other hand, Welsh is taught extremely well in some schools. The result is that when children enter secondary schools their levels of attainment in the second language vary enormously. The pupils who are well ahead virtually start again and become understandably bored and discouraged.

[11] Central Advisory Council, p. 221.
[12] Report to Development and Finance Sub-Committee, 12.12.73.

Pupils who are taught Welsh indifferently respond at best grudgingly. In many cases they develop a hostility to the language. The policy has tended to dissipate resources instead of concentrating them on schools where they would be most effective.

The degree of success in learning depends in no small measure on parental interest and support. The success of the bilingual schools illustrates this point. No consultation has ever been undertaken in Glamorgan with parents and the teaching of Welsh has been denied the motivation which parental backing can provide.

Mr. Brace went on to advocate the dropping of compulsory Welsh. A row resulted, but not as great as would have been expected a few years ago. Perhaps even hardline nationalists are beginning to realise that compulsion is a waste of time; they may come next to realise that even the Welsh schools and Schools Council bilingual streams will be insufficient to pull Glamorgan's Welsh language bacon out of the fire.

It was the *Gittins Report* which described the situation of Welsh in primary schools as the " more or less ineffective teaching of a second language as if it were a language foreign to the country to which it belongs ".[13]

The Schools Council experiment (which looks like becoming pretty permanent) is either a great success or a moderate failure, depending on standpoint. The project, which started in 1969 with 28 schools, involved 56 by December 1974, and further growth has occurred since.

As I write, the formal report on these schools has yet to appear, but a success rate of no more than 50 per cent. has been estimated by a senior educationist for one of the better schools. By success is meant ability to pass to a Welsh-medium secondary school.

These bilingual schools teach about half the time and half the subjects in the junior section through Welsh. They had been suggested by Gittins as perhaps the only method of attaining " full and adequate bilingualism ".[14] Yet the three pre-conditions for success which the committee set have been consistently broken, although not all schools have sinned in all respects.

[13] Central Advisory Council, p. 244.
[14] ibid., p. 245.

The conditions were :

1. The area should have residual Welsh, yet this hardly exists in Rhiwbeina, Cardiff, for instance;

2. Good relations with parents are vitally important, but when Glamorgan set one up in Sully there were considerable protests and it emerged that there had been very little contact with parents; and

3. Three teachers from each school should be seconded to a special training course. In fact, training had to be in-service on the basis of special visits by Schools Council staff. In any case, in some schools there was a marked lack of enthusiasm on the part of staffs, and not infrequently the aim of 50 per cent. of higher-level teaching in Welsh was not reached.

In the case of Cardiff schools, an essential not mentioned by Gittins is absent. This is the availability of a Welsh secondary school. Few parents have been willing to allow their children to attend the school at Llanhari, 14 miles away by bus. The children who opt for the local secondary school will thus waste what they have learned : for them, and for the 50 per cent. who did not in any case make the grade, the experiment will be nigh futile.

Welsh education has so far thrived, but on success. Can it thrive also on failure? In any case, why the pussyfooting? Prof. Lambert's work with a bilingual project teaching French to English speakers near Montreal was a resounding success. But while Gittins advocated starting with not too much Welsh, and eventually teaching only lesser important subjects through that language, Lambert started with the vast majority of subjects in French, including maths, and only in the seventh year allowing English to overhaul French.

7

The Rural Primaries

UNDER THE SHADOW OF THE BLUE BOOKS

The true enemy has been the " worm i' the bud " — neglect and indifference in the camp.[1]

It takes a lot to wipe away almost 130 years of history, and the job is still not complete. For there still lies over some Welsh-speaking country districts the shadow of those disastrous Blue Books of 1847. Every now and again, a parent tells a headmaster : " Don't you bother with the Welsh, we'll teach him that at home. You just get on with teaching him English; that is what he'll need when he leaves school ".

The last 15 years have seen this situation change beyond belief. Even in 1966 it could be said that the unlikeliest of a number of generally gloomy futures for Welsh was that Welsh speakers could decide " they are not going to be pushed back any further ".[2] Today we are entering that position, which thus firmly marks off the heartland from the anglicised east. A major effort and the heartland schools can integrate all the newcomers and give the old society new life.

It was an HMI who made the comment about the shadow of 1847 : " The further west you go into the countryside, the deeper is the shadow. It reaches even up to headmasters, who tell of

---

[1] " Scottish Gaelic ", by J. R. Morrison, *The Welsh Anvil,* July 1952, p. 57.
[2] Gerald Morgan, *The Dragon's Tongue* (Cardiff, 1966), p. 134.

87

parents urging them to concentrate on English. But when I press for details of the requests, it generally turns out they are getting about one every ten years.

" But the attitude still lingers even if it is not formulated. People can be so blind in those districts : it is just the fatstock market prices which interest them, never the census returns. As long as the people next door speak Welsh, they imagine there can be nothing wrong with the health of the language."

This attitude has its parallel in the long-serving Cardiff journalist who asked me what was the fuss over the language, as he thought more than ever were speaking it!

The most difficult areas in which to break through are the council estates housing many immigrants, such as Penparcau, at Aberystwyth, where the lack of the Welsh language is blamed on wartime arrivals from Liverpool and other areas who stayed. Welsh speakers were so affected by their attitudes that, although a few sent their children to Ysgol Gymraeg Aberystwyth, hardly anyone arrived at Penparcau Primary School Welsh-speaking.

The situation now has changed. " The number of Welsh-speaking children I have is increasing and has now reached about 30 (15 per cent. of the school)," says headmaster Mr. Dilwyn Jones. " Despite this, I am still shaken when I discover that the parents of some pupils can, in fact, speak Welsh, although very often it is a case of one parent being fluent and the other not. In these cases I have asked the fluent parent to use the language with the child : I have had a fair response."

What has vanished is the idea that Welsh is a waste of teaching him : parents realise that possession of the language will aid their offspring to good jobs. But even at Penparcau the success rate is not high. Of the 54 pupils who left in July 1974, about 10 could have gone to the Welsh learners' class at Penweddig, Aberystwyth's Welsh comprehensive school (in fact, only one did). Of the 10, about five would have had a Welsh background at home, although only two would have been Welsh speakers.

Although the attitudes of the heartland are changing, much still depends on the local head teacher, a leader in the community and expected by the education authorities to act as one.[3] It has been said that nothing is more private than what goes on in a classroom and there is no doubt that, in the absence of strict instructions from County Hall, a head has much power over both the teaching and official language of his school.

Many allegations are made that certain head teachers are " not healthy ", but it was a survey by Cardiff Welsh teacher Mr. Owen John Thomas which really put the cat among the pigeons.[4] The pigeons squawked loudest in Pembrokeshire, where Mr. Thomas published a list of " Murder Machine Schools ", English-language schools in Welsh-speaking districts.

To be fair, the list provoked very strong reactions from several headmasters.[5] The schools Mr. Thomas listed, based on information supplied by the education authority, were Newport (where the village was 74.1 per cent. Welsh-speaking in 1971), Mathry (71.8), Manor Owen (66.7), Cilgerran (78.4) and Wolfscastle (92 per cent. in 1961).

Interestingly, if one is to try and regionalise the continued presence of the Shadow of the Blue Books, this area might appear quite black on the map, for it is here that

> so frequently the headmaster is accused on being "a !!! Welsh Nationalist", or "he teaches too much of that !!! Welsh ". So many in education have acquired a degree of unpopularity with some for their efforts on behalf of the Welsh language and culture and giving it the place is deserves in our society.[6]

Perhaps one should not be too hard on the head teachers, as they have to reflect in some way the society in which they live. Caernarfonshire, and to a lesser extent the rest of Gwynedd, however, shows a different face to the world. A strong policy from the education department, backed up by strong councillors with parents

---

[3] The row in the 1960s over whether headmasters should have to occupy school houses in Ceredigion was due to the county council's belief that they should take an active part in the life of the community.
[4] Owen John Thomas, " Welsh in Schools ", *Welsh Nation*, Vol. 45, No. 1, Carmarthenshire, 45.3 Flintshire, 45.4 Caernarfonshire, 45.5 Anglesey, 45.6 Powys, 45.7 Pembrokeshire, 45.10 Denbighshire, 45.11 Gwent, and 46.31 Glamorgan.
[5] *Welsh Nation*, 4.1.74.
[6] ibid.

in agreement spells the recipe for success. But even here there are problems, with some teachers unwilling to continue pushing Welsh in linguistically mixed areas.

The crunch came for them when they saw pupils they had worked hard at turning into bilinguals enter the almost wholly English secondary schools. Within a couple of months their command of Welsh was vanishing because there was no chance to use it officially at school. Indeed, one southern headmaster told me of a Gwynedd grammar school which, in 1974, performed its first-ever play in Welsh.

The point is spelled out in a document urging bilingual secondary education for Dyfed :[7]

> The disadvantages of the present (secondary school) system flow back into the primary schools and on into higher and further education. Since facilities for teaching through Welsh are either ineffective or non-existent in the secondary school, the standard of literacy in Welsh has been rapidly declining at primary level, because there is no *educational* purpose to spur on the teachers. This is killing the language far more effectively than the factors which usually get the blame — television and English-speaking immigrants.

Gwynedd County Council find that the attitude of teachers can make or mar a school's contribution to bilingualism. One official said : " Everything stands or falls by the conviction and determination of the teacher, and his flare for second-language teaching." The council has done almost everything it can to provide the materials, indeed almost spoonfeeding them. Some schools have then succeeded with the most primitive of aids, and others have failed with the best.

That the primary school in the Welsh-speaking area is a powerful medium for teaching Welsh to non-Welsh speakers is vividly borne out by the language survey carried out by Gwynedd education department in January 1975. In precisely half the secondary school catchment areas, 79 per cent. or more of the children aged 8-11 were judged by headmasters to be capable of receiving secondary education through Welsh.

---

[7] J. Davies and G. Matthews, *Better Education for Dyfed* (Carmarthen, 1974, duplicated), p. 5.

But often the figure bore little relationship to the total of Welsh speakers in the area. At Blaenau Ffestiniog, 91 per cent. of the pupils were suitable, but only 69.5 per cent. were native speakers. At Dyffryn Nantlle the figures were 89.5 and 82; Brynrefail 89 and 78; Botwnnog 88 and 80; Dyffryn Ogwen 85.5 and 70.5; Caernarfon 84.5 and 72.5; Llangefni 83 and 75; Pwllheli 81.5 and 69.5; Porthmadog 80.5 and 69; and Bala 79 and 74.

In other words, in each of these areas between five and 22 per cent. had been taught Welsh thoroughly enough at primary level to attend a bilingual (Welsh) secondary school.

This trend is reflected in the census figures for 1971 (see table). In every county, as would be expected, there are far fewer pre-school children speaking Welsh than the county average. But two counties — Caernarfon and Meirionnydd — managed to teach the language so successfully at primary school that the percentage aged 5-9 speaking Welsh *exceeded* the county average.

PERCENTAGE SPEAKING WELSH, 1971

	All ages	Age 3-4	Age 5-9
Wales	20.9	11.3	14.5
Meirionnydd	73.5	63.9	78.6
Ceredigion	67.6	54.8	67.2
Caernarfon	61.6	55.8	64.4
Anglesey	65.7	49.2	59.9
Carmarthen	66.5	43.7	52.1
Carmarthen (excluding Llanelli)	70.6	48.7	58.4
Denbigh	28.1	14.4	19.4
Montgomery	28.1	15.8	19.3
Brecon	22.9	10.9	15.1
Pembroke	20.7	9.8	14.4
Flint	14.6	5.6	10.4
Glamorgan	11.7	3.9	5.6
Radnor	3.8	1.9*	1.4*
Gwent	2.1	0.8	1.0

* These figures are statistically not reliable.

In Ceredigion, the figures are within an ace of the county average; poor Anglesey, though, is probably still suffering from its recent influx of population. Of the anglicised counties, only Flint has put up a really good show.

The difficulty of making much impact on the situation is revealed in the Gwynedd figures for catchment areas where half or less of the pupils are native Welsh speakers. Bearing in mind that almost every school catchment area will include very Welsh areas, the success rate for anglicised areas is exaggerated by most of the figures. Even so, the schools centred on very Welsh areas can on average convert 11.2 per cent. of their pupils into fluent Welsh speakers. The other schools can manage only eight per cent., and the true anglicised area conversion figure may be nearer the three per cent. of Llandudno.

Advance in these anglicised, often middle-class, areas can be difficult. To a middle-class parent, the most important achievement for his child is learning to read, and often considerable opposition has had to be overcome when immersion-type programmes have been introduced in these schools, involving pupils learning to read in Welsh.

As one education official commented : " It needs guts to forestall this type of criticism." It is fair to add that a lot of the relevant officials would do nothing rather than incur this type of criticism, especially when they know the row will immediately reach the local MP and be rapidly escalated to involve the Welsh Office and the English daily press.

For years the policy in the heartland counties has generally been to allow English speakers to be naturally integrated into the local school, as a minority is integrated almost anywhere. The policy began to break down when the immigrants exceeded the native speakers. Fortunately for the sake of the language, many of the families who entered areas such as Llŷn in the last ten years have proved transitory and a school which one term was half English is the next almost entirely Welsh again.

To deal with the many who stayed, the most successful method seems special lessons from peripatetic teachers, as employed in Ceredigion and south Caernarfonshire. It is sad to hear, however, of opposition within Gwynedd County Council to such methods. Of course they are costly, but the problem is too serious to be left to luck and the ordinary classes at the local school, where the teachers may be hard-pressed already, without having to deal with youngsters who cannot understand the lessons.

Yet it is a sign of the times that in the whole of Gwynedd there was last winter only one primary school in which every pupil was a native Welsh speaker. That school, with just 21 pupils on the register, was at Ysbyty Ifan, on the remote upper reaches of the River Conwy.

It is indeed Gwynedd which is the only county to have really faced up to the situation in the primary schools. In June 1975 the authority gave its officers proposals to teach Welsh to every child in anglicised areas, beginning with nursery classes. Equal time would be given to each language, with the initial concentration on teaching the language orally, leading gradually to reading and writing, so that children will have gained complete mastery by the age of seven.

The policy document did not go into detail, but what is being proposed is very similar to the School Council bilingual project schools which are becoming increasingly common in the south-east and north-east.

The council also intend to make all incomers in the rural areas bilingual " as quickly as possible " so they can take part naturally in lessons. Unfortunately, the methods are not spelled out, and the £42,000 a year estimated for the entire project will not go far.

The most promising method of dealing with immigrants has still still to be tried, although the idea was apparently accepted in principle by Cardiganshire education committee. The plan, put forward by Undeb Cymru Fydd (New Wales Union) in 1967, involved setting up Welsh learning centres in the main towns of Aberystwyth, Tregaron, Aberaeron, Llandysul, Cardigan and Lampeter.

To these centres would be sent newcomers of junior school age for one-month intensive Welsh courses — shades of the Ulpan intensive learning courses started recently for adults. Transport would be no problem — the existing secondary school buses would be used.

Even late arrivals in the primary schools would then be able to integrate, rather than turning the language of play in the school yard to English, as so often happens. In the last couple of years, this idea has been resurrected by campaigners in Ceredigion fighting for Welsh-medium secondary schools.

8

The Secondary Schools

THE LINGUISTIC BLIMPS ARE STILL HALE AND HEARTY

While Celtic language maintenance has declined consistently on the periphery, this apparently has not been a direct consequence of industrialisation, but rather the result of political intervention by central government, in providing for compulsory public education on a monoglot basis.[1]

To describe the present policy of conducting almost all secondary education in the heartland areas through English as " linguistic imperialism " may seem harsh. But this was precisely the aim of the educational reformers of the mid-19th century, an essential part of the process of maintaining Wales as an internal colony of England.[2]

In many areas of life, the policy has been relaxed, but scarcely here. Indeed, in some ways it has been intensified, witness the recent appointment which ensured a monoglot English head and deputy head for a Carmarthenshire grammar school with a high proportion of Welsh speakers.

Having made some progress with official forms, road signs, courts and broadcasting, this is the field to which language campaigners have belatedly turned their attention, particularly in Dyfed, the county which is considered to have the fewest good intentions.

---

[1] M. Hechter, *Internal Colonialism, The Celtic Fringe in British National Development, 1536 - 1966* (London, 1975), p. 167.
[2] ibid. for a very full discussion of the situation in Wales, Scotland and Ireland, embracing in particular economic development, religious affiliation and culture.

In primary education, the taint which followed the Treachery of the Blue Books of 1847 has largely been eradicated : where it lingers can usually be blamed on human frailty, a factor difficult to legislate against.

The switch to Welsh-language instruction in the primary schools in the Welsh districts was indeed largely forced by the pressure of monoglot youngsters. The aim has always been, and still is, to ensure that every child is fluent in English by age 11 : only a few Irish cultural extremists have ever reached the corridors of educational power to argue otherwise.[3]

As a result, the argument that education *must* be in Welsh even after age 11 cannot hold water. Thus there has been no need for the grammar and secondary schools to change their age-old policies, although, to its credit, even a school such as Queen Elizabeth Girls' Grammar School, Carmarthen, bowed sufficiently recently to run a special class in English for native Welsh speakers.[4] Fundamentally, though, old 19th century policies are unchanged.

These policies were drawn up in a society much given to anti-Celtic racism :[5]

> From the 17th century on, English military and political control in the peripheral regions was buttressed by a racist ideology which held that Norman Anglo-Saxon culture was inherently superior to Celtic culture. English denigration of Celts and their culture survives today in at least one form, the ethnic joke.[6]

In 1846, the House of Commons sent its three monoglot English and Anglican commissioners to inquire into the state of education

---

[3] See Department of Education, *Report of the Council of Education on the Function of the Primary School and the Curriculum to be Pursued* (Dublin, 1954), p. 120.
[4] Mistakes to be eradicated included such as " I have pulled a picture ", a direct translation of " 'Rydw 'i wedi tynnu llun "
[5] Hechter, p. 269.
[6] ibid., p. 342. Hechter then goes on to quote from a review of Ned Thomas's " The Welsh Extremist " which appeared in the *New Statesman* (81, 2101 (1971)): " In the golden days of Oxford, when Balliol was remarkable for the number of niggers it took, and drunken Trinity louts had a chant which challenged Balliol to ' bring out its white men ', one scoffed at Jesus (College) for its connection with Wales. It was said that if you walked into the front quad of the college and called out ' Jones ' a face would appear at every window; if you then added, ' I mean, the Jones with the toothbrush ', all the faces would disappear."

in the thirteen counties. Sentence was pronounced before the three gentlemen even crossed Offa's Dyke : in his Commons speech requesting the investigation, Mr. William Williams, of Llanpumsaint, Carmarthenshire, made his aims quite clear :[7]

> If the Welsh had the same advantage for education as the Scotch, they would, instead of appearing as a distinct people, in no way differ from the English . . . The people of that country laboured under a peculiar difficulty from the existence of an ancient language . . . It should be borne in mind that an ill-educated and undisciplined population, like that existing among the mines in South Wales, is one that may be found most dangerous to the neighbourhood in which it dwells, and that a band of efficient schoolmasters is kept up at much less expense than a body of police or soldiery.

The commissioners naturally lived up to what was expected of them :

> The Welsh language is a vast drawback to Wales and a manifold barrier to the moral progress and commercial prosperity of the people.
> It bars the access of improving knowledge to their minds.
> Because of their language, the mass of the Welsh people are inferior to the English in every branch of practical knowledge and skill.

By continuing the commissioners' policy in secondary schools in the Welsh-speaking areas, today's education authorities are ensuring that, although the handicap of being " inferior to the English " is overcome, another is introduced, that of the inability of a proportion of their native-speaking alumni to take jobs requiring Welsh language qualifications.

At best, a Welsh speaker is forced to adapt English-language secretarial skills, for instance, with varying degrees of success. At worst, the Welsh-speaking former pupil finds that his or her command of the native tongue has been so little developed at the crucial secondary school level that he or she is debarred from jobs.

That something is hideously wrong is shown by the distribution of Welsh-medium comprehensive schools : In January 1975 there

[7] G. Evans, *Land of my Fathers* (Swansea, 1974), p. 367.

4. The daddy of all Cymdeithas yr Iaith sit-downs . . . the blocking of Trefechan Bridge, Aberystwyth, on February 2, 1963. Post Office vans are now bilingual.

(*Western Mail*)

5. Earlier that afternoon, language society members had plastered the town post office with posters demanding use of the language and official status.

(*Western Mail*)

were seven : Glan Clwyd, St. Asaph; Morgan Llwyd, Wrexham; Maes Garmon, Mold; Rhydfelen, Pontypridd; Ystalyfera; Llanhari; and Penweddig, Aberystwyth. Only the last serves a mainly Welsh catchment area. It is thus much easier to obtain Welsh-medium secondary education in an anglicised area than in the heartland. The deep-felt objections of parents who have to move children from the Welsh atmosphere of Pontypridd to the English one of our country towns is a deep reproach to the consciences of our councillors and their fidelity to the 1947 Education Act and its provisions for freedom of parental choice.

If education is one seamless garment, as is often argued, deep rents are introduced if Welsh primary education is followed by English secondary teaching. It has already been noted how this split can discourage effective Welsh teaching in primary schools.

The battle has been joined first in Dyfed, perhaps because Welsh is obviously in a perilous position in Carmarthenshire, but also because of the lack of commitment from the county council.

This campaign raises fundamental questions about the future pattern of secondary education in rural areas. If the education authority continues to prevaricate, it could lead to the forced closure of schools such as Tregaron because of lack of pupils caused by parents in the Aberystwyth side of the catchment area opting for Penweddig. The fundamental question is the right of Welsh speakers to live as complete a life as possible in their own districts. Thus the Glamorgan and Flintshire expedients of busing children perhaps twenty miles becomes unacceptable.

Such a method can only be accepted for a minority. But in Ceredigion, Preseli and much of Carmarthenshire it is the majority which is demanding the new-style education. In parts of Llandysul area, 90 per cent. of parents have opted for it.

With figures such as this, there can be no doubt about the demand. Yet the first campaign for a Welsh secondary school in Dyfed, for Carmarthen town, started fighting the county council as long ago as 1967, following the Urdd Eisteddfod. It came to a climax at the National Eisteddfod in the town in 1974, but still no date has been fixed for the opening.

Yet these seven years did far more to reveal the extent of opposition than physically to prepare the ground. Mr. Gwynfor

97

Evans, then and now once more MP for the constituency, took a leading part, and it is sad to relate, because it shows the lack of principle among the opposition, that senior educationists have said that had he played no part the school would by now (1976) be open.

In towns such as this, with more than one existing school, Welsh-medium education can easily be introduced. As at Aberystwyth, one school stays English-medium; the other goes Welsh. In Carmarthen the demand has been proved both by the parents' action group and by the education authority. Unfortunately, the lackadaisical education reputation that was Carmarthenshire's has been inherited by the new county of Dyfed.

Labour-controlled for so long, Carmarthenshire was, however, one of the Welsh counties least advanced on the comprehensive road. It was argued : " But we are all socialists and our hearts are thus in the right place," even if it meant dimmer kids still being pushed into sec. mods. and along the path to failure. And now that the county is belatedly trying to push forward its comprehensive plans, it has run into money troubles : the U.K.'s economic troubles means the Welsh Office has refused to allow the council to borrow the cash for the new buildings considered necessary for the change-over.

Never mind that one senior educationist with wide experience of Welsh schools is amazed at the excuse, considering it just another delaying tactic, overcomeable by any authority which is sufficiently determined. After all, this is scarcely an area of rapidly-growing population, the only factor, apart from extensive arson campaigns, which could really place a strain on school accommodation.

The excuse does, however, delay introduction of bilingual education in Carmarthen, Teifi Valley and the Gwendraeth valley, areas still with grammar schools. Yet there is no guarantee that comprehensive and Welsh schools will arrive together, because the authority wants to deal with comprehensive education before it comes on to the " thorny " topic of Welsh-medium.

The real problem arises in areas which are already comprehensive — the upper Tywi valley, mid and south Ceredigion, and north Pembrokeshire. All are sparsely populated districts, with schools typically 15 miles apart, each with between 400 and 600 pupils. In English terms, all are too small and too costly to run per pupil-unit. They have survived because of distance and local sentiment.

At two in particular, efforts have been made to reflect the local community (the correct implication is that the others have made little effort). But at both Tregaron and Crymych the weight of both monoglot English pupils and tradition has gravely weakened their stand for the language. That these schools are *not* Welsh is proved by the parent who, although he lives well within the Tregaron catchment area, insists on sending his children to the newly-founded Ysgol Penweddig at Aberystwyth.

At these schools, and in the Gwendraeth valley, Welsh streams have been introduced. This is an easy solution for the education administrator at County Hall, but it is no answer to the language problem. A Welsh-medium school — which does indeed teach some subjects, principally in science, through English — succeeds because it nurtures a completely Welsh atmosphere with Welsh the language of every member of staff, of the morning service, the societies, the notice-board, the games field and of every committee, concert and play.

Introduce a single English stream and the idea of Welsh as the official school administrative language must go for a burton. As the monoglots cannot be kept in pariah within the buildings, teachers will find it easier to switch to English on most occasions outside the classroom.

Equally unsatisfactory is the introduction of Welsh streams in an English school, a policy which Dyfed is considering extending. Whether intended or not, this has the result of pushing Welsh " under the counter ". In a school teaching everything through English, Welsh streams are obviously a luxury, particularly in smaller institutions.

Few children will draw attention to themselves by opting for the minority class, particularly in their first days in a large institution when everything is unfamiliar :[8]

> Even if they have come from a primary school which has worked hard to give them the necessary standard of literacy in Welsh, the inferior status, the inferior teaching material and

[8] *Better Education for Dyfed*, p. 5.

the implicit contempt from the more conservative on the staff will drive the children into the safe anonymity of the large classes.

Few children will, however, get even that choice, for how is linguistic streaming to be introduced in a comprehensive school of only two-form entry? Even when introduced, perhaps in a larger school, how often will it be possible to offer a realistic course throughout the school? There will be grave danger of falling into the Irish trap : many schools in the Free State offered teaching through Irish, often compulsory, but so often Irish lessons one year were followed by English the next, even in so-called Irish-medium schools. Recently the number of such schools and courses has fallen heavily,[9] and it is difficult not to lay part of the blame on this educationally-unsound practice.

In Wales, one can see difficulties arising from conflicts over administrative convenience, class size, subject choice and language streaming. Much will depend on the character and dedication of a particular headmaster, not a very sound basis on which to establish the linguistic character of a school. Doubts have also been raised about the amount of work involved in teaching the same subject in two languages, especially as the teacher through Welsh must rely less on teaching aids.

One must also asked, which subjects are available in which language? How often are the lessons available through Welsh (in addition to Welsh), subjects such as religious instruction and history? R.I. is quite widely available, but it is a topic which is hardly likely to appear near the top of the pupils' popularity charts. Thus as soon as Welsh starts to climb out of one ghetto, it is pushed into another. In usefulness to the children and general prestige, the language has moved hardly at all :

> In describing the influence of teaching some some subjects in one language on a person's bilingualism, it is important to determine which subjects are taught in which language. If one of the languages is used for religion, history and literature, the influence is likely to be different than it would be if this

[9] Comhairle Na Gaeilge, *Irish in Education* (Dublin, 1974), p. 17.

language were used to teach arithmetic, geography and biology instead.[10]

The very lack of interest by both parents and pupils in this sort of solution (see, for instance, the complaints by the headmaster of Lampeter Secondary School, *Cambrian News*, 3.10.1975), will push principals and administrators towards the only acceptable solution, the full-blooded one.

In these rural areas there are two choices : a couple of central Welsh-medium schools, or the conversion of the existing institutions. To bus Welsh speakers in the heartland is abhorrent to many and would probably force the closure through loss of pupils of whichever of Tregaron, Aberaeron and Lampeter were not chosen for the site. Closure of Tregaron school would be an economic disaster for the town.

To bus the English speakers to perhaps Aberystwyth and Cardigan would cost less and should not endanger even Tregaron school. The numbers involved should be low, as the old Ceredigion authority, unlike Carmarthenshire, has made real efforts to integrate incomers. Gwynedd County Council's survey shows that in the stronger Welsh-speaking areas surprisingly few pupils are unable to benefit from Welsh-medium secondary education.

The main opposition to converting the present schools into naturally Welsh institutions has come from the existing teachers. Some are admittedly too old to change their ways and should be left in peace; others need reassuring with intensive courses and, say, a five-year change-over period. All need a promise that their jobs are guaranteed : as a change of linguistic character such as this entails issue of closure notices, and as Ceredigion staffs are appointed to an individual school and not to the authority, some teachers have partly justifiable fears about their futures.

There is next to no hope of the Welsh Office pushing reluctant local authorities towards Welsh secondary schools. Mr. John Morris, Secretary of State for Wales, is quite blunt. He say : " In education, local authorities get an enormous amount of guidance. But they also have a great amount of expertise. If I were to tread on the toes of county education committees I would be in very great difficulty."

[10] W. Mackey, "The Description of Bilingualism", in J. Fishman (ed.), *Readings in the Sociology of Language* (The Hague, 1968), p. 562.

But if the Government is more than willing to tread on their toes to force introduction of comprehensive education, on what grounds can a British Government stand aside and allow a county to be derelict in its duty towards the historic language of Wales in its heartland?

Problems exist, too, in the Welsh-medium secondary schools, but they are of a diffcrent order. A lot of them revolve around the standard of Welsh of the learners who arrive from the Welsh primary schools. The teaching of the basic skills of language is usually considered the task of the primary, not the secondary, school. When the task involves teaching these skills in a second tongue in a school in an area where that language is scarcely heard and with scarcely a classmate speaking that language, the immensity of the job can be realised.

As the years have passed, the problem has worsened with the increase in popularity of Welsh education, both swamping the native speakers and demanding far more staff. There is no doubt that good teachers succeed in inducing this linguistic change, but there is a limit to the number of dedicated teachers, and it is often said that some teachers are in Welsh primary schools " just because it's another job " — which is just what it isn't.

One of the basic rules in such teaching is that the teachers use only the second language, even between themselves, and if they have to use the pupils' first language to a visitor, either a pupil translates or the teacher leaves the room with the visitor.[11]

But the combination of poorer teachers and a slap-happy attitude that " We've succeeded before with such children, so why bother too much with the rules " is leading to poorer products being turned out, to the secondary schools having to do part of the primary schools' job. Thus we have had primary teachers speaking to pupils, both in and out of class, in English, and even almost entire lessons, including blackboard work, being done in that language when it is Welsh that should have been employed.

The sheer dedication at the secondary level does, however, overcome these problems. After all, Clwyd has recently, as an

---

[11] A. Cohen, " Successful Immersion Education in North America ", *Working Papers on Bilingualism, No. 5* (Toronto, 1975), p. 41.

experiment, started admitting pupils to Welsh-medium secondary schools straight from English-medium primaries.

The lack of solid state backing for Welsh schools shows up at several levels. Complaints come from many sides about the lack of suitable training teachers have been given for second-language work. Although the colleges of education will vehemently deny the charge, one very senior educationist dealing with the second-language field went as far as to say : " I would dearly love to know what the training colleges have done to change their methods to enable them to cope with teachers who will instruct English children in the bilingual schools. I get the impression that it is just about nothing. Certainly some of the methods they are teaching are as old as the colleges themselves."

This complaint is borne out by the Welsh Joint Education Committee :

> There are complaints that some teachers leaving college have not attained satisfactory standards of fluency in Welsh or competence to teach Welsh. Some of them are unaware of the exact nature of the courses prepared at the National Language Unit, by the Schools Council and by the local education authorities, and of their relevance to Welsh language teaching, and few know how to use correctly the tapes and filmstrips produced at the unit.[12]

When his report calls for " the closest possible co-operation between the teaching staffs of the training institutions and the advisory staffs of the local authorities ", it is because present co-operation just is not good enough.

These critics know that among the staff in the colleges whom they are criticising are men and women of unimpeachable loyalty towards the language. Perhaps the fault in these colleges lies at a slightly higher level, in other words, with the principals and governors. After all, to them the Welsh section is just one of many, and there are a host of other problems to deal with as well.

The answer can only lie in a college which sees the Welsh language as its *raison d'etre,* in which the problems of Welsh are

---

[12] Welsh Joint Education Committee, *Report on the Teaching of Welsh in Primary and Secondary Schools* (Cardiff, 1974).

central rather than peripheral. After all, if Welsh does not get this priority treatment in Wales, it won't get it anywhere else. Although the demands for a comprehensive tertiary level comprehensive college (combining university, training college and polytechnic provision) have inclined to rest on language rights and the demands of students, it is in the sphere of what the language *needs* that the case is perhaps strongest.

This same WJEC survey also revealed that the present set-up was just not delivering enough teachers. In the secondary field, the numbers coming forward were enough to set up one new school a year, but no more. The survey revealed a shortage of 59 nursery teachers (for local authority schools), 135 primary teachers, and 30 secondary teachers. Ominously, it added that the situation was worsening, which raises important questions about the ability of Welsh-medium education to expand in the anglicised areas.

This problem for these areas will only worsen if the heartland concept catches people's imagination. Already, in the primary sector, schools in the less attractive valleys of the south have difficulty attracting teachers : they are having to take anyone who can speak Welsh, even as a second language, despite the Bullock Committee warning that to speak English was not a qualification for teaching that language.

If the heartland concept catches on, they could not only fail to get newcomers, but could also lose some of the old stalwarts. Although there are a number of " unknowns " in the valleys situation, such as the numbers who have passed through Ulpanim courses and can be added to the Welsh teaching stock, the weaknesses are obvious.

9

Local Government

ALREADY A WELSH GAELTACHT

The four council clerks were asked for their views about the future of the Welsh language in local government. All thought it had no future.[1]

How right, and wrong, were these gentlemen can be vividly seen 12 years later. In the south-east, local councils are refusing to answer letters in Welsh; in the north-west, other councils are happily spending ratepayers' cash ensuring that nothing for general distribution leaves the offices in English unless it is in Welsh too.

To some extent, this situation certainly reflects a conspiracy against the language by some councillors. But it far more reflects a far deeper and, at the same time, more obvious situation . . . the numbers of Welsh speakers in a council's area. Too few in Wales have ever taken note of this fact when trying to draw up plans for the very labour-intensive industry that is local government, but it was a cardinal point in the deliberations of the Canadian Royal Commission on bilingualism.

Consider first the plight of councils in the anglicised districts. Certainly, some of them are just asking for a sit-in at their council chambers by members of Cymdeithas yr Iaith Gymraeg infuriated at them flouting one of the fundamental freedoms of man.[2]

---

[1] Council for Wales, *Report on the Welsh Language Today* (London, 1963), p. 48.
[2] Article 1 of the Charter of the United Nations states that the purpose of the U.N. is to " . . . promote and encourage respect for human rights and for fundamental freedoms for all without distinction as to race, sex, language, or religion ". The Declaration of Human Rights is based on this.

Actions such as those by Taff-Ely Borough Council (covering the Pontypridd area) seem especially designed to exacerbate the situation and produce the Northern Ireland situation which some councillors see just around the corner. The council's formal pronouncement sounds more like the last trumpet call from a dying empire than a communication from newly-reorganised Welsh local authority :

> By minute 3083 of Council meeting on 25.3.75 it was decided that if the public wish to write to the Council in Welsh, the letter should also be written in English.[3]

This is not an isolated example, because the neighbouring Rhymney Valley District Council follows the same policy. Presumably it has not occurred to the councillors who passed these policies that they are blatantly flouting the Declaration of Human Rights : that this was done in the name of the Labour Party only emphasises the low level to which this party, renowned world-wide for its fight for the rights of man and the dismantling of empire, has sunk in the valleys it dominates. Both authorities can get away with this policy only because of the very low proportions of Welsh speakers in their areas (Taff-Ely 6.7 per cent., Rhymney Valley 7.3 per cent.) : there just are not enough Cymdeithas members around to cause much bother.

Behind these councils' attitudes lies, however, a more realistic view of the situation than that propounded by certain members of Cymdeithas yr Iaith, who call for the pursuit of policies as Welsh as those demanded in the heartland. What is sadly lacking among the members of both these councils is a wish to see both language communities to live together in a peace other than that of the dominator and the pacified; if they have not the qualified staff to deal with the very occasional letter received in Welsh, I am sure the Welsh Office translation unit would be delighted to oblige.

It is the question of staff which lies behind many of the reasons given for refusing to accede to linguistic requests. Some will articulate this as a fear that all the jobs will go to Welsh speakers; the more sensible, who realise that there is not a hope on this earth of getting bilingual staff to man these anglicised authorities, fear the burden which could be imposed.

[3] *Y Cymro*, 10.6.75.

Mr. D. Windsor Morgan is the clerk to Rhymney Valley Council. A Welsh speaker from Aberdâr, he is quite capable of understanding correspondence in Welsh and of writing the reply. But that is the problem; he would almost surely have to write and type the letter himself. Of the council's 400 staff, only five others, none of them chief officers, can speak Welsh.

Politics do, of course, come into it. Plaid Cymru election successes have served to focus attention on things that party is supposed to stand for, and some Labour councillors have dubbed Plaid " the language party ", very unfairly, as the local branches for long blatantly ignored successive national conference decisions calling for bilingual literature.

As Welsh is seen as a Plaid weapon, most things connected with the language have been opposed as part of the cut and thrust of party battle. The situation has been exacerbated by the letters that the council has received only in Welsh having come from a local person whom they consider a member of Cymdeithas yr Iaith. As the society centrally had for a time dropped the policy of sending communications bilingually to local councils, the authority considered the letter an attempt to get them to use Welsh against their will.

There is a loophole in the policy : if Mr. Morgan receives a letter in Welsh, but where there is no political motive, he would translate it himself. Quite how far this extends is unclear; the example given by the clerk is of old people whose Welsh is better than their English. Similarly, the clerk would correspond with these few in Welsh, after having a word with the ward member just to check their bona fides !

There is a strong taste here of the situation in the courts prior to the passing of the Welsh Language Act of 1967; before that date " the Welsh language may be used in any court in Wales by any party or witness who considers that he would otherwise be at a disadvantage by reason of his natural language of communication being Welsh ".[4] Despite the wording of the Act and a specific statement from the Home Office, a legal figure as notable as the

[4] Welsh Courts Act, 1942.

Lord Chief Justice himself ruled that this was a matter for the court, and not the Welsh speaker, to decide.[5]

Which seems just about the position taken by Rhymney Valley Council.

If staffing is one reason for pursuing a policy which many would consider anti-Welsh, another is the small percentage in the valley still using the language. While excuses of cost do not hold much water, as even the Welsh Office avow in their circulars to local authorities, the excuse that it is a waste of effort as hardly anyone will read it bears far more weight. Why produce something which can be understood by only one in 14 of the population, especially as many of these by force of habit or lack of understanding of official terms in Welsh will voluntarily read the English version?

Much literature from any council goes to only a fraction of the population. With only 5,700 Welsh speakers in the Rhymney Valley, how many would be receiving copies of some of the more obscure forms? Can anyone really imagine officials sitting down and translating such forms for a handful of readers, especially if, as so often happens, they are returned in English? As the council obviously has not the staff, is a translation department really a feasible policy for such an authority?

A survey by the Council for Wales found that in 1960 three-quarters of the local government staffs cited as needing Welsh worked in education departments.[6] The vast majority of these are teachers; in the department offices the situation can be vastly different. For instance, the administrative staff at Mid-Glamorgan's education offices in Cardiff are almost 100 per cent. English speaking. The Director of Education says he has been trying for some years to get a bilingual secretary.

A limited amount of bilingualism is practised, however, with some forms available in both English and Welsh. And Glamorgan County Council used rigorously to give all its schools the correct Welsh forms of place-names. But, again, any considerable increase in the amount of Welsh used causes difficulties, with the director having to type letters himself. Even a vigorous recruitment campaign

[5] R. Lewis, *Second Class Citizen* (Llandysul, 1969), p. 33.
[6] Council for Wales, p. 42.

would probably have little effect — beyond pushing up the amount institutions like the BBC pay to keep bilingual staff — because Cardiff area produces far too few bilinguals and the demand is too great. Some organisations make a particular point of concentrating their advertising on newspapers like *The Cambrian News,* Aberystwyth, trying to tempt native speakers away from their homes.

It is not that Welsh speakers are boycotting these councils : In 1965 a survey found that only one of the 179 administrative and clerical staff of the Newport and East Monmouthshire Hospital Management Committee spoke Welsh.[7] For some other anglicised districts the figures were : North Monmouthshire, none out of 70; Cardiff, two out of 174; Merthyr and Aberdare, two out of 69; Clwyd and Deeside, 28 out of 121; and Welsh Border, four out of 17.

The Canadians chose 10 per cent. of minority-language speakers as the proportion for determining bilingual provinces and districts. The Royal Commission commented :[8]

> In a province where the official-language minority formed only five per cent. of the population . . . it would be difficult for it to supply the number of skilled personnel necessary to establish a bilingual provincial system (for example, in the judiciary and in education).

The predilection in the Welsh-speaking areas for the brighter youngsters to go in for teaching means that education should cause no problem in any Welsh bilingual districts : if 5 per cent. were the break point, there would, however, be considerable difficulties over administrative and executive staff, in central as much as local government.

Central government keeps no detailed records; all that can be used are the lists of candidates taking Welsh in the Civil Service Commission's written examinations.[9] The numbers are consistently very small and the impression that there are very few Welsh speakers occupying positions of any importance seems borne out by the figures.

[7] Welsh Office, *Legal Status of the Welsh Language* (Hughes Parry Report) (London, 1965), p. 74.
[8] Royal Commission on Bilingualism and Biculturalism, *Report, Book 1, The Official Languages* (Ottawa, 1967), p. 99.
[9] Council for Wales, p. 37.

Of those taking the executive class examinations, no more than 10 in any half year submitted Welsh. In the 10 years surveyed that 10 also provided the highest proportion of the U.K. total — 0.9 per cent., just under the one per cent. that would be expected were Welsh speakers to be represented according to their proportion in the U.K. population. Typically, the figure varied between 0.3 and 0.6 per cent., with a low point of nil.

It's a brighter situation among clerical class candidates, with a high point of 52 candidates in one half year, giving a proportion of 2.1. Consistently the one per cent. " fairness figure " is breached. The impression, however, is that the Welsh speakers provide the coolies for the civil service, while the English send in the mandarins.

Leave the anglicised areas for the heartland districts and the jobs position radically changes. Not, though, because of any positive policies by local authorities but just because most people who apply for jobs will naturally be Welsh speaking. Even Gwynedd County Council, with a thorough-going Welsh policy, does not usually specify the language as a qualification, except for chief officers.

The siting of the headquarters in Caernarfon (86.5 per cent. Welsh-speaking) has enormously helped the policy because of the linguistic nature of the staff catchment area. The alternative siting which was being urged (at Bangor) would, on the other hand, have been a near disaster, as only 53.4 per cent. of the city's populace speak Welsh, and I have already noted the " anti " views of some.

Difficulties do arise, though, especially over higher technical staff, a long-time problem. The general shortage of staff in some departments is allied with the shortage of training facilities in Wales, plus the major growth of these professions in major urban centres (which means England), to produce the necessity for even the most language-minded council to employ monoglots.

The real problem in the Welsh areas is, however, the weight of tradition in favour of English, a tradition so strong that the Council for Wales report on the language, issued under the chairmanship of Professor Richard Aaron, concluded, after a review of a thoroughly dismal situation, " It seems that relatively few Welsh-speaking persons choose to transact their business with the administration, including that conducted in writing, in Welsh."[10]

Mr. Ioan Bowen Rees has commented that the biggest problem in getting a bilingual policy going in Gwynedd County Council, where he is county secretary, has been the lack of official tradition. And this is in the area, the districts longest under independent Welsh rule, where what tradition there is is strongest. Yet it had painfully atrophied, to the extent that, when the old Caernarfonshire County Council was beginning to go bilingual, only 30 forms were available in Welsh or bilingually in 1969.[11]

It was during the 18th century that English really made big inroads into governmental administration on a local level when, under an Act of 1730-1, the use of Latin was abolished in courts in favour of English. Parish registers followed, but in parts of the North the switch was not from Latin but from Welsh.

A feeling in favour of Welsh lingered on, though. When county councils were set up in 1889, Meirionnydd decided it wanted to keep its minutes in Welsh. The matter was referred to the Attorney-General, who said the " claim to keep records of counties and other resolutions and orders in the Welsh language cannot in my judgement be admitted as legal ".[12]

In the event, Meirionnydd was still, when it went out of existence, keeping to that old legal judgement. Some councils, though, never got around to asking the Attorney-General.

Thirteen district councils, in the event, kept their minutes in Welsh. Every one was in Gwynedd.[13] Dyfed, many areas of which have as high proportions of Welsh speakers, has no place in this table of Welshness. Similarly, it was only in Gwynedd that every local council replied in Welsh to a letter written in Welsh.[14]

Outside these limited spheres, English has ruled almost supreme. So often, fluent Welsh-speaking councillors switch to English immediately they enter the council chamber and then struggle to participate in the debate, or, more likely, say nothing. The Council for Wales and Hughes Parry reports both, by implication, criticised

---

[10] ibid., p. 51.
[11] R. Lewis, *Y Gymraeg d'r Cyngor* (Bangor, n.d.), p. 8.
[12] Welsh Office, p. 13.
[13] Council for Wales, p. 40.
[14] ibid., p. 45.

Welsh speakers for not making proper use of their rights. So often, councillors and officials expressed a preference for English, sometimes arguing they did not know local government terms in Welsh.

Much store was laid on the recent council reorganisation. In Gwynedd, the opportunity was indeed seized to give Welsh its rightful place. The foundations were simultaneous translation of council and committee meetings, official forms, and councillors and officials who believed in the language.

They were determined to succeed, in the knowledge that if they muffed it in Gwynedd, the language would get no second chance in local government in any other area. Cost has been no bar — yet the total for a thorough-going policy is only £73,400 a year, equal to 0.18 per cent. of the budget, or a charge on the ratepayers, after deducting Government grants, of one-fifth of a penny rate. In any case, the policy is seen as a worthwhile investment in defusing the situation and giving justice to both Welsh and English speakers (GCC Policy and Resources Committee, 31.7.1975).

Of the 750 forms issued to the public or to staff by February 1975, about 670 had been translated or were in the course of being translated. Least-used forms are being left until last, with preference being given to bilingual versions : separate Welsh and English versions are unpopular because of cost and the necessity for either displaying both or asking which version a person wishes, a question which could, in view of tradition, so easily be dropped in favour of simply handing out the English form.

That the policy has the full backing of staff and public is revealed by the completely unselfconscious manner in which it is being carried out. Councillors have taken to their translating equipment like ducks to water; most now speak in Welsh and a considerable improvement in the standard of debate has been noted.

Significantly, in this era of rising rates and inflation biting into wages, the policy has brought complaints that not enough is done in Welsh. Forms still not translated have been an especial target. Few complaints have been registered from the " antis ". The provision of Welsh is increasing the appetite for more. It has also reversed a trend among parish (now community) councils which had been slowly switching to English.

6. The start of another major Cymdeithas yr Iaith campaign, one which is still under way . . . members assemble at Wybrnant, near Penmachno, before painting out the first of thousands of English-only road signs. *(Geoffrey Charles)*

7. Law-breaking often led to jail . . . society members protest outside Swansea Prison in May 1966 at the imprisonment of their secretary, Mr. Geraint Jones.

(Western Mail)

8. The often cynical purchase by rich outsiders of rural homes, sometimes needed by local people, led to a series of cottage occupations by members of Cymdeithas yr Iaith. This one occurred in January 1973. *(Western Mail)*

9. The BBC came in for a lot of stick for broadcasting each week 480 hours in English, 70 in Arabic, and 18 in Welsh. Inside Cardiff newsroom on November 30, 1968.

(Western Mail)

Most of the translation is done by the translator and four translator/trainee administrators, rather than by departmental officials, because of the elitist view about correct Welsh, a line not taken about the horrible standard of English often found on government forms (although academics do like complaining about journalese!). The staffing necessary to service the council lends no credence to fears that equality for Welsh will mean armies of translators tramping the country. About three-quarters of the time of the translator/trainee administrators is spent on translations, a figure which will probably fall once the bulk of initial work is completed.

Gwynedd is the only one of the new county councils which is linguistically-speaking a success. One of the disasters of the re-organisation was that the langage was hardly taken into account, civil servants being far too concerned with tidy, equal patterns, acreages and rateable values.

Thus Powys has landed up with strongly Welsh-speaking areas at its northern and southern extremities. A very Welsh area of the old Meirionnydd County Council was handed over to the Flintshire and Wrexham-dominated Clwyd. The district council boundaries are even worse, with only six councils having a certain majority of Welsh speakers. In Preseli, for instance, the completely differing Welsh and English-speaking sections of Pembrokeshire were joined. Anglicised Llandudno stayed in Aberconwy instead of being joined with Colwyn Bay, while Colwyn District Council stretches from the colonists of Lancashire on the coast into areas where more than 80 per cent. of the population speak Welsh.

Glyndŵr suffers from stretching from semi-anglicised areas near Denbigh right up into the mountains. Montgomery manages to encompass Llanfyllin and Machynlleth, as well as Welshpool and Newtown.

Much trite rubbish was spewed out beforehand about the effects of such mergers on the language. We were told the Welsh areas would have a beneficial effect on the English districts. Common-sense, often absent when politicians are pushing a policy affecting the Welsh language, said otherwise, and few would disagree today with the commonsense view.

113

The worst situation in a heartland area is undoubtedly that in Dyfed, where the county council, which had the linguistic base to formulate a strong language policy, has done very little. While Gwynedd adopted a policy and then waded in, Dyfed has put its toe in the water, found the temperature not quite to its liking, and withdrawn for contemplation.

After considerable consideration, one translator was appointed, who slowly moved in on the pile of county council forms. He is not being allowed anywhere near weightier items like prospectuses, or council minutes. Not that a decision has been taken about whether all forms will be bilingual — that has still to be considered by the council, some of whose members are concerned about costs.

It was the £8,000 cost for simultaneous translating equipment for the council chamber that caused the item's deletion from the estimates for 1975-6. For the benefit of the rate-conscious councillors, that was 0.01 per cent. of the budget. Even had it been installed, it might have had to stay unused because there was no provision for money to pay an interpreter, the translator being unable to do the job.

For Ceredigion, the Dyfed set-up is quite a step backwards. In their final months, Cardiganshire Education Committee had started sending out its minutes in Welsh. The education department sent all its circulars to teachers bilingually, and the normal language of the office was Welsh. The same cannot be said of Dyfed's offices.

In Dyfed, the tradition of Welsh-speaking councillors using English on council business continues with a vengeance. Many of them will drop Welsh immediately they enter an official's office. Cost to them is just an excuse; many of them do not seem in favour of the principle. Perhaps, significantly, it is in Dyfed that officials are most prone to look to the future and wonder how long before the new Welsh Assembly makes them superfluous : Dyfed seems to be an amalgamation no one is happy with, perhaps because of the stresses and strains of a county council deeply unsure of its linguistic basis, with wide areas perhaps on the verge of losing their Welsh.

The battle in Dyfed County Council is going to be long, bitter and slow when a Welsh-speaking councillor can go as far as to complain about a county council telephone being answered in Welsh.

In Ireland, despite Irish being the official first language of the state, local authorities give no lead to Wales:[15]

> So far, the language has achieved only an insignificant place in the system of local government. It is rarely used at meetings of local authorities and their subsidiary bodies, even of those in counties which contain Gaeltacht areas. While advances have been made in the use of written Irish in such things as street names, public notices, inscriptions, forms, correspondence, etc., the practice of using Irish in these is by no means universal and serves merely to underline the failure to advance in other areas.

The strongest recommendation of the Government commission for reviving Irish was that Irish versions of all documents be made available in the Gaeltacht: the Government's action was to " commend " the recommendation to the local authorities and " encourage " them to implement it.[16] By the following year, letters had been sent to the various councils telling them how they could implement the decisions.[17] But little has been done, and no one seems to expect changes.

It was regarded as a small victory that Galway County Council refrained from cleaning road signposts on which the English version of Gaeltacht names (which are considerably larger than the Irish) had been obliterated with paint. In the rural areas, the county is the lowest level of government, and each Gaeltacht forms only part of a county.

The whole Irish effort has, indeed, been too mechanical. According to regulations, a wide range of posts in the Gaeltacht were open only to Irish speakers. As the necessary doctors and so forth were not available, non-Irish speakers have had to be appointed. Out of all local appointments made in the Gaeltacht by the Local Appointments Commission (who deal with many posts which in Wales would be covered by local councils) in the year ended March

---

[15] Commission on the Restoration of the Irish Language, *Summary in English of Final Report* (Dublin, 1963), p. 31.
[16] *Restoration of the Irish Language, Progress Report to 1965* (Dublin, 1965), p. 38.
[17] *Restoration of the Irish Language, Progress Report to 1966* (Dublin, 1966).

1962, only 49 out of 91 had a competent or good knowledge of Irish. Such appointees are, according to Government regulations, supposed to acquire the language within three years, but amendments to the regulations have made them a dead letter.[18]

Outside the Gaeltacht, the Government made Irish necessary for all the top local government jobs, and priority for other jobs was given to Irish speakers. The commission sadly commented, however, that the system had not ensured a knowledge of Irish, never mind its use. Their recommendations that the regulations be brought into full use and non-Irish speaking Gaeltacht officers sacked if they did not learn the language were, hardly surprisingly, rejected.

The situation in Canada could hardly be more different, mainly because the demands for linguistic equality come from the grass roots. Quebec for long had been the only bilingual province in the dominion. Bill No. 22 changed all that by enacting French as the official language.[19] Some areas of the province are mainly English speaking, but their local authorities are now compelled to do everything in French. Admittedly, if at least 10 per cent. of the population is English-speaking and it has been the practice to issue documents in English, this must continue, but only the French version is authentic.

Every communication from a local authority or state organisation to the provincial government has to be in French, unless most of the persons administered are English speaking, in which case either language may be used. The working language is also laid down as being French, except in English-majority areas.

Despite the presence throughout Quebec of monoglot English speakers, the Bill also provides that public notices need be published only in French.

Bitterly attacked though this Bill was, with hints that it was unconstitutional, it has been put into full operation. Thirty-two municipalities in western Quebec, just across the river from Ottawa, the federal capital, and English-speaking Ontario, were told that in future they would have to deal with the Outaouais regional

[18] Commission on the Restoration of the Irish Language, p. 32.
[19] National Assembly of Quebec, 30th legislature, 2nd session, Bill No. 22, Official Language Act, assented to 31.7.74.

government in French only.[20] The information flow in the reverse direction would also be exclusively French (except for brief English summaries), the regional government would not hire anyone unable to speak French, and monoglot English speakers would not be promoted.

Bill 22 was passed with the intention of protecting French from the encroachments of English. If the Quebecois, who have wide areas of their country mainly peopled by French speakers who know no English, consider legislation necessary, how much more needed is that form of protection in Wales!

[20] *Montreal Star,* 15.11.74.

10

Central Government

THE MURDER MACHINE

The decree went forth
to destroy the language — " not cariad "
they said, " love ".[1]

As the growth of central government inexorably marches onwards, fuelled by citizens' demands for increased and better services, the Welsh language is being eased into a corner from whence it can be exhumed for the extremist or two who demands the occasional form or leaflet that is available in the language.

The role of governments in the decline of the language is gigantic, not so much for what they did, but rather for what they have not done. Much emphasis has been laid on the " murder machine " of compulsory English education; too little has been said about that other " murder machine " which now permeates every slice of life — the government.

The Victorian age has often been described as the " glorious age " of Welsh literature, when dozens of newspapers appeared in the language, when massive multi-volume encyclopaedias were sold and books proliferated. The language was even then being undermined, including by one of the factors which did so much to give it strength and bring about this literary revival — industry and associated immigration.

---

[1] From R. S. Thomas, " It Hurts Him to Think ", *What is a Welshman?* (Llandybïe, 1974), p. 12.

But of the now ever-present government there was scarce a trace :[2]

> The individual a hundred years ago hardly needed to know that the central government existed. His birth, marriage and death would be registered, and he might be conscious of the safeguards for his security provided by the forces of law and order and of imperial defence; but, except for the very limited provisions of the poor law and factory legislation, his welfare and progress were matters for which he alone bore the responsibility. By the turn of the century the position was not much changed.
>
> Today, however, the individual citizen submits himself to the guidance of the state at all times. His schooling is enforced; his physical well-being can be looked after in a comprehensive health service; he may be helped by government agencies to find and train for a job; he is obliged while in employment to insure against sickness, accident and unemployment; his house may be let to him by a public authority or he may be assisted in its purchase or improvement; he can avail himself of a wide range of government welfare allowances and services; and he draws a state pension on his retirement.

At the end of the last century, there were not more than 50,000 non-industrial civil servants; in this century there has been a tenfold increase, while the population of the U.K., which has itself lost Ireland, has increased only by half.

If democratic government is supposed to proceed from the people, the government suffered by Welsh speakers verges on a dictatorship, with an occasional sop thrown to the masses in the shape of a bilingual form to keep them quiet and blur the real situation.

It is difficult to disagree, other than marginally, with Cynog Davies :[3]

> Despite some marginal alleviations in the sphere of education, despite literary and scholastic revivals, in the fundamental context where the Welshman came face-to-face with authority, where his rights and duties as a citizen and as an individual were in question, Welsh had no place whatsoever.

[2] Royal Commission on the Constitution, *Report, Vol. 1* (London, 1973), p. 76.
[3] Cynog Davies, " Cymdeithas yr Iaith — The Manifesto ", *Planet* 26/27, p. 106.

119

This was realised by the framers of the Welsh Language Petition of 1938, who gained 394,860 signatures calling for Welsh to have " the same rights as English in all aspects of the administration of the law and public service in Wales ".[3a]

The result of the petition was the Welsh Courts Act of 1942. To Nationalists this was a great betrayal, increasing the status of the language only in that a legal right now existed for use of Welsh in courts by any person who " might otherwise be at a disadvantage ", and that the Welsh speaker would no longer have to pay for his translator.

Wales has often been incredibly naïve in its efforts to obtain concessions from Parliament; it seems that few saw that this bid for official public service status was being outflanked from the very beginning. The petition itself followed as a result of the court hearings against the Penyberth three (Saunders Lewis, Lewis Valentine and D. J. Williams), and one of the earliest people to take up the cry was Alderman William George, younger brother of David Lloyd George, from the chair of Undeb y Cymdeithasau Cymraeg, which eventually led the campaign. But he referred only to status in the courts.

There is no doubt that by the time the politicians got hold of the idea it was only this they were concerned with. At a meeting in Cardiff, presided over by the Deputy Lord Mayor, both Mr. James Griffiths, MP for Llanelli, and Captain Ernest Evans, MP for the University of Wales, waxed eloquent, but only in the cause of the poor man in court. The chairman concurred.[4]

Prior to the rise of governmental power, the main outside body with which the man-in-the-street or in the fields came into contact was the church. And here Welsh was undoubtedly the official language, to the extent that the Acts of 1563 and 1662 were held to prohibit the holding of English services.[5] Hughes-Parry commented :[6]

It was the status enjoyed by Welsh and its regular use as the official language of worship in the Established Church (and

[3a] Western Mail, 23.10.41.
[4] Western Mail, 25.3.39. See J. E. Jones, Tros Gymru (Abertawe, 1970), tt. 207-10, for the official Nationalist view.
[5] Legal Status, p. 12.
[6] ibid.

later among the Dissenting congregations) which has marked it off from its sister Celtic languages in Great Britain and Ireland. It appears to be the principal reason why Welsh held its ground so successfully in contrast to the much swifter decay of languages like Irish, Gaelic or Cornish.

Today, the same status is needed in the new spheres of importance :[7]

> The main crippling disability remains : Welsh has not obtained proper and full official status. No language can maintain itself in the modern world without such recognition.

That the language does not have that status is manifest. Very rarely are government services actually *offered* in Welsh, although it may be possible to demand them, if you don't mind wasting what could be a lot of time and risking considerable unpopularity from staff who have never before dealt with such a request. Despite advances of recent years, the comment by the Hughes Parry Report probably needs little updating : Welsh is hardly used by government departments except to provide a limited number of forms and correspondence with members of the public who so request.[8]

This is the situation in which Mr. John Morris, Secretary of State for Wales, says that the language has been facing a crisis for years, and that to translate 400 forms into Welsh (in 10 years) is " a tremendous achievement ". Mr. Morris, a native Welsh speaker, has considerable and genuine feeling for the language and for Wales (he was deputy general secretary of the Farmers' Union of Wales), but his solutions are very weak, although not perhaps to some of the anglomaniac backwoodsmen of his party.

Asked if a crisis package were needed, he replied significantly in money terms : " I have inherited my job at the time of a money crisis. I only wish I were minister at a time of great affluence. Welsh books, for instance, got £1,000 a year in 1961; now it is £25,000." After being held for three years, it was raised in February 1976 to £45,000, almost exactly in step with inflation.

Not that advances have been absent : Mr. Morris probably has not been given due credit over the decision in principle to use the fourth channel for Welsh-language television. When cash is not

---

[7] W. B. Lockwood, *A Panorama of Indo-European Languages* (London, 1972), p. 70.
[8] *Legal Status*, p. 30.

121

involved and Mr. Morris has a free choice, he puts Welsh above English, as on new personal Welsh Office letterheads, and he forcibly told British Railways that whereas for safety reasons he was putting English first on bilingual roads signs, that argument could scarcely apply to railway stations.

But, as Labour Party apologists so often say, letterheads and road signs don't save a language.

Even when urging other people to pursue, and thus pay for, a policy, the Welsh Office is very weak. It took them over two years to issue a circular to local authorities (No. 82/69) on the effects of the passing of the Welsh Language Act, 1967. Circulars are often larded with phrases such as " the Government expects "; the equivalent phrase in this circular was " local authorities will no doubt wish to consider ".

Every phrase such as " making full use of the Welsh language in public business " is weakened by a qualification, such as " having regard to local considerations and the resources of each authority and to the need for the appropriate economy of expenditure ". The only " strong recommendation " is that persons sending corres-pondence in Welsh be not charged for the translation, a rather academic matter, because anti-Welsh councils are far more likely to just send the letter back or ignore it.

With Mr. Morris at the helm, the Welsh Office has given the area health authorities a much tougher set of guidelines (circular WHSC (IS) 117), but, again, it is only policies they " might " take. The handiwork of Cymdeithas yr Iaith Gymraeg in radicalising the linguistic situation is clearly seen however :

> The health service also has a responsibility to the community which it serves. Use of the Welsh language alongside the English can make a significant contribution to the attitude of a visiting family and, indeed, of the community at large to the work of the particular hospital or service.

It is sad, though, that when a health authority looks to see the example it is presented by the Government, it sees a policy that is a sham. Indeed, although these circulars are bilingual, are they really meant to be read in Welsh? Their method of printing and stapling ensures that, unless restapled, they are suitable only for English readers.

The sham is worst in the field of Government forms. The number issued in Welsh or bilingually has indeed risen : from 40 in 1967 to 240 in 1970, over 300 in 1973 and 400 in 1975. Quite what they are, no one seems to know because the only list is dated February 1973, contains 356 forms and has not been updated.[9]

But what is important is not so much the total but the proportion which have been translated. In spring 1975, Plaid Cymru MPs Mr. Gwynfor Evans and Mr. Dafydd Wigley tabled Commons written questions of every Government department, asking how many official forms, pamphlets and leaflets, magazines, booklets and books were published by or on behalf of the department and were currently available to the public or sections of the public; and how many of each class were in Welsh or bilingual form.

There must have been something embarrassing about the questions, because almost every minister gave an identical answer : " I regret that the information is not readily available and that the cost of obtaining it would not be in the public interest." That few departments even bothered to give the total of Welsh or bilingual forms strongly suggests collusion. Questioning has, however, elicited that none are issued by the Defence, Trade or Foreign and Commonwealth departments, and the only Industry material was that issued through the Small Firms Information Centre in Cardiff.

Cause of the embarrassment is apparent when the 35 listed Health and Social Security forms are compared with the total issued by that department of 2,340, a percentage of 1.5.[10] The 400 has to be compared with the total of public forms issued by central government. Even if as few are issued as by the Canadian Federal Government (as the U.K. is a unitary state, the figure is likely to be far higher), that would still give a total of 7,000 and a percentage of five, without taking into account the 36,000 internal forms the Canadian Government has need of, and the 25,000 manuals[11], both categories presumably issued in Wales only in English.

[9] Y Swyddfa Gymreig, *Ffurflenni Cymraeg a Dwyieithog* (Caerdydd, 1973).
[10] I. B. Rees, " The Welsh Language in Government ", *The Welsh Language Today* (Llandysul, 1973), p. 213.
[11] Royal Commission on Bilingualism and Biculturalism, *Book 3, The Work World* (Ottawa, 1969), pp. 137-140.

Mr. Morris demurs when asked if public demand is the criterion for issue. Hardly surprising, in view of the 87 forms issued for magistrates courts and juvenile offenders. I can imagine offices swifty running out of Form 83, Order in respect of original offence on commission of further offence during probation period or period of conditional discharge, or of Form 6, Order for taking finger-prints and palm-prints of defendant!

It is easy to see the reason for issue: once inside, a Welsh language protestor has not much to lose by demanding everything in Welsh. It is more difficult to see the reasoning behind issue by the Privy Council Office of Declaration of Deputy Sheriff forms.

The pity is, there is probably little rhyme or reason. Departments are supposed to liaise with the Welsh Office: they don't, and one London civil servant admitted, in an off-guard moment, that Welsh forms were a joke, to be prepared only if departments were forced to. Departments often ignore official guidelines: how many forms include a note that a Welsh version is available; how many, indeed, are bilingual, as is urged; in how many offices are notices promin-ently displayed listing Welsh forms available?

How often are they " deliberately " not available, as happened to the motor tax documents which were on display for only weeks before going under the counter on instructions? After Mr. George Thomas, then Secretary of State, issued in the Commons his list of the small numbers issued of certain forms, I rang various important Government offices in Cardiff, asking for copies of the forms in question.

Usually I was met with blank incomprehension and a piteous variety of excuses, such as " We have run out " (after they had never heard of the form), or " We can get them to send you a copy from Newcastle-on-Tyne if they have any."

If it is any consolation, similar difficulties used to be experienced over French forms in Canada, which were disliked in some pro-vinces. Would, though, that Wales could see more of the ingenuity displayed by the federal authorities: faced with opposition to extension of bilingual family allowance cheques to partly French-speaking New Brunswick, the government eventually agreed to distribute them, on the understanding that if a hue and cry ensued, a bureaucratic slip would be pleaded!

124

More significant than publication of almost unheard of forms is the amount spent by the Stationery Office on publishing material in Welsh or bilingually. For printing in English, the cost rose from £2,230,000 in 1965-6 to £6,614,000 in 1974-5. Spending on publishing material in Welsh or bilingually dropped from £2,697 to £2,241 (0.3 per cent.). The high spot was £7,125, and the low were three years when nothing was spent.[12]

The case of the Highway Code, one of the most important Government publications to the ordinary man, emphasises that the Government treats Welsh as a, perhaps, inconvenient extra which is certainly non-essential. As I write, the only Welsh edition available was printed in 1968 by the old Ministry of Transport; the English version, on the other hand, was reprinted in 1974.

Omitted from the Welsh version, therefore, are a host of regulations introduced since 1968 :

1. Pedal cyclists must not, when approaching an uncontrolled zebra crossing, overtake the moving vehicle nearest the crossing, or the leading vehicle which has stopped (Zebra Pedestrian Crossing Regulations 1971);

2. Motor-vehicle drivers (a) must use headlights at night on unlit roads (Road Vehicle Lighting Regulations 1971);

(b) must not exceed 70 m.p.h. (Road Traffic Regulations Act, 1967);

(c) must not drive a vehicle with an unsuitable or defective silencer (Motor Vehicle Construction and Use Regulations 1973);

(d) a variety of prohibitions were introduced by the Zebra Pedestrian Crossings Regulation 1971;

(e) must not park without lights on a road with a speed limit higher than 30, or if the vehicle is other than nearside to the kerb, or if it is within 15 yards of a road junction (Road Transport Act 1972 and Road Vehicles Lighting Regulations 1972);

3. Motor-cyclists and pillion passengers must wear an approved safety helmet (Motor Cycles, Wearing of Helmets, Regulations 1972); and

4. Motorway drivers must not exceed 70 m.p.h. (Motorways Traffic, Speed Limits, Regulations 1974).

[12] *Y Cymro*, 18.11.1975.

125

Details of all these regulations are included at the back of the English code. As ignorance is no excuse at law, should one assume that the Government doesn't really expect Welsh speakers to rely on their own version of the code?

Scarcely touched on in Wales is a civil servant's right to work in his own language, if it is other than English. This right, considered fundamental by the Canadian Royal Commission,[13] has made no impression on the British Civil Service in Wales : in its entire domain, the only work done in Welsh (without having been translated from English) is the keeping of minutes of some meetings of H.M. Schools Inspectorate. Even these gentlemen's reports on Welsh schools are presented first in English.[14] Even letters in Welsh from John Morris are carefully translated.

Although Canada differs from Wales in having a block of monoglot French speakers in Quebec, the practical importance of this is lessened in the Civil Service where every French-speaking middle rank employee is, in fact, bilingual.[15] They have had to be because, for instance, the Quebec office of the Department of Munitions and Supply had no Francophone officials, and federal offices in the province never used to be supplied with French-language telephone directories. For years, linguistic considerations were ruled out in making appointments, even for Quebec offices.

The commission states :[16]

> Unless a language can flourish in the world of work, legal guarantees of its use by government services, courts and schools will not be able to ensure its long-term development. Formal linguistic equality is of little importance to those living under a system that always places them in inferior social and economic conditions.

This problem in Ireland has produced one of the few successes of their language revival. They were faced with the traditional unilingualism of one of the most hide-bound of the professions (as in Canada and Wales), resulting in only a tiny amount (1 per cent.) of Irish being used in the civil service.

[13] *The Work World*, p. 3.
[14] *Legal Status*, p. 30.
[15] *The Work World*, p. 122.
[16] ibid., p. 3.

The first stage was spreading the knowledge of Irish through the schools system. According to theory, this knowledge would then seep into life in general and the anglicised would gradually be reclaimed. Nothing of the sort happened : instead, the government has switched to concentrating Irish-speaking staff in units which would work through Irish. Usually, a pilot section was first set up in the establishment branch of a department.

Government directions to the departments emphasised that these sections had to be engaged on important and interesting work. Certain departments, such as the Department of the Gaeltacht, work entirely through Irish, even to the exclusion of English-language signs on doors . . . most confusing![17]

This has been Canada's line, too, with bilingual units being set up wherever French is, or could be, viable. Where the numbers are too small, a cluster of French workers would be established. With the federal capital right on the border between Quebec and Ontario, it has been easy to demand French clusters at a department's headquarters, and a French chain of command. Thus not only would a French group work in French, they would also deal with their directorate and other departments in French, although they might receive material from other departments in English.

The road to these French-language units has been eased by the acceptance of the doctrine of " receptive bilingualism ". This does not necessarily require complete familiarity and ease with all facets of the second language, but rather the ability to read the other language and understand it when it is spoken, an ability significantly easier to acquire than total bilingualism. It enables a person to review documents and understand oral presentations in the other language, and is particularly useful for superior officials with whom French units have to deal.

" It's a rough road," remarked one newspaper reporter, and it has been expensive, too, but evidently cheaper than the costs of the break-up of the federation that was threatened. Scarcely anywhere does the Royal Commission mention the violence and politics which were coming close to tearing the dominion asunder, but it has ever been the unspoken thought.

[17] But see Appendix 3 for spoken use of Irish in these units.

127

Six years (until 1978) were given for the creation of a bilingual civil service.[18] About 50,000 posts (19 per cent. of the total) have been designated as bilingual : where a monoglot incumbent refuses to transfer or take language training, double-banking may be resorted to, involving the appointment of an extra official to share the work.

To increase the number of bilinguals, the federal government set up a series of language schools costing £6m a year to run. They have been costly in human terms, too, with only a 10 per cent. graduation rate and drop-outs and absentees leaving them running over 30 per cent. below capacity. To some extent, this has been because of faulty teaching methods : only after a couple of years of relative failure has the method of teaching the second language through three courses a year, each of three weeks, repeated for perhaps four years, been phased out in favour of " continuous language training ".

This involves a non-stop course for almost the whole year. The cost in teaching is about the same, £2,000 per student. But to this has to be added the civil servant's salary, and that of the man who has to take his job for the year. And it is a cardinal point that bilinguals get extra pay for what is a valuable qualification.

It seems that civil servants are the same the world over, for similar arguments were heard against bilingualism in Canada as I imagine are being honed for use here. I have already noted the small proportion of Welsh speakers entering the middle and higher reaches of the service; a similar shortage exists in English-language journalism and a similar force may be at work. In neither field would a person of Welsh cultural background feel thoroughly at home; in journalism, this would be because of the anti-language line promoted by most newspapers, and in the civil service because of the English cultural background and partial public school image, both accentuated by the policy of directing staff to posts outside their home area, thus bringing " typical upper middle class English-men " into the heart of very Welsh areas.

Not enough Welsh speakers available with qualifications? With goodwill, that can be overcome, as Canada proved.

[18] *Toronto Globe and Mail,* 7.6.73.

10.   With his placard, reading Life to Welsh, upright to the end, a member of Cymdeithas yr Iaith is carried from Guildhall Square, Carmarthen, in April 1971 after a protest against the conduct of a case involving leaders of the society. Only days previously, 50 members and supporters of the society were jailed for contempt of the court.   *(Western Mail)*

11. The eye of the law . . . a police photographer is caught recording the faces of members of Cymdeithas yr Iaith during a road signs demonstrations outside the Welsh Office in Cardiff in May 1973. (*Western Mail*)

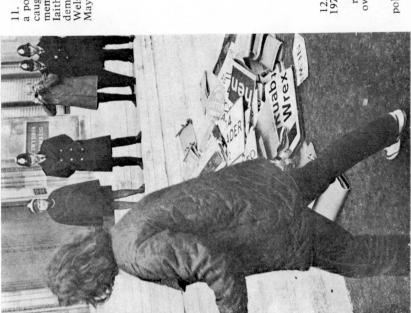

12. Carmarthen ministers in 1971 show their disagreement with the ban on bilingual road signs by erecting their own. The 36 members of the cloth then trooped off to give themselves up to the police. (*Raymond Daniel*)

Of course, the policy of moving staff is justified on the grounds of efficiency, as if every civil servant is efficient! Linguistic ability can be excluded from the efficiency equation simply by ensuring no one deals with the public service in Welsh.

There is much to be said for not preparing one grand plan for the language . . . it could so easily go the way of other grand plans and gather dust on a very high shelf in Cathays Park. But having an aim and a strategy is a different matter. Britain is one of the world's most centralised states, perhaps because of the English liking for uniformity and strong governmental control. The result is that even in Wales local government expects a lead from Cathays Park or London before it will move. Hence, even though powers to assist the language may exist, few authorities will use them without a lead. Pusillanimous they are, of course, and even the recent reorganisation, of which so much was expected, has achieved very little.

Often, of course, no move is possible without that lead. The system discourages initiative in that every local government action has to be justified by reference to Act of Parliament or regulation — breach of this leaves officers and members liable to surcharge. To suggest adoption of the overseas system, with authorities free to do anything unless it is illegal, is to introduce apoplexy at both central and local levels! Local government has, indeed, for years regarded itself, consciously or unconsciously, as an extension of central government.

In addition, local government has to put up with such a degree of central supervision and instruction that Cathays Park and Whitehall seem to view district and county officials as either incompetent or rogues :

> During the 22 working days up to the end of December 1969, the clerk to the council of a certain small county received no less than 135 communications of substance from the central government.[19]

In this situation, the Government's neglect of the Welsh language is doubly criminal. Hardly any local council is going to overthrow

---

[19] I. B. Rees, *Government by Community* (London, 1971), p. 51.

centuries of tradition without a lead. Significantly, the county which has gone closest is Gwynedd, controlled by Nationalists and their allies. In Dyfed, the votes on Welsh language issues have been close : officials there consider a lead from the centre essential to tip the balance and get bilingualism off the ground.

In Gwynedd, indeed, there is considerable concern that the effect of the county's bilingual policy is being seriously weakened by the great preponderance of English-only material being pushed out by central government agencies, the health authority, and nationalised industries in the area.

Even if the debilitated nature of Welsh local government did not require a lead, the prestige of central government justifies one :

> One can hardly overestimate the importance of some official status in maintaining a language. It gives it social status among its native users, and serves in part as a barrier against self-deprecation and embarrassment. A little of state support in the form of official printing presses, court proceedings, and school use, can, at times, do more to establish a language than can a vast amount of energetic activity by language loyalists.[20]

[20] N. Glazier, *The Processes and Problems of Language Maintenance*, quoted in M. Ó Murchú, *Language and Community* (Dublin, 1971), p. 32.

11

The Press

STOP PRESS FOR WELSH?

I merely state
That the language, for us,
Is part of the old, abandoned ways.[1]

English-language newspapers in Wales have generally been only fair-weather friends to the Welsh language. At the height of Cymdeithas yr Iaith's unpopularity a few years ago, to find a paper which refrained from labelling them " hooligans " and which tried to probe the injustice below the surface was like finding an unbiased report in *Pravda* — rather unusual and a shining example to the rest.

But have the Welsh-language papers of the past, in their different ways, been any better? Of the nine papers listed in *Benn's Newspaper Press Directory* for 1967 with Welsh-language titles, only four had not succumbed to the blight of bilingualism, a form of palsy which usually leads to death.

Eight years later, the four which kept to Welsh are still with us. Of the others, three are dead, gone to the heaven (or is it a hell?) where there is always a welcome in the hillsides for newspapers which will abandon their right to a Welsh title at the drop of a hint that there might be a potential reader down the street who cannot, or cannot be bothered to, read Welsh.

---

[1] From Herbert Williams, " The Old Tongue ", in J. S. Williams and M. Stephens (eds.), *The Lilting House* (Llandybïe, 1969), p. 183.

In this field, as in so many others, it has taken youngsters with a strong political commitment to their country and their language, and with no rose-coloured spectacles to tint the view, to disprove the contention that equates English with profits and Welsh with Carey Street and Westgate Street, its Cardiff equivalent. The new papurau bro (district papers) have rescued the language from the clutches of the literateur and returned it to the manual labourer in the council house up the street who is far more interested in the state of his sewers than in the latest poetic gem from the minister in the manse in the next county.

The worst example of a Welsh-language paper being murdered by a commercial decision taken with blatant disregard for the language was *Y Seren* of Bala. The paper had been started in 1885 as a typical small-town affair, with the publishers also printing and editing it. The owners were Liberals at the time when everyone in the area was Liberal too, and its circulation was strong enough at the turn of the century for a really ambitious proprietor to have had a chance of giving it a national circulation.

But this was a family business and there was a weak link in the line of inheritance. In the late 1950s the then owner, Mr. Robert Evans, decided to sell. It may have been small-town politics, or a desire to get as much cash as possible irrespective of national interest, a not uncommon failing among businessmen, but it is alleged the company was not advertised for Welsh eyes to see.

It must be borne in mind what sort of newspaper was being sold. Over the years, small items had crept into the paper in English. In the issue of January 6, 1940, for instance, two out of the 12 district notes from Bala were in that language : it is usually in little towns like this that some of the correspondents are either too lazy to write in correct Welsh, or develop a soft spot for the newcomer down the road who can't speak the language (and, therefore, would never buy *Y Seren,* preferring one of the big English-language weeklies which have a small sale in the town).

The only other English items were one and a half columns of rather crude war propaganda (" Watchman, what of the night? ") and a tiny poem.

Right up until June 6, 1959, almost the entire paper was in Welsh. The change was sudden and complete. On July 4, a small

132

item announced that Mr. R. S. Evans had resigned as managing director and Mr. A. J. Chapple had taken over. In fact, Mr. Chapple, billed as " a newspaperman of many years' experience ", had taken over the previous issue.

Mr. Chapple, who had come from Staffordshire (" I hope very soon to speak and write to you in your own language"), immediately made his presence felt. Page one was, as usual, entirely advertisements. The lead story on page two was in Welsh, but everything else on the page was in English. Page four was almost entirely English. Significantly, the short news paragraphs set in bold type, which were Mr. Chapple's trade-mark, were all in English.

The editorial with which Mr. Chapple announced his plans was hardly the hallmark of an Englishman intent on integrating into a Welsh-speaking community. Apart from the throw-away line about learning Welsh, his long consideration of the problems of the world did not mention Wales once. " We believe in Britain," he trumpeted, adding, with a hint of condescension in his words, " Your dear old *Seren* must change."

It certainly had changed, although for a couple of weeks Mr. Chapple did make slight obeisance to the Welsh language : the headline and first paragraphs of the front page lead story were in Welsh before switching to English.

In the issue of July 11 what proved in later years to be a general disapproval broke to the surface in a letter from an unnamed reader :

> " I can only regret that a paper which used to be almost entirely Welsh is now two-thirds English. Surely the raison d'être of *Y Seren* . . . was the very fact that it was Welsh. I can assure you that the great majority of your readers are Welsh reading and that their desire is that *Y Seren* continues to be a Welsh paper . . . The current editorial policy of *Y Seren* is going to cause harm rather than good to the locality and to Welsh in general. May I urge you to re-establish *Y Seren* as a real Welsh paper. A hybrid production is of no use to anyone. I cannot recall any local English paper, even in the London area, which prints two-thirds of its news in French simply because a handful of French people live in the area."

The letter was printed in the editorial, and Mr. Chapple replied underneath :

We hasten to assure our correspondent that we had no intention of printing more than was necessary in English and that the only reason for using English at all was the inability of the present writer to write Welsh . . . We pointed out that in spite of our desire to encourage the Welsh language, that the first requirement of *The (sic) Seren* is that it must secure sufficient revenue to pay for the cost of printing it. Let us say unashamedly that the first reason for publishing *The Seren* is to provide a modest living for *The Seren* staff and its manager. Only after that can we talk about defending and furthering the interests of the Welsh language.

In the sale of the paper, cash had come before the language, and so it continued. But those last sentences were the death warrant for the paper and the jobs necessary to keep it going. Although the letter of protest had come from a person outside the circulation area, and there was apparently little convulsion in the heart of Meirionnydd (except in the editorial columns of *Y Faner,* which was printed, although not edited, in the town), the readers gradually registered their disapproval, despite the quite high English journalistic standard of the paper.

After Mr. Chapple's sudden departure from Wales, the paper was sold to Mr. Gwyn Evans and his brother, proprietors of *Y Faner* and *Y Cyfnod.* They said the circulation had by then slumped to only 200.

It is not, though, that the history of *Y Cyfnod* is a light shining in the gloom. This paper was founded on January 5, 1934, with an issue that was entirely in Welsh, except for a report concerning Bala town silver band and the football notes (sport has been a consistent weakness in language journalism). By the following year the paper had formalised its policy with the back page (p. 8) entirely in English (including the all-important town council meeting report). But the rest of the paper was Welsh, including every one of the Bala district notes inside.

The paper's Welshness suffered serious harm during the war when paper rationing reduced the journal's size to four pages. But the entire back page remained in English, set in small type. The advertisements were crammed onto the remaining, Welsh, pages. By the end of 1946 the English was spreading from page four on to the other pages, and from January 22, 1947, the tagline to the

CYMANFA GANU GWERIN CYMRU.

PAFILIWN CORWEN, NOS IAU, AWST 11, AM 7 45.

CROESAW MAWR I HOLL GANTORION CYMRU I YMUNO YN YR WYL.

A REAL FEAST OF SONG.

Ie, Nos Iau, Awst 11eg, am 7-45, cynhelir Cymanfa Ganu Gwerin Cymru a Chyngerdd Uwchraddol ym Mhafiliwn Corwen. Disgwylir dros 2,000 o Leisiau i ganu Hen Emyn-Donau Cymreig:—Aberystwyth, Moab, Trewen, St. Gertrude, Huddersfield, Cwm Rhcudda, Rachie, Saron, Telyn Seion, etc., hefyd Chantio Psalm cxxi, " Dyrchafaf fy llygaid i'r mynydd." Cenir yr anthem bendig:dig " Teyrnasoedd y Ddaear "; a'r rhangan anfarw l " Bydd melus gofio y Cyfam. mcd." Cenir Caneuon Gwerin gan Cor y Berwyniaid. Detholiad gan Pedwarawd y Chwarelwyr. Gwasanaethir gan Seindorf Arian Rhyl dan arweiniad Tal Morris, Ysw. Manylion llawn yn ein nesaf. Bring your English Friends and Visitors they will enjoy this mammoth musical Festival. Forget the Hard Times—Come and Sing them through at Corwen Pavilion on Thursday, Aug. 11th. at 7 45. Massed Choirs of about 2,000 voices. together with Rhyl Town Silver Prize Band. The treat of your lifetime Admission to all parts including the stage 1s., children 6d. Proceeds will be given towards deserving causes. Programmes 2d. each, D. R. Morris, organiser Many Welsh musicians from abroad (on holiday in Wales) intend to be present at this festival which will be bigger and better than those of previous years. Several Welsh Choral Societies and Church Choirs have kindly promised to assist. " Pob perchen anadl unwch yn y Cydgan Mawr." Cynhelir rehearsals yng Nghorwen a'r cylch.

The ultimate in bilingualism? A page one report from *Yr Adsain,* July 12, 1932.

paper's title was changed from " Papur Newydd y Bala a'r Cylch " to " Newyddiadur Wythnosol Cymraeg a Saesneg ".

Thus it has remained, supposedly half Welsh and half English. The owners firmly believe that to eject the English would lead to sales plummeting, and the circulation of their group of four papers at 4,000 is not high enough for any but a very brave man to take the risk, especially as, for years, profits from other activities have helped to subsidise *Y Faner,* the nationalist weekly which, of course, prints everything in Welsh.

But bilingualism is more than a commercial necessity. It is considered a " healthy " policy, the way in which to attract the Anglo-Welsh. Unfortunately, while there may be sentiment behind such arguments, they fly in the face of facts. When has such bilingualism gained the only convert to Welsh who is really worth having, the one who has learned the language? If a monoglot attends a bilingual function he knows he is not really out of the swim and there is no real need to bother to learn Welsh because in a moment everything of importance will be translated for his benefit. I know this, as I speak from experience.

To maintain such a bilingual balance is difficult, as *Yr Adsain* —sub-titled Newyddiadur at wasanaeth Corwen a'r Cylch — discovered. This little eight-page weekly even managed a dateline entirely in Welsh, but then gave up. In the issue for July 12, 1932, for example, only four news items in the paper were in Welsh, compared with 21 in English and one bilingual hybrid, which should be enough to end all talk of mixing Welsh and English (see page 135). What monoglot would want to read that?

Eventually the paper legitimised the situation and changed its name to *Corwen Chronicle.* But it seems the good folk of the town did not like even the new guise, and in 1947 *Y Dydd,* of Dolgellau, took it over. *Y Dydd,* run now as a sideline to a printing works, has a very honourable history, being founded in 1868, principally by one of the great men of Wales, the Rev. Samuel Roberts (S.R.). Its early history was very much bound up with the Independents and it gained a very extensive circulation,[2] being printed for a time in Merthyr.

[2] T. M. Jones, *Llenyddiaeth fy Ngwlad* (Treffynnon, 1893), t. 29.

In 1946, Alfred, the son of the first publisher, Mr. William Hughes, put the paper, by now selling only locally, and works up for sale. Fearing a take-over by outside interests, followed by closure of the works and printing of the paper elsewhere, a local group, prominent among them nationalists, took over. Their venture into Corwen didn't work, but the paper continues, although squeezed in size to only six pages some weeks by the forces of economics.

Economics is certainly the main reason why the proportion of Welsh in the paper has dropped drastically of recent years, but whether it is due to lack of money to translate items which arrive at the office in English, or fears of a drop in circulation, is unclear.

The symbols of commercial caution in *Y Dydd*'s office stands in stark contrast to the stand of principle taken by the papurau bro (although these newcomers have low costs, they also refuse to maximise their advertising potential). Although *Y Dydd*'s management reckon there has recently been an upsurge in Welsh-language items arriving in the office, there has been a big drop compared with 1965 when the issue of June 18, for instance, printed 189 inches (87.9 per cent.) of news and features in Welsh and only 26 inches in English.

The issues of May 9 and 16, 1975, contain an average of only 60 per cent. in Welsh, although the front page *("O Gader Idris", gan O.M.L.)* is entirely in that language. It could be argued that it is the Welsh content that has kept the circulation as high as it is (1,600), because the entire area is saturated by *The Cambrian News*. That *Y Dydd* is sold the other side of Barmouth, and that 50 copies each are sent to Barmouth and Tywyn would indicate a loyalty based purely on *Y Dydd*'s Welshness and the Welsh-language items printed from these areas.

Even today it is difficult to see how the paper could appeal to an English monoglot. Indeed, the paper's policy of occasionally translating items received in English (such as some funeral reports, because they will appear in English in *The Cambrian News*, and the minutes of the now defunct urban council) indicates a weakness in the sales argument.

Absence of editorial staff certainly causes difficulties, as does the habit of some correspondents of submitting copy in English. Prominent offenders are the local post office in Barmouth, a major

137

Dolgellau correspondent, the National Council of Women, North Wales Naturalists' Trust, certain W.I. branches and the county federation (the same group that constituted a major reason for the breakaway that led to Merched y Wawr), and local sports clubs.

But it seems that also lacking is the will, in a world overrun by English, rigorously to maintain the paper as Welsh, and not bilingual.

There is certainly a will to maintain *Herald Cymraeg* and *Herald Môn,* if only because, with parallel English papers, there is no room for a language change. The Welsh papers claim a circulation of one-third of the group circulation of 30,000; although the sales of *Herald Cymraeg* are slipping, those of *Herald Môn* are holding well. To many Welsh speakers, these papers are to be viewed down the length of one's nose — "How much more important it would be if *Taliesin* or *Barn* sold a few more copies " — but it is, in truth, difficult to disagree with the comment of their editor-in-chief, Mr. John Eilian Jones, that their disappearance would be more of a blow to the language than most realise.

Not that the papers are perfect : all the staff can write Welsh, except the recently-departed news editor. Both Welsh papers suffer from an all-too-common fault in the vernacular press, far too much emphasis on the world of literature, culture and eisteddfodau. Certainly, these causes are strongly espoused by cultured Welsh speakers, generally the only ones to make themselves heard, but I refuse to believe that the latest couple of lines of cynghanedd springing off the linotype are what your average Welsh reader of a local paper wants to contemplate over the marmalade pot.

While such work certainly has an important place, an editor is surely asking for trouble when the reader of *Yr Herald Cymraeg* is presented with massive reports on Eisteddfod Gadeiriol y Felinheli and Eisteddfod Mynydd y Cilgwyn, while the reader of the *Caernarvon and Denbigh Herald* is titilated with " Justice for the forgotten men of farming ", " More spy charges ", " Young mother on drugs charge ", " Trouble with squatters ", " Three fined after street scuffle ", etc.[3]

[3] *Herald Cymraeg,* 13.5.75, and *Caernarvon and Denbigh Herald,* 9.5.75.

The same weakness is found on the main news page of *Herald Môn,* where the main lead is " Cyhoeddi Eisteddfod yr Urdd " (Proclamation of the Urdd Eisteddfod), and the third lead " Rhagolygon am ŵyl Môn dda " (Prospects of a good Anglesey festival). *The Holyhead and Anglesey Mail* entices readers with " Plans for a big Menai Bridge celebration " (150th anniversary of the suspension bridge) and " Was Llywelyn's palace here? " (at Aberffraw).[4]

The overwhelming impression is a lack of effort with the Welsh papers. The issue of *Yr Herald Cymraeg* published during the week of the Cricieth National Eisteddfod in 1975 insisted in filling itself with farm show results, with scarcely a word about the festival most readers would be attending. *Yr Herald Cymraeg* seems to get what is left over from the English papers, and the events which occur each week just too late for the *Caernarvon and Denbigh Herald,* the circulation-pulling sports reports, are ignored.

While the Welsh-language papers of the 19th century were often dull, their proprietors, long before the days of the *Daily Mirror,* knew well the attractiveness to readers of sex, scandal and sudden death.

Thus *Y Byd Cymreig,* the national weekly published in Castell Newydd Emlyn in the 1860s, had a regular column entitled " Damweiniau, Llofruddiaethau " (Accidents, murders) culled not only from correspondents in Wales but from any English newspaper that came to hand. As this was 60 years before the English dailies began to reach into rural Wales, plenty of space was given to foreign news, generally played straight, although with a wide eye open for the oddity, such as " Halen yn lladd defaid " (Salt kills sheep, in Vermont).

Either as the world has got older, we journalists have got more serious, or, more likely, our readers will already know of such events from the dailies or television.

The most glaring gap in the coverage of today's Welsh papers is sport, carried regularly only by *Y Cymro.* The excuses — that people talk about sport only in English and that reports are untranslateable cliches — have themselves the sound of cliches. It is true that some of the poorer reporters on weeklies do little but

---

[4] *Herald Môn* and *Holyhead and Anglesey Mail,* same dates.

string together a series of hack phrases dredged up from past editions.

Certainly, there is a problem of "charged holy words and expressions",[5] but it is a worry that arises primarily with length, when the reporter has his eye on the lineage payment account or on a big run of type in the paper. Restricted to 250 words in a rugby game with a 25-15 scoreline, and you might be lucky to get all the scorers in, never mind the cliches. Significantly, the papurau bro, which have tight limits on copy, express surprise that there should be any difficulties.

The omission of both sport and most of the situations vacant adverts from both *Herald Cymraeg* and *Herald Môn* opts both papers out of two of today's most important newspaper functions. The fact that the owners do not insist on offering Sits. Vac. only on a group basis (they could get away with it as they occupy a near-monopoly situation), also slims the Welsh papers by an average of a couple of pages a week, a factor guaranteed not to help circulation.

With their claimed joint circulation of 10,000, they dwarf both *Y Cymro* (7,500) and *Y Faner* (4,000). *Y Cymro,* likewise, owes its continuance to membership of a profitable group, this time the highly professional North Wales Newspapers based in, of all places, Oswestry in Shropshire.

The strength of the *Heralds* are the columns of district news paragraphs. Their absence is *Y Cymro*'s weakness : staff are coy about discussing past circulation figures, but there is no doubt that the economic decision to scrap district men (who had operated in Blaenau Ffestiniog, Anglesey and Caernarfon : the circulation and adverts they were pulling in did not cover costs) hit the paper hard. Editor Mr. Llion Griffiths reckons their reinstatement would double circulation, which gives credence to tales that *Y Cymro* used to sell 13,000.

The paper, as with all other Welsh papers in both languages, certainly suffers at times from the lack of something to write about. National papers are hit worst as there is no real national centre

---

[5] D. Tecwyn Lloyd, "The Welsh Language in Journalism", *The Welsh Language Today,* p. 163.

of activity to focus on. *Y Cymro, Y Faner,* the *Western Mail,* and, perhaps, other papers too, all have their eyes firmly fixed on the journalistic opportunities that will arise with the opening of the Welsh Assembly. Perhaps, then, the Welsh-language nationals will have stronger raisons d'être, accompanied by stronger circulations.

The important field of local news over most of Wales has by now been left vacant for the papurau bro. Most districts, indeed, never had Welsh local papers, even after the great expansionism of the Victorian era. Dyfed was almost devoid. One bright spot was Lampeter from 1892 to 1901 with *Y Brython Cymreig.*

The paper was almost a one-man-band, and when Mr. H. Tobit Evans had to pack in because the travelling to and from the office in winter was affecting his health, the paper died, too. Not that, after its first year, it was losing money.[6] Although its circulation, as evidenced by editorial campaigns, advertisements and letters to the editor, seemed concentrated around Lampeter, news coverage embraced much of Carmarthenshire and Ceredigion.

Much space was given to British and world news, with contemporary events often covered at length, including in editorials. Such was the Welsh-language press at the turn of the century. Survival was no real difficulty because the London " national " press was in no position to offer a challenge. High-speed printing and type-setting, the prerequisites of a mass circulation, had not long been in existence, and the new " popular " journalism did not start until 1896 with the *Daily Mail.* But the run-up to World War I saw the grave being dug for a vernacular press without real local news roots, trying to exist in an increasingly bilingual society. Between 1900 and 1914 were founded the first of the tabloid picture papers, the *Daily Graphic, Daily Sketch* and *Daily Mirror.*

World War I was just the story for which the London press was waiting. The demand for news doubled circulations, and left the Welsh-language weeklies standing. The coming of radio to Wales in 1923 merely confirmed that only a Welsh-language daily could compete. In 1900 the circulations of morning and evening papers printed in London was not more than 750,000 a day, and the total

[6] *Y Brython Cymreig,* 27.9.01.

for all dailies in the U.K. was only one million.[7] Most of Wales could hardly have been touched.

By 1939 the London total was 10,500,000 daily[8], and Wales was considered completely integrated with England.[9] The conquest was complete.[10]

The launching of the monthly papurau bro (seven between September 1974 and the 1975 National Eisteddfod), based almost entirely on a formula of local news, is thus one of the most significant developments ever in Welsh-language journalism.[11] Each is rigidly controlled. Print orders range from 500 to 2,000, near saturation for these areas.

Small in size, certainly, but the May 1975 edition of *Papur Pawb* (Talybont, Ceredigion) contained 5,500 words of editorial, and *Llais Ogwan* (Dyffryn Ogwen) over 10,000, compared with only 4,000 in *Y Dydd* (Dolgellau) of May 9. The pad that has launched these four or six-page papers into circulation has been the new technology of web-offset production.

Freed of the constraints and costs of metal, a number of nationalists have over the past decade set up small one or two-man printing works. Some have succeeded and the profit motive has ensured their growth. For the first years it was almost a case of living off business from your friends. It is on the basis of their owners' and workers' strong commitment to the language that it has been possible to start the papurau bro.

The aim has been to provide Welsh reading : it was estimated by Gwilym Huws, the editor of *Papur Pawb,* that whereas only 10 to 20 per cent. of the people around Talybont were reading Welsh, his paper boosted the figure to 90 per cent. Significantly, the idea of bilingualism has been rejected as being disliked by both language groups : one of the reasons for the failure of *Llais*

---

[7] F. Williams, *Dangerous Estate* (London, 1959), p. 113.
[8] ibid., p. 177.
[9] PEP, *Report on the British Press* (London, 1938), p. 242.
[10] It was, however, not until the 1950s that the London and Manchester papers managed to reach some of the non-main road villages in counties such as Ceredigion. Even today there are, no doubt, settlements served only by the vehicles of the *Western Mail* and *Liverpool Daily Post.*
[11] At July 1975, they are *Llais Ardudwy* (Harlech area), *Yr Ancr* (Llanddewi Brefi), *Clebran* (north Preseli), *Papur Pawb* (Talybont, Tre'rddol and Taliesin), *Pethe Penllyn* (five parishes of Penllyn), *Llais Ogwan* (Dyffryn Ogwen), and *Lleu* (Penygroes).

Ceredigion, a give-away monthly run by Plaid Cymru members in the county, was readers' dissatisfaction about its bilingualism.

Ultimately there is only one reason for running a newspaper : public demand. Worries on this point delayed the launching of *Llais Ardudwy* for months; to his surprise, editor Martin Eckley then had to increase the size of the second edition and plan for 12 a year instead of 10.

Today's high wage costs are beaten by volunteers collecting, typing and laying out the news. Almost all the income is from a rather high cover price of 5p or 7p; advertising, the basis of almost every newspaper in Britain, seems to be taken only on sufferance, with little, if any, active selling of space.

What of their future? Some will fail as enthusiasm among the staff wanes. But, as Plaid Cymru found with *Welsh Nation,* the value of a weekly is more than that of four issues of a monthly. As I write, *Welsh Nation* has been running for over four years without a single paid member of staff, although it has taken up time of full-time party officials.

One man could run one, or even two, weekly papurau bro; or a paper could be run as a sideline by a member of, say, a community association staff. Or a secondary school could take the plunge. A carefully-handled expanded circulation area could provide the cash to pay an editor. It would be ironical if, where Victorian commercialism failed, 20th century idealism succeeds in founding truly local Welsh weeklies throughout the heartland.

12

Dyfed and Gwynedd

WHICH IS HEADING FOR A FALL?

> *I have walked the shore*
> *For an hour and seen the English*
> *Scavenging among the remains*
> *Of our culture, covering the sand*
> *Like the tide and, with the roughness*
> *Of the tide, elbowing our language*
> *Into the grave that we have dug for it.*[1]

According to the orthodox, the Welsh language has been half-murdered by the British Government, with the oppression starting with the Norman conquests, fuelled by the Satute of Rhuddlan (1284, which abolished the independent courts of law), the Act of Union (1536, which banned non-English speakers from public office), and the Blue Books education system.

Much political rhetoric has been expounded on the iniquities of the English, too little on the willingness with which so many Welshmen accepted these policies. The ease and rapidity with which the Welsh changed from Catholicism to Protestantism, for instance, contrasts vividly with the upheaval and threatening postures adopted in some areas of England, and the rebellion in Cornwall.[2]

---

[1] From R. S. Thomas, " Reservoirs ", *Selected Poems, 1946-68* (London, 1973), p. 117.

[2] See G. Williams, " Carmarthen and the Reformation ", *Carmarthenshire Studies* (Carmarthen, 1974), p. 136, for the story of one of the few areas where there was unrest. In Cornwall the reformation was one of the final nails in the coffin of Cornish. It is said (see A. S. D. Smith, *The Story of the Cornish Language* (Cambourne, 1969), p. 9), that people were offered the Prayer Book in Cornish, but they refused it in any language. What may have been good for their Catholic souls was bad for their tongues, because they were then forced to accept the Prayer Book in English.

13. Carrying a sign reading
Aberteifi (Cardigan) members
of Cyfeillion yr Iaith
(Friends of the Language),
a supporters' group of older
people, march through
Aberystwyth in April 1971
before erecting it in the town.

(Raymond Daniel)

14, 15.   Portraits of fighters: The family of coalminer Trefor Beasley, of Llangennech, first sufferers in modern times for the language; and Dafydd Iwan, the singing chairman of Cymdeithas yr Iaith, with Huw Jones and Heather Jones at the launching of the highly successful Sain record company.
(Y Cymro and Pete Davis)

16.   (Below) Local people stop the car of Englishman Mr. Brewer Spinks of Blaenau Ffestiniog in July 1967 in protest at his ban on the use of Welsh in his factory. *(Western Mail)*

As another crisis arrives in the history of one of the oldest languages in Europe, once again the question must be asked : will the Welsh fight, or will the resistance be only token? Has the retreat of the language border stopped, or are their worms at work in the fabric of the heartland, in the minds of the language's speakers, that will bring the edifice crashing, despite the efforts of the enthusiasts in so many fields to shore it? Are there regions where the Blue Books mentality lives on?

I wrote earlier that there were few signs the language was declining in its rural heartland, where 70 per cent. or more of the population spoke Welsh. In some areas, indeed, there is considerable hardening of views, witness the increase in " monoglots " in parts of Meirionnydd and Caernarfonshire. In south Ceredigion and north Carmarthenshire, campaigners for a bilingual secondary school have been finding up to 95 per cent. of parents in favour.

I hinted, however, that one index caused concern : the proportion of Welsh speakers also able to write the language. In view of the lack of Welsh-medium education, these numbers are surprisingly small, except in two types of areas, the zone of rapid decline, plus Carmarthenshire and Pembrokeshire.

In the 1971 census returns, while 20.84 per cent. overall said they were Welsh speakers, 17.23 per cent. declared they were able to read the language and 15.25 per cent. that they could write it. This national variation masked local differences between speakers and writing from 0 to 33.3 per cent.

This state of illiteracy leads Professors Bowen and Carter to an analogy with a colonialist situation,[3] the same conclusion that Professor Hechter has reached using more of an economic base for his thesis. Bowen and Carter write :

> The parallel to be sought would be in under-developed countries, but although that would be meaningless, there would certainly be clear associations with colonial situations where the vernacular remained a means of oral communication and the colonial language became that of all formal, official and written transactions. The explanation . . . would adopt the

[3] Bowen and Carter, " Distribution of the Welsh Language ", p. 9.

view that Welsh was a peasant language intimately associated with rural communities, where the spoken word was the basic means of communication. It has not become a means of bureaucratic communication in an urbanised society.

The notion that Welsh is a private, as opposed to an official, language would certainly help to explain the lack of literacy in the Carmarthenshire industrial areas. With written communications forming an important part of life for a fair section of the working population, English had to be accorded considerable importance, and written Welsh fell by the way.

In the rural areas, English did not have this importance, and Welsh was thus able to develop nearer full flower.

To a small extent, ability to write Welsh depends on age, with more of the youngsters than of the older folk displaying the ability, presumably because of the slightly greater importance given to Welsh in schools over the last few years (see table).

PERCENTAGES OF WELSH SPEAKERS/WRITERS IN EACH AGE GROUP

Age group	Percentage of all Welsh speakers in each group	Percentage of all Welsh writers in each group
3-4	1.80	0.38
5-9	6.01	6.16
10-14	6.49	7.75
15-24	11.34	12.77
25-44	21.54	22.54
45-64	31.17	30.39
65-plus	21.65	20.02
Total	100.00	100.01

(From Bowen and Carter, *Distribution of the Welsh Language.*)

Neither of these factors, however, fully explain the geographical distribution of the illiteracy areas, closely grouped as many of them are around the line where 70 per cent. speak Welsh.

The existence of this belt, however, provides the anwer. This is the area where use of the language falls off dramatically, where the tongue is visibly decaying, where parents will often not be

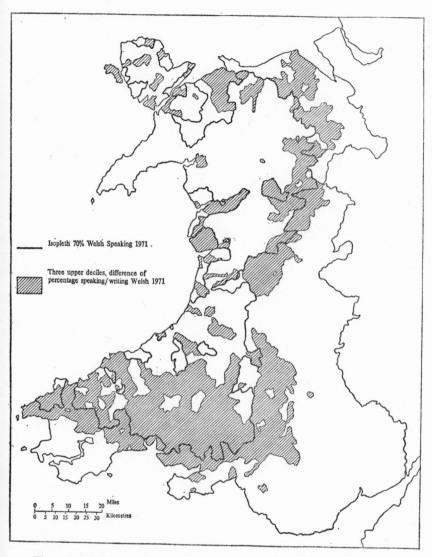

Isopleth 70% Welsh Speaking 1971 .

Three upper deciles, difference of
percentage speaking/writing Welsh 1971

0   5   10   15   20 Miles
0   5   10   15   20   25   30   Kilometres

The relation between the Welsh-speaking areas and the speaking/writing
differences. (From *Geography*, January 1975, page 12.)

teaching it to their children, often as not because a Welsh speaker has failed to find a Welsh-speaking marriage partner.

Once decay sets in, morale drops, the cultural tradition weakens, the Welsh-language chapels lose their hold, and whatever commercial value the language has anywhere swiftly disappears. Welsh is in these areas in the position it occupied throughout much of the heartland only a few years ago : it becomes the language of the hearth, for use with relatives and close friends. It then no longer is necessary, or considered worthwhile, bothering to learn to write. With whom will one correspond, particularly in this age of the telephone and the $8\frac{1}{2}$p post? Each family, in effect, carries out its own cost-benefit study on the language.

That many in this marginal zone have given up speaking the language altogether is evidenced by the rate of decline which is, for a significant number of areas where between 70 and 40 per cent. speak the language, at least twice the national average.

Decay of alarming proportions is revealed by the language survey carried out by Carmarthenshire County Council in 1970.[4] Throughout the county there were only three areas where Welsh speakers were in a substantial majority in the primary schools : these were Castell Newydd Emlyn (78 per cent.), Llanybydder (74 per cent.) and Gwendraeth (65.6 per cent.).

In Rhydaman, the figure was 54.2 per cent., in Llandovery and Llandeilo 53 per cent., in Whitland and St. Clears 38 per cent., in Carmarthen 37 per cent., and in Llanelli a dismal 18.5 per cent. Close examination of the census goes some way to confirming this evidence. In all counties, the lowest percentage speaking the language is among children aged three to four. There is usually then a big increase during the school years. If the figures for Carmarthenshire, less Llanelli borough, are examined, the drop among the nippers is shown to be considerably more than in counties where a similar overall percentage speak Welsh. The increase at school still leaves the percentage of 5 to 9-year-olds speaking Welsh far below the average for all ages, in stark contrast to counties such as Caernarfon and Meirionnydd, where it is among school pupils

[4] See *Welsh Nation*, 21.9.73, for details.

that the highest proportion of Welsh speakers of any age group, including pensioners, is found (see table).

This contrast certainly places Carmarthenshire's education policy in rather a poor light, and supports allegations that teachers in that county are just not bothering to do what they are paid for. Numerous are the tales of head teachers, Welsh-speaking themselves, who do not care about the language, letting matters slip at the first hint of a few problems.

Undoubtedly there are teachers in the north of Wales with the same predilections. But while slippage there will earn a visit from nasty-minded county hall officials, no one expects such pressures in favour of the language to emanate from Guildhall, Carmarthen.

PERCENTAGES SPEAKING WELSH, BY AGE, 1971

	Carms. except Llanelli	Pembs.	Cards.	Meirion	Caern.	Anglesey
All ages	70.6	20.7	67.6	73.5	61.9	65.7
3-4	48.7	9.8	54.8	63.9	55.8	49.2
5-9	58.4	14.4	67.2	78.6	64.4	59.5
10-14	63.7	15.4	71.7	77.3	64.8	67.0
15-24	65.7	16.8	52.2	72.9	55.8	62.4
25-44	68.7	20.2	67.2	73.0	65.0	63.6
45-64	77.0	25.0	72.2	73.0	64.8	70.9
65-plus	80.0	27.3	76.5	73.0	58.4	71.1

Percentages in italics are for age groups which exceed the average Welsh-speaking percentage for the county.

But teachers generally only reflect the society in which they work, as, to a lesser extent, does county hall. Both Pembrokeshire and Carmarthenshire deserve to be damned for allowing their counties to own the most unhealthy possible profile for Welsh speakers, one in which the largest percentages are always nearest the grave. This is precisely the same situation, although not as exaggerated, as in Glamorgan, where the language has almost completely collapsed.

It is often said among southerners that northerners are dour and unfriendly towards outsiders, even Welsh speakers from the south, while the typical southerner is supposed to give an open-armed

Croeso to every tourist. All such generalisations are exaggerated, but they do contain some truth.

It is significant that almost every minority language group in Europe is hostile to tourism, because of its supposed erosive powers. With tourists ever searching for the quaint, unusual and isolated, speakers of the major languages of Europe are pressing into the heartlands of the minorities. It has been isolation and lack of contact with outsiders which so often preserved the small languages.

These qualities are often synonymous with poverty, and such areas are urged by governments to increase their income by cashing in on the mobile hordes, by letting rooms, selling products, etc. The lure of money (excellent English has to be spoken to get the best jobs) has been a powerful factor in the history of the minority languages, and the increasing awareness that ability to speak Welsh can pay off in hard cash terms has given the minority languages movement a powerful impetus.

But tourism is an industry of servility, of pandering to the flickle, ever-changing needs and wishes of a clientele largely ignorant of the traditions of the areas they visit. Certainly they want to see Welsh, or Irish, or Breton, but in a gilded cage, if you please, as a pet to be fondled and cooed over with comments like : " Oh, how quaint ! "

This feeling of quaintness can so easily be transferred to the speakers of the language. And who wants to be a living museum piece, or a walking tourist attraction? It is possible for the tourist and his language even to take over in the home, once the sanctified stronghold of the old language. Let a tourist walk through the door looking for bed and breakfast, and servility can enter, too.

Such an attitude, with the visitors in the best rooms and the family camped on the sofa, ill accompanies a campaign to give dignity and strength to the local language.

Tourism, regrettably, is here to stay. It seems, though, that its damage will vary. If Welsh is to be maintained, the attitude to be decried is the open-hearted Croeso to " our cousins from across the dyke ", an attitude more typical of the south.

To be encouraged is the hard-hearted cynicism of " fleecing the Sais ". It was an elderly and well-known northern solicitor, not known to me for his connections with Plaid Cymru, who most vividly put this view to me. In Llanberis I can well remember the shopkeeper who decided my request in Welsh for a newspaper justified ignoring a queue of tourists who had arrived first. I also vividly recall the workmen who walked into a cafe crowded with visitors and, in loud voices to the woman behind the counter, poured scorn in Welsh on her customers.

It has been argued that the death of the last monoglots will be followed several generations later by the death of the language. There is certainly much evidence of the language being impoverished as outside influences flood in without a defence line of Welsh-only speakers, on whom English can have hardly any effect, to maintain its purity.

If the death of the monoglots is to be followed by the demise of the language, the peril will be greatest in Dyfed. If seven per cent. is the lowest point at which monoglots have significant effect on the language of the district, that point was reached in Gwynedd and Ceredigion in the 1950s, but in Carmarthenshire 20 years earlier. In 1911, while the other counties showed percentages in the mid-30s, Carmarthenshire was way down at 20.5 per cent.

Why this was so can only be surmised. Certainly, when the attitude of the Labour Party is considered later in this chapter, isolation is found to be important, but the start of this loss of monoglots pre-dates the arrival of easy transport.

In Gwynedd there is, of course, a considerable tradition of being the last bastion of independent Wales. I have already noted how it was only in Gwynedd, plus one council in Denbighshire, that local authorities either met in Welsh or kept their minutes in that language. It has often been remarked that no council in Dyfed would have followed the course of Llangefni U.D., which continued to meet solidly in Welsh, even though one of the newly-elected members did not understand the language at all.[5]

In rural Carmarthenshire even today the shadow of the Blue Books hangs heavily. In Llangadog Community Council, for instance, to speak Welsh is considered a sin, even when all the

---

[5] *Western Mail*, 12.11.69. A Labour councillor, originally from Maesteg, was involved. He later lost his seat to a Plaid Cymru member fighting almost solely on the language to be used in the council chamber.

fellow members present are Welsh-speaking, and anyone attempting to use Welsh for any more than a couple of words at the beginning and end of a speech (the sort of concession made by so many politicians, even when simultaneous translation is available, just to show their heart is in what they consider the right place) is apt to bring a reminder of the time-honoured custom of the authority.

In Gwynedd, perhaps, it is the shadow of Lloyd George which lies heavier, for he was well-known to use only Welsh with his family, and in politics, too, at times, despite his seduction by the glories of the imperial capital.

The differences between the two parts of Welsh-speaking Wales are mirrored in people's willingness to use the language on public or semi-public occasions. When reporting for the *Western Mail,* I have often noticed the frequency with which a telephone is answered in Welsh in Gwynedd, not only by nationalists but also by local councils and members of the Labour Party.

South of the Dyfi, answering a phone in Welsh is a sure sign of a member of Cymdeithas yr Iaith Gymraeg or Plaid Cymru, although even members of those groups living in the heartland will reply in English.

One trained observer of the scene reports that he was 50 per cent. less likely to hear someone using Welsh in a public meeting in north Pembrokeshire than in Gwynedd, although both areas were equally Welsh-speaking. Labour councillors from Llanelli would be absolutely fluent in the language in chapel, but would never utter a syllable in the council offices.

Some would continue using the language inside county hall, even discussing the business of the committee in Welsh. But immediately the chairman raised his gavel, the Welsh language left through the door. Such councillors will speak Welsh outside the office of a council official who is fluent in the language and wants to use it; but immediately they are ushered into his presence they chose to make it English only.

While Gwynedd County Council has gone all-out for simultaneous translation, and Welsh is now the main language of debate, Dyfed council deferred plans for similar equipment, and to speak Welsh in a meeting is rare and regarded by some members as the height of bad manners.

The north-south split seems to occur again in the very tradition which reposes in the language in these areas, with Ceredigion, as in so many of these comparisons, occupying the transitional position. In Gwynedd, there is a continuous, strong and continuing literary tradition, which flares again into activity in south Ceredigion, but which is largely absent in Carmarthenshire.

It is said that sales of books and, indeed of records, are lower south of the Teifi than to the north. There is no doubt that the rate of loan of Welsh books is lowest in Carmarthenshire, but is this merely because of the undoubtedly poorer library service of that county? Regional sales figures of books are difficult to obtain, but there are only two good outlets for Welsh books in Carmarthenshire, compared with five in Caernarfonshire.

Is the poor state of the local literary world the result of or the cause of the illiteracy of the two southern counties? But the production of literature is, even in Wales, primarily the work of an elite which would not worry too much whether the woman down the street read their works.

This lack of tradition seems deeply ingrained, for, even in the last century local newspapers were founded south of the Dyfi in areas now Welsh-speaking only in Castell Newydd Emlyn, Ystalyfera and Lampeter, while centres in the north included, within living memory, Dolgellau, Corwen, Bala, Blaenau Ffestiniog, Pwllheli, Caernarfon, Denbigh and Llangefni.

Although *Y Cymro's* circulation is now spread pretty evenly throughout Wales, this has happened only since the paper abandoned its attempts to get mass readership, going, instead, for the " upper classes ". It was sometime in the 1950s that the paper tried to extend its circulation, then concentrated in Gwynedd, into the Amman Valley, an urban area very suitable for a sales campaign. The campaign was given considerable editorial backing, and in the first couple of weeks about 2,000 new sales were obtained. But hardly any of them stuck . . . the people could not read the language.

This situation has led many to the conclusion that Welsh in Carmarthenshire has always been based on the chapels. This certainly seems true today, with rather horrible consequences in store for the language as the chapels decline. But closer examination shows that Dyfed once led Wales in Welshness.

The first printing press in Wales was set up Isaac Carter in 1718 in Adpar, just across the river in Ceredigion from Castell Newydd Emlyn. In 1725 it moved to Carmarthen, where Nicholas Thomas had started Wales's second press in 1721 and where James Breden followed with the county's third in 1730. It is said of one of their successors, John Ross, that during the 18th century he printed and circulated nearly as many books as the rest of the printers of Wales combined.[6]

There was good reason for this concentration on Carmarthen, for it was at Llanddowror, near St. Clears, that the great circulating school movement of the Rev. Gruffudd Jones was born in 1736. Between 1737 and 1761, over 158,000 scholars received instruction, almost half of the population of the time, sufficient to make Wales one of the most literate nations in the world.[7]

But the effect of these schools was very strongly regionalised. By 1740-1, only three had been set up in the north, and the majority were in the three counties of Dyfed.[8] Throughout the high years of the movement, until 1776, these counties remained the strongholds, and it is impossible to doubt that 90 per cent. of the population of these areas must have been associated with these schools.[9]

Yet, within a century, when the time came for Victorian entrepreneurs to set up weekly papers, the effect had vanished in the south (although papers were opened in Merthyr and Aberdâr in the very different conditions of the Valleys).

A hint of the present weakness of Carmarthenshire shows in the detailed distribution figures for Y Wawr. Of its 4,898 circulation, only 413 copies go to Carmarthenshire and reach only 47.2 per cent. of the members of Merched y Wawr, the lowest penetration but one in any of the organisation's 14 regions.[10]

But it is the regional spread of the movement's membership that gives one of the clearest clues to the relative strengths of the

[6] J. & V. Lodwick, The Story of Carmarthen (Carmarthen, 1972), p. 131.
[7] G. Evans, Land of my Fathers, p. 329.
[8] W. Rees, An Historical Atlas of Wales (London, 1959), p. 61.
[9] G. Evans, p. 347.
[10] Y Wawr, Gaeaf 1974.

154

language. Unlike many Welsh organisations, Merched y Wawr has not had an appeal just to the elite, the *crachach*, and the possessors of B.A. degrees in Welsh. In a number of places, entire W.I. branches have come over, and the membership certainly crosses every strata of society.

Detailed examination of membership[11] shows, however, little interest in the organisation in Carmarthenshire — about half what would be expected from the number of Welsh speakers in the county, while it is twice the expected figure in Gwynedd. The willingness of women to move from the predominantly English-language Women's Institutes to the all-Welsh Merched y Wawr tells an eloquent tale of their attitude towards the language (see table).

MERCHED Y WAWR MEMBERSHIP

District	Number of members	Percentage of total membership	Number of Welsh speakers	Percentage of total Welsh speakers
Gwynedd	3,606	42.6	135,090	24.9
Clwyd	1,390	16.4	73,980	13.6
Powys	535	6.3	23,950	4.4
Ceredigion	1,096	12.9	35,780	6.6
Pembrokeshire	275	3.2	19,490	3.6
Carmarthenshire	875	10.3	103,825	19.1
Glam. & Gwent	698	8.2	150,305	27.7

A potent factor in the current weakness of Carmarthenshire is the Labour Party, a very different creature from the party of Gwynedd. In the south, the party has been very British, dominated by the English language, and powerful. In the north, its power has been far less and the party has been indigeneous and Welsh-speaking. Although the distinctiveness of Gwynedd has been considerably weakened, particularly since World War II, Welsh-speaking party members from the two areas still have very different views on the language.

In Carmarthenshire, most Welsh-speaking Labour members of Dyfed County Council are violently against bilingualism when it

[11] ibid.

155

comes to spending money. One even complained when a telephone in the council offices was answered in Welsh. The language question is considered an ugly creation of the Nats, who are ready to pounce and sidetrack the council from its socialist path at the slightest opportunity.

The most eloquent spokesman for their point of view is Councillor D. H. Cooke, from Ammanford. To him, bilingual schools are the creatures of a certain political party which cares not about the cost to ratepayers.

His views represent, he says, pretty fairly the views of the group. Welsh should be taught as a subject : to provide Welsh schools is duplication. In any case, why bother so much with Welsh as it will not help the pupils in later life. The language will not survive through road signs, he says, adding (it was 1975, after all) that he has no objection to replacing damaged signs with bilingual versions.

A harder line sets in, though, over council administration. He asks how many could use the simultaneous translation equipment the authority has been considering buying : only four or five, he guesses. Questioned about council minutes in Welsh, he draws attention to the size of the typing pool which would be necessary, and then quiety adds that it could come eventually.

This " anglicisation " of the Labour movement in the south dates back more than a century. As far back as 1846, the commissioners who produced the Blue Books noted that all the political unrest in the coalfields was due to incoming Englishmen, thus anticipating the anglicisation of the Labour movement which was to bring Keir Hardie from Glasgow to lead the Welsh.

The growth of the Labour Party was closely associated with the unions, and in the south that meant the South Wales Miners' Federation and the National Union of Railwaymen, joint maintainers of the Central Labour College, which was especially active in the Valleys, arranging classes locally and giving scholarships for younger men to attend the college in London. In political activity it seems to have had pride of place.[12]

---

[12] H. Morgan, *The Social Task in Wales* (London, 1919), p. 75.

Its doctrine was the class struggle and economic materialism, seen as opposed to Welsh poetry, the eisteddfod and language, interest in which was castigated as nationalist.[13]

The Labour Party emphasised the ties linking the working class and socialist movement throughout the British Isles and was dominated by the centralist ethos of the Webb tradition, which looked with suspicion on anything rendolent of Welsh separatism.[14] The unifying effects of the great depression completed the work of the Central Labour College, and talk of " separatism " (and thus separate Welsh policies) was largely abandoned.

By the time Labour was in the ascendant, the Valleys which formed the party's base were rapidly changing language, and the internationalist code would have ensured almost exclusive use of English. But what was there to protect the western Welsh-speaking part of the coalfield from the influence, dominance even, of the much larger English-speaking districts?

Nothing, and thus Carmarthenshire Labour inevitably slipped into the expanding English-language sphere of life. As Labour was for years the only properly-organised political party in the county, with only a motley collection of Independents for opposition on the county council, the party could thus more easily extend its influence and ideas into the non-industrial areas, even of Ceredigion. It is noticeable, for instance, how Ceredigion's Labour Party, before UCW, Aberystwyth, grew to its present size, relied extensively on personnel and ideas from the south. Not until 1964 did they get a parliamentary candidate resident at the time in the county, in highly respected farmer Mr. D. J. Davies.

In Gwynedd, the tradition was, and remains, different.[15] An isolated area, the growth in trade unionism in the quarries after 1890 was no reflection on the New Unionism of England and the increased interest further east in socialist doctrines. And the unionism did not result in backing for the ILP, but for the radical wing of the Liberal Party.

[13] ibid., p. 73.
[14] K. O. Morgan, " Welsh Politics ", *Anatomy of Wales* (Peterston, 1972), p. 128.
[15] See C. Parry, *The Radical Tradition in Welsh Politics* (Hull, 1970).

The only voice of strength in Gwynedd unionism was the North Wales Quarrymen's Union, covering an industry which is even today solidly Welsh in speech. The union was no exception. Fabianism made no impact because it was seen as essentially English in character, as well as being alien to Welsh radicalism.

It was only after a determined effort was made to link socialism and Welshness that the ILP gained any footing. But even the ILP kept its distance from the London headquarters, with its leaders feeling that the radical tradition in Welsh politics involved the recognition of nationalism as of political value.

The affiliation in 1918 of the North Wales Labour Council to the Labour Party was looked at askance by some local union leaders because of the different cultural background. Although half a century has passed, this tradition has not been wiped out, as it was in the south by the depression and regular immigration from England and, later, the depression.

When the party gained MPs in the area (the first in 1945 for Caernarfonshire), it was with local men steeped in the tradition. The result today is that in Gwynedd an observer can fairly claim that Labour men are sometimes stronger on language questions than Plaid Cymru and friends, the controlling group on the county council.

13

Politics

WITH FRIENDS LIKE THESE, WHO NEEDS ENEMIES?

The Conservative Party has done more than any other to assist the Welsh language.[1]

Ask a Welsh politician of any party what his organisation's policy on the language is in detail and almost the whole room will shudder. This is the one topic most would love to forget. The language lobby is now strong and vociferous enough for the four parties represented in Parliament to take centrally a pro-Welsh stance. But with most voters English monoglots, and thus supposedly deeply concerned about job prospects and their children's education, great care is taken not to harm the susceptibilities of any but the most rabid anti-language fanatic.

The politicians' way out is to issue a vague general statement omitting to fill out the detail. Such is the path taken by the Tories and Liberals.

Plaid Cymru is rather like the Labour Party in Carmarthenshire — who were so obviously socialist that they didn't bother to abolish grammar schools. In the Blaid's case, so many of their members and parliamentary candidates speak Welsh that they haven't a policy at all worth the name.

[1] Wales and Monmouthshire Conservative and Unionist Council, *A Conservative Manifesto for Wales and her People* (Cardiff, 1974).

Which leaves Labour, who did their research in some detail. There was just one fault: they did a Nelson and clapped their telescope to the blind eye.

The Labour Party's policy is quite recent, having been prepared between 1973 and 1974. In the old days, the bogey when dealing with a Welsh issue was that of separatism. The bogey today for a language policy is " non-Welsh speakers, the bulk of our population ". Labour's basic difficulty is its need to encompass the widely differing views of the south-east and of Gwynedd, of the Cardiff councillor who wanted to push the language down the sewers, and of Gwynedd members who see their county's language policy as crucial to the entire future of the language.

Each area has its aberration, such as Councillor Paul Flynn, of Newport, or Mr. John " Linguistic Apartheid " Davies, secretary of Bangor Labour Party.[2] Sometimes, as in the call for a fourth television channel for Wales, the anti- and pro-Welsh can have a common end in view.

But generally the sheer numerical preponderance of neutrals or enemies of the language ensures a policy than can never be satisfactory to a language activist in the party. In drafting their current policy, they tried to strike a balance, but the extreme they were balancing was not the Welsh-only demands from some elements in Cymdeithas yr Iaith Gymraeg, but rather " those who will not be satisfied until Welsh is used alongside English everywhere in public ".

What is to Labour an extreme is to experts such as Professor W. B. Lockwood,[3] as well as world-wide minorities strong enough to threaten a state's existence, no more than a basic demand. Against this demand they have balanced the old bogey of jobs fears, one that is never quantified for fear of being laughed out of court were the tiny proportion of Welsh-essential jobs ever revealed. Throughout the great mass of industry and commerce — ranging from mining, through transport, steel, plastics, and engineering — the Welsh-must is surely unknown.

Indeed, the total of Welsh-essential jobs cannot exceed 20,000 in a working population of almost one million (two per cent.), and

[2] *North Wales Chronicle*, 20.3.75.
[3] W. B. Lockwood, *A Panorama of European Languages*, p. 70.

17. The first Welsh-medium primary school, opened by Urdd Gobaith Cymru as a private venture in September 1939. The room used now houses the switchboard at the Urdd's headquarters in Aberystwyth. *(Urdd Gobaith Cymru)*

18. The Welsh-medium nursery school which resulted from the strains of trying to maintain the Welsh language in an anglicised city such as Cardiff. This school at Llysfaen (Lisvane) insists that most of its pupils be Welsh-speaking.

(Western Mail)

19, 20.   The advance of the Celtic languages. Above, the first-ever camp of Urdd Gobaith Cymru, at Llanuwchllyn in 1928. The organisation is now the largest youth movement in Wales. Below, the towering mast and low buildings in the heart of the Connemara bogs which herald Radio na Gaeltachta, the Irish-only radio station at Casla.   *(Urdd Gobaith Cymru and Radio Telefís Éireann)*

6,000 of these are in education, with about 2,500 in other local authority departments.[4] Yet Labour continually talks of "ensuring not the slightest discrimination against the non-Welsh speaker". There is no hint of reassuring the majority that the only threats to their future lie in their minds.

The party takes great pride in the increase in forms translated by Labour Governments — great work, indeed, unless it is compared with that left undone. But even on the production of forms, concern is felt about the danger of "inequities" arising : perhaps someone might tell me how they might.

The crux of the matter is that Labour sees the language as a potential threat to non-speakers. To English monoglot activists in the party, the ones whose voices are heard in the party's councils, Welsh may appear a threat. But these activists no more represent the general public view than do the activists in any party.

The older leadership in some areas is English by ancestry; in others the party is under the control of left-wingers steeped in an internationalist philosophy, to whom the Welsh language is a dying relic of a past best forgotten, as, after all, there are plenty of things from days gone by — housing, industrial conditions, poor living standards — which are willingly consigned to limbo.

Labour Party members are seriously under-represented, for instance, in the Welsh primary schools in the Valleys, a growth which has truly come from the people, and not from a middle-class elite. But it is Plaid Cymru badges which adorn so many of the cars of parents able to afford to buy a vehicle, and Labour gets little sympathy from parents after it loses a bye-election. Not that these schools are nationalist cells, just that a Labour Party badge seems as out of place as Lucifer in Heaven.

Crucial to formulating a reasonable policy on Welsh is a correct diagnosis of the situation. Dealing with education, the party sees as the threats : an indigenous, traditionally English-speaking population; parental indifference or opposition to teaching Welsh as a first or second language; and mobility of population in an industrial area.

---

[4] *The Report on the Welsh Language Today* (p. 30) states that only 0.3 per cent. of vacancies notified through Wales by the Ministry of Labour specified Welsh essential.

161

Points one and three are valid, but where, apart from a few extremists in part of Carmarthenshire, are Welsh speakers opposed to their children being taught in their home language? How out of touch can you get? But what of television, and the greatest threat of all, English parents moving into Welsh-speaking areas? Absence of the latter should cause no surprise, because it touches on one of the most delicate subjects in Wales today, the difference between the Welsh and the English.

The Scots, who have only a dialect to distinguish them from the people of the south, overcame their feelings of inferiority some years ago. In the Welsh-speaking rural areas, many an anti-comment will be made about the incomers, but one sometimes feels that to express these feelings in print in a newspaper is to risk being labelled a nasty Nat, instead of a reporter of social trends and conditions.

To wish to be British rather than Welsh is a legitimate desire, provided the dislike of many of the English for the Welsh and their language is realised. But when this feeling of Britishness and we're-all-the-same-really is transferred to the language front, with suppression of facts which do not fit in with the desire, the damage to the language can be mortal.

What Labour ends up with is a policy which stresses the need for the "willing and enthusiastic" support of the English-speaking majority. On education, every child should have the opportunity to be taught throughout primary school in his mother tongue, and to learn the second language, which should be used in reasonable measure as a medium of instruction. There should be no compulsion on parents, although it would be the duty of local authorities to provide the facilities.

To achieve the aim, the central government should allocate extra finance, particularly to set up the fourth television channel. In publishing, steps should be taken to ensure that public resources should reflect the most important priorities.

Plaid Cymru's stand on Welshness should be uncompromising, what with Gwynfor Evans titling a major section of his history, *Aros Mae*, " Wynebu'r Prydeinwyr " (Facing the British). But ask for a copy of the party's language policy and there are embarrassed apologies. Ask for details of motions passed by conference, the party's supreme body, and no one seems to have them. Not that they would tell too much : until recently seldom were motions properly debated, thus allowing the slack, imprecise wording which was the rule to pass unchallenged.

Even today, the sheer weight of motions submitted to the conference steering committee (159 for the January 1975 conference) and the number eventually placed on the agenda (34, one of which had 39 amendments) militates against full and detailed consideration. In any case, a conference, with its restrictive rules of debate, plus the inevitable confusion in the minds of some delegates, is no place to hammer out a policy. The job of the annual meeting of delegates is to confirm, or reject, propositions worked out in great detail beforehand.

For social and economic policies, this has been done in admirable detail. But these initiatives have come so often from southern-based left-wingers. No such drive towards a party line has come from the linguistic group which not only founded the Blaid but has since maintained and enlarged it not only in the Welsh-speaking areas but in many English districts as well.

Partly this is due to the youngsters among this group, those who would have the push to drive the elder statesmen towards formulating a policy, transferring their energies to Cymdeithas yr Iaith, although they remain workers for Plaid at election times. Cymdeithas yr Iaith can be criticised at times for not knowing quite what route it is taking and for some rather odd priorities. Even this organisation is only now producing a detailed plan for the future, having preferred to pinpoint individual targets, often on the basis of attainability or prominence in public life rather than on the basis of significance.

But in their manifesto they have produced one of the most thorough, closely argued and significant documents of this century on the language[5] and the causes of its decline : it is an indication of how out of the swim the Labour Party is on the language question that there is no evidence of this booklet, part of the mainstream of Welsh political thought, having been studied prior to the production of that party's policy.

[5] *Maniffesto Cymdeithas yr Iaith* (Aberystwyth, 1972), translated in *Planet*, 26/27.

As well as "stealing" some of Plaid's best members, the lawbreaking activities of Cymdeithas yr Iaith caused that party to sharply de-emphasise what language policy it had. With the society getting a real mauling from the English-language press in Wales, and with real public feeling on the issue rather unknown, the party had every reason to play for caution.

Gwynfor Evans, the party's president, blamed the society's activities for his loss in 1970 of his Carmarthen parliamentary seat, although more powerful factors were likely to have been his self-casting as "the Member for Wales" (with valuable time taken pushing the message in England, of all places), lack of activity on the constituency front (although local authorities refrained from seeking his help at Westminster, in contradistinction to their usual policy, which would have given him and their complaints much publicity), and mishandling of the election campaign (the emphasis was on "The night you made history" at the bye-election and on Wales-wide policies, rather than on Labour's bribes because of the Nationalist Member[6]).

Cymdeithas yr Iaith were blamed both for creating an anti-language backlash in the anglicised areas and for upsetting the applecart in the rest of the country. Whether Welsh was a bogey or not, both sides believed it was. No agreement was possible before the February 1974 election on Cymdeithas yr Iaith standing down for the duration. But afterwards it was different, with another election due very soon and Gwynfor Evans only three votes from victory in Carmarthen. A top-level meeting was held beween the two groups. Although the direct plea from Plaid Cymru was rejected,[7] the society knew what not to do, despite grumbles from some members, who were rather disenchanted with Plaid's language policy.

The Post Office campaign (Carmarthen GPO had recently been invaded) slithered to a near halt. The society was pledged to obliterate any bilingual road signs which gave precedence to English, expecting them to appear in the autumn. The first went up near Mr. Evans's home in the spring. It went untouched.

---

[6] *Welsh Nation*, June 1970, Carmarthen Special Edition.
[7] *Western Mail*, 10.7.74.

The society was, in any case, floundering a little at this time; knowing the crucial importance of Plaid victories, what little fight members had in them was stilled. Until October, that was. As a cartoon in that month's *Tafod yr Iaith,* the society's official magazine, pointed out, now the booths were closed the paint brushes could come out!

The extreme extent to which Plaid was willing to go to disown the language probably reached the depths in the Caerffili bye-election of 1968. Plaid was terrified the language fighters would do considerable damage : they countered this by playing up that both the candidate, Dr. Phil Williams, and his wife were monoglots. To ignore the language in policy documents would be to play into the hands of their opponents : the problem was solved by including in a newspaper distributed to very house little more than a long description of the Welsh primary schools in the constituency.[8]

On the back page, Dr. Williams pronounced his Welsh policy : " All children should have the chance to go to Welsh primary schools *if the parents wish it* " (his emphasis). What a far cry from the conference decision of 1942 that " the learning of Welsh should be compulsory in every branch of education in Wales " !

The word " compulsion " is enough to send George Thomas & Co. into an apoplexy. In later declarations, Plaid learnt how to get around the difficulty : their aim of a bilingual Wales by the early years of the next century was to be achieved through education . . . but " this means that the language would have to be more than a mere compulsory subject like mathematics and geography, it would probably have to be used as a medium of instruction for specified periods ".[9] Compulsion by any other name?

It seems a mental aberration when " Welsh should be a normal part of the curriculum, at least up to O Level ", crept into the February 1974 election manifesto,[10] a sentence entirely absent from the October popular version.[11]

---

[8] *Welsh Nation,* July 1968.
[9] *Welsh Nation,* June 1970, election specials.
[10] Plaid Cymru, *Rich Welsh or Poor British* (Cardiff, 1974), paragraph 2.28.
[11] Plaid Cymru, *Nerth i Gymru* and *Power for Wales* (Cardiff, 1974).

Plaid Cymru certainly has a long list of language demands, mainly formulated in response to particular problems or language society initiatives. Thus equal status — which can mean almost anything — is demanded, with all official documents bilingual, instantaneous translation equipment in all official debating chambers, and officials capable of doing business in Welsh available in every public department.

The language should be a part of the schools' curriculum, with crash courses for adults and public officials. More money should be spent on books, plays and films, and, to ensure fair and effective implementation, a permanent Language Commission should be set up.

But it is only on television that a detailed and coherent policy has been worked out, by both Plaid and Labour.

The nearest Plaid Cymru has got to a detailed overall policy is that expounded by Mr. Chris Rees and adopted in substance by a 1971 national council. Covering 37 points, it has, nevertheless, failed to gain general acceptance (full report, *Welsh Nation,* May 1971).

Although presented to the executive and amended, it was discussed without enthusiasm. Why, it is difficult to say, unless it be that a cardinal feature, that Wales should be zoned, with linguistic provision varying by area, was unacceptable to key figures in the party hierarchy. Certainly Gwynfor Evans is vigorously opposed to such an idea, and in Plaid Cymru the amount of weight to be accorded a policy (or, indeed, whether the documents should be pushed onto a dust-covered shelf) is decided not by conference, or by the executive committee, but by discreet phone calls and meetings encompassing the " inner cabinet " (now the Parliamentary sub-committee) of about half a dozen. Indeed, on some matters the word of Gwynfor Evans, who has his finger very closely on the pulse of the Welsh-speaking areas, is sufficient.

But there is one way in which the language continually crops up in conference agendas — in demands that branches observe party policy that election literature should be bilingual. Many an election has passed, even at parliamentary level, in which scarcely a word of Welsh has been used by candidates fluent in the language. In exasperation, Cathays branch in Cardiff sent a motion for debate at the January 1975 conference demanding that "the executive committee and/or constituency committee refuses the nomination of any candidate who will not undertake to carry out this direction [to use approximately equal amounts of Welsh and English]".

A particular black spot used to be Caerffili constituency. The legion of linguistic faint-hearts in the party should be reassured, though, by the overwhelming victory of the party in the Tirphil council bye-election. The ward, fought for the first time ever, gave the Plaid candidate two-thirds of the votes . . . with every bit of literature bilingual and despite a Cymdeithas yr Iaith smear tried by the Labour candidate.[12]

Perhaps the change which has come over Caerffili may spread to the rest of the Valleys. Not that there was much sign of that at the party's October 1975 conference. One hopes that the groans that came from a number of southern left-wingers when the conference voted to add to its agenda a motion from Carmarthen calling for bilingual schools is not typical of nationalist feeling in that area.

It was not as if the agenda was overladen with language motions : of the 71, only two mentioned Welsh, one to demand the "rightful place" for Welsh in the Royal Welsh Show, and the other to urge a 1977 start for the fourth Welsh-language television channel.

One must certainly doubt the commitment of a few in the Valleys towards the language. More serious, though, has been the party's chase after a left-wing image, which has led to a downgrading of language issues. Of 20 motions submitted on the language question, only two were chosen by the steering committee for debate, although conference itself, by vote, added two more. With 172 motions submitted and 68 chosen for debate, the failure rate is rather high.

There were signs, however, at the October conference of the leftward drift being halted. The party is unlikely ever to return to the days when Welsh was the only language heard in its meetings, but the recovery of their equilibrium by the representatives from the Welsh-speaking north and west after several years of intense Left pressure should return Plaid to a more even keel linguistically.

[12] *Welsh Nation*, 11.7.75.

Not that friction between the two groups will cease : it is probably inevitable, primarily due to lack of understanding of the other's problems. Yet, although Valley nationalists have been heard decrying the language, how often have the other group poured scorn on the fight to save Ebbw Vale steelworks?

At the highest level in the party — Plaid's three MPs — there is not the slightest doubt about commitment to the language. As I write, Mr. Dafydd Wigley, Caernarfon, is engaged in battle with Gwynedd's health administrators on two separate language issues — the matter of a doctor's note in Welsh, which elicited a reply in Hindi, and the decision to appoint a new general practitioner for Y Felinheli (Port Dinorwic, a very Welsh area) without requiring knowledge of or willingness to learn Welsh : the advertisement emphasised the scenic beauties of the district. In the Commons, the language can have no three better friends.

The Liberal Party, whose last strongholds are in the Welsh areas, start with the disadvantage that they don't know what to call their party in Welsh. A printed, all-Wales Common Market leaflet pushed through doors during the referendum campaign referred to the party as " Plaid Ryddfrydol Cymru " at the head of the sheet, and as " Plaid Ryddfrydol Cymreig " at the bottom.

But in Ceredigion their MP, Mr. Geraint Howells, treats the language as of importance. A real man of the *werin,* a keen and natural *eisteddfodwr,* his attitude on the language question helped win him the seat in February 1974. Very close to Plaid's Welsh speakers on several cardinal issues, he attracted enough votes from strong nationalists to ease out Mr. Elystan Morgan who, although (or perhaps because) he sent a child each to Welsh and English-language schools in Aberystwyth, failed to disassociate himself from the vociferous stand by town members of the Labour Party against founding a Welsh-medium secondary school in the town.

But in reality the Liberals are deeply split on the language, and their Gwent councillors have on ocacsion headed vigorous attacks on it. This, combined with the party's chronic weaknesses in organisation and research, accounts for their shying from the nettle of a language policy.

A discussion document circulated by Mr. Emlyn Hooson, MP for Montgomery, in December 1971, urged spending not on

" prestigious matters ", but " in a way which will really persuade people to learn and love the language ". He wrote : " If the money now being spent in Wales on translating official forms, which are hardly ever used or read, were to be spent on improving Welsh education or television, then it would be money much better spent from the point of view of the future of the Welsh language ".

Far more promising was a press statement of September 17, 1973, by Mr. Terry Thomas (at the time of writing prospective parliamentary candidate for Carmarthen) on the then proposed Welsh Language Council. He wrote : " An essentially advisory council is not the answer to our problems. What we need is a council with power to initiate steps, to actively promote the language, and this means a council with a substantial budget ".

The party which believes in preserving the best from the past, the Tories, gave their Welsh language policy in the 1974 elections in just 26 words :[13]

> The Conservative Party has done more than any other to assist the Welsh language. A new Conservative Government will continue this support of language and culture.

But this is piety, not policy, and all that can be expected from a party even whose leaders attack it in public for lack of concern for things Welsh. Change will not come easily, for this party is at its most English in the counties where most Welsh is spoken. In Meirionnydd they freely admit that almost every office holder and party worker is an English immigrant, generally retired. They are not proud of this, just unhappy that the few indigenous supporters they have keep firmly out of sight.

Only in Pembroke has the party strength, and there they equally freely admit that Welsh is of no consequence in election campaigns, even in the Welsh-speaking north, a point echoed by the Liberal Party.

Not that this has prevented Mr. Nicholas Edwards, Conservative MP for the county and Shadow Secretary of State for Wales, from diving in at the deep end recently, emerging from the pool with the epithet " anti-Welsh " neatly attached to his forehead, according

[13] *A Conservative Manifesto for Wales and her People.*

to some. His strongest comments were about proposals for Welsh-medium secondary schools in the rural, Welsh-speaking areas :[14]

> What is proposed is that Welsh-speaking children should be bussed over quite long distances to attend these schools, and the English-speaking children should be bussed over equally long distances to English-speaking schools. What is proposed is that an iron curtain be erected between those of our children that speak English and those that speak Welsh. I would like to go on the record as being wholly opposed to this concept.

The previous Conservative Secretary of State took a rather different line. It was under him that the first such school, Ysgol Penweddig at Aberystwyth, was set up, despite choruses of protest from several local groups. No matter how much Mr. Edwards protests that he wants to see more Welsh teaching, particularly on the lines of Ysgol Preseli, the secondary school in the north of the county, where half the pupils are taught through Welsh, he cannot avoid the anti-Welsh stigma.

And yet, on economic policy he speaks sense :[15]

> Over a very large part of Wales the ability of communities to thrive and prosper, and thus to sustain their cultural life, their ability to retain their young men and women, and, therefore, their hope of the future, is almost entirely dependent on the health and strength of the private sector and of small businesses. The restoration of rural Wales is dependent above all on a restoration of the private sector and the small businesses that, given the right conditions, could thrive and develop there. There are some who believe that what is wanted are Agencies and Plans and Subsidies. I don't believe it . . . It is only a Conservative Government that can restore rural Wales. It will not be done by the Labour Party, which does not care about the countryside.

Whether Mr. Edwards heeds the calls for caution, only time will tell. Should he become Secretary of State for Wales, I would certainly expect him to turn a few educational somersaults : his arguments clash with his party's " freedom of choice " beliefs and he is, in any case, probably too late to stop this ball game.

---

[14] *Cardigan and Tivyside Advertiser,* 12.12.75.
[15] Speech at Birmingham, 2.2.76, issued by Conservative Central Office (Wales Area).

Much of the present state of the language can be justly blamed on its neglect by the British political system and Parliament " which no more expects to discuss the problems of the Welsh culture than the problems of Fiji ".[16] Over recent years " the oldest language of Britain " has certainly secured more notice in " the only parliament Wales has got ". But while Plaid Cymru, the nearest thing the language has to political guardians, persists in fearing that any initiative on the question will tar them with the " ram Welsh down throats " brush, the supreme body in the United Kingdom will remain very much a sideshow on this issue.

Fortunately, efforts to " take the language out of politics " and make it " non-partisan " are at long last doomed, and those with solutions to the crisis no longer have to seek the emasculated middle way. But while the political parties stand a good few steps behind public opinion, failing to recognise the extent to which it has been radicalised by Cymdeithas yr Iaith direct action and the Welsh schools movement, the torch which carries the message " Cenedl heb iaith, cenedl heb galon " (A nation without a language is a nation without a heart) will never be borne by our political leaders.

[16] *The Welsh Question,* p. 334.

14

The Wide World

BILINGUALISM BITES THE DUST

All forms of compulsory bilingualism are to be condemned.[1]

Listening to the arguments of many nationalists, it would seem they have never left Britain. That is a fair conclusion after hearing of the bilingual traffic signs throughout Belgium and the trilingual ones in extensive areas of Switzerland.

Now, it is true that Belgium has two official languages and Switzerland three, but these are not the linguistically liberal states our Pleidwyr fondly imagine. For both countries have rigorously rejected the idea of national bilingualism, defined as the knowledge of both languages throughout the territory of the state. Equally, they have rejected the principle of personality, that a person should be able to demand the full range of central and local government services throughout the country in his own language.

Instead, they have plumped for territoriality, that in each region one language will be supreme, and residents and immigrants will be expected to conform to the local majority language. It is rare to find a country where this principle is not paramount : even Quebec is unilingually French in many of its government functions. Perhaps only Finland, among those countries where the minority language has a history which encompasses the entire country's land area, approximates to the principle of personality, and even here it stops where too few speak a particular language.

---

[1] R. Senelle, *The Revision of the Constitution, 1967-71* (Brussels, 1972), p. 15.

The other countries where the principle of personality is adopted are those where there is no real minority language, such as white South Africa (Africaans spoken by 58 per cent., English by 38 per cent.), with both groups inter-mixed (in each of the four provinces, the proportion of whites speaking the minority language ranges from 23 to 39 per cent.).

Only Ireland, which does not, in any case, give full rights to Irish, approximates to the Welsh situation with the native language spoken by a majority in a limited area as well as by many, but a minority, over a wide area. But I have already argued that from the point of view of their importance to Welsh, these minority areas can be largely disregarded, especially as they are districts of rapid decline.

The trend towards monolingualism in Ireland and Wales is just one facet of a world-wide movement, which has been reversed and resulted in bilingual states only in very special circumstances. Usually this has followed war (especially civil), revolution or federation. In South Africa the impetus towards the breach of the hegemony of English in official life came from the rising educational level and aspiration of the Afrikaners, but also, and, more important, from their rise to political prominence after the defeats in the Boer War.

Welsh has nothing to approximate. Although the Afrikaner is face to face with the world's most powerful language, politically there is no doubt that he is boss. At the same time, the inter-mingling of the two groups has produced a significant bilingualism : between 60 and 70 per cent. of each group can speak the other's language, which makes relatively easy the provision of bilingual services throughout the republic.

Were Belgium, Canada and Finland to try and introduce the principle of personality, the lack of individual bilingualism, which is in the region of 12 per cent. in Canada, would militate against. And in Wales, as in Canada, it is predominantly one group which is bilingual, the Welsh and French-speakers, thus effectively limiting adoption of the principle to these areas.

The Belgians have no doubt where they are going. A basic tenet of their constitution is to bring harmony between the two main language groups by preventing either of them imposing their will on the other. Their first constitution, of 1831, was based on only limited interference of the state in the life of the citizen; French was then considered the natural language for state machinery, and within a generation or two it was expected to supplant Dutch.

Today, strict equality is the rule in the framework of a country with a language boundary virtually unchanged for ages. Friction is reduced to a minimum by accepting the principle that the Walloon and Flemish communities should be homogenous and people settling in the other's community must be absorbed. To ensure this, the entire cultural (which includes educational) system in Wallonia must be in French, and in Dutch in Flanders. Only Brussels, the predominantly French-speaking capital city in the Dutch-speaking area, has parallel institutions.

The rejection of bilingualism by the French-speaking Walloons extends even to their insistence that there should be complete freedom in choice of second language in the schools. The result is that in the French-speaking areas a not-insubstantial number of parents opt for German or English rather than Dutch.

The 1970 amendments to the constitution took the rejection of bilingualism to its logical conclusion. The unitary state of Belgium was abolished and replace by a community state. The ramifications extended even into the cabinet, which has to have an equal number of Dutch and French-speaking members.

For each division of the country, cultural councils have been set up with a wide range of powers covering the use of languages, education, literature and the fine arts, libraries and museums, mass education and leisure activities, youth organisations and activities, radio and television, historic monuments and beauty spots, cultural relations with foreign countries, and those organisations whose activities are concerned with these subjects.

The decrees issued by each council have the force of law. Running parallel are councils covering the same areas with power to issue regulations over regional economic development, housing, employment, public health, tourism, etc.

The Flemish cultural council has already taken steps to enforce use of Dutch, rather than French or English, in commercial institutions in its area, in pursuance of the aim that all intellectual life, education and administration must be unilingual.

Switzerland gives official status at federal level to three languages, French, German and Italian (Romansch is official only at cantonal and lower levels), all spoken by major states the other side of the frontier. The possession of a powerful neighbour who might one day raise something like the pre-war German rallying cry of "Ein Volk, Ein Reich" is a powerful incentive towards giving linguistic minorities considerable rights, particularly if they are clustered near the frontier.

In Switzerland, it is, though, the tradition of cantonal autonomy which has preserved equal language rights. But the equality extends only to the federal sphere. Of the 26 cantonal units, 22 are unilingual, with the language in the schools, for instance, the language of the canton. Even the bilingual cantons are made up almost entirely of unilingual districts. In the few areas where there is a truly mixed population, monolingualism is maintained as much as possible by running two separate schools systems.

But elsewhere the principle is maintained that the immigrants who knows only a foreign language has no personal right to introduce its use in official organs or public services (except, of course, those run by the federal government). He is granted the means of integrating as regards language, but it is his responsibility to learn the official language of his place of domicile.

The creation of unilingual districts was one of the first moves in Canadian attempts to deal with the language problem. Early Canada was entirely French. The applecart was upset in the massive loyalist immigration after the American War of Independence. The newcomers settled upriver of present Quebec, and demanded primacy for their language. The U.K. Parliament preserved tranquility by splitting Old Quebec into Upper Canada (now Ontario and English-speaking) and Lower Canada (the present French-speaking Quebec).

Upper Canada quickly became more unilingual than was intended — in 1792 the local legislative assembly scrapped French civil and property law. In 1839 the assembly abolished the right to use French in debates, in the courts and in public documents. By the time of the British North America Act of 1867, only the federal and Quebec legislatures and courts had to be bilingual.

In its early history the district which became Manitoba was bilingual in its administration and justice. But this was only a temporary phase. The Manitoba Act of 1870 maintained this bilingualism, and later Acts extended it to some municipal activities. In 1890 it all came to an end : an influx of English speakers led to the English Language Act making English the sole language of the legislature and courts.

In the North-West Territories, official bilingualism suffered a similar fate. After being sanctioned in an amendment to the North-West Territories Act in 1877, it was abolished in 1892.

In fact, even in the two areas — Federal and Quebec — where bilingual rights are entrenched, it is only the majority in the relevant field which gets a fair deal. At federal level, English private bills are never printed in French until the annual volume of statutes is published, and vice-versa in Quebec.

Bilingualism really breaks down at the level of subordinate legislation — only a proportion is issued in the secondary language. In federal courts outside Quebec, the shortage of bilingual justices and stenographers leads to problems for the French speaker. Interpretation is often weak and is admitted to be liable to lead to miscarriages of justice. At the municipal level, even in Quebec, where there were legal bilingual obligations, the numerical strength of the majority often led to monolingualism in French.

The predominance of English has long been recognised in those Canadian provinces where it dominates. Quebec is now taking the same path, with, as its goal, French as the common (but not necessarily only) language of all Quebecers. With the proclamation of French as the sole official language (Official Language Act, 1974), and demotion of English to national language status, yet another bilingual province has bitten the dust to counter the additional rights given to French speakers throughout Canada by the Official Languages Act of only six years before.

BIBLIOGRAPHY

Government of Quebec, *The Position of the French Language in Quebec* (Quebec, 1972, three volumes).

Royal Commission on Bilingualism and Biculturalism (Ottawa, 1965-70).

Official Languages Act, 1968-9 (Ottawa, 1970).

Official Language Act, 1974 (Bill No. 22) (Quebec, 1974).

I. B. Rees, *Government by Community* (London, 1971).

State of South Africa, 1974.

South Africa Official Yearbook, 1974.

R. Senelle, *The Revision of the Constitution, 1967-71* (Brussels, 1972).

F. Coppieters, *The Community Problem in Belgium* (Brussels, 1971).

Bilingual Traffic Signs, Report of the Committee of Inquiry under Roderic Bowen (Cardiff, 1972).

15

The Heartland

RIGHTS OF A COMMUNITY

*Some good, solid people, trained to be docile, have stopped
looking on obedience and poverty as a national vocation.*[1]

To most English speakers in Wales, it is the rights of the individuals
that are paramount. You or I must be able to obtain our needs,
and the more liberally-minded will concede that, if wished, this
obtaining must be possible through the use of Welsh.

To suggest that communities, nations or language groups of
themselves have rights, must be fed with the means of succour and
aided in organic development smacks to some of the ideologies
of Adolf Hitler and his grandiose plans for a Greater Germany.

Members of a strong grouping like that of the English-speakers
of England can without fear for the future speculate about the
desirability of the withering of nations and lessening of differences.
Almost any stirring of the human melting pot will find them at
the top.

For Welsh speakers it is different. In many parts of the historic
area where Welsh once ruled, the strands which merged to form a
Welsh-speaking community have all but disappeared. Even in the
heartlands the fibres are wearing bare. Without a community there
can be no language : thus the group comes to have an importance
unimagined to an English speaker.

The Welsh are not alone in this position. The same gulf separates
English and French-speaking Canadians, with the latter taking the

---

[1] Royal Commission on Bilingualism and Biculturalism, *Preliminary Report*
(Ottawa, 1965), p. 110.

view that to enable an individual to develop fully it was necessary first to secure fully a majoritarian French-Canadian society and culture.[2] The extent to which French Quebecers have pushed their demands is revealed in the three-volume government commission report, *The Position of the French Language in Quebec.*

Although French speakers are spread throughout Canada, it is Quebec, where 75 per cent. speak only French, that has seized the giant's share of attention in the dominion's battle of the languages. Some French-speaking Quebecers have even been disposed to forget the minorities of their own tongue strung across the prairies and into British Columbia.

For they take the view that only in Quebec is a fully-French life possible, only in the heartland where an overwhelming proportion speak the elder of Canada's two main tongues can a French society develop in all its glory. The difference between life in and outside the heartland in both Canada and Wales must be emphasised.

The Canadian Royal Commission was forced to spell it out in detail : it was no use, it told its readers, for English speakers to look at their local French minority and imagine that was just a smaller version of life as lived in Quebec.[3] For they were not seeing the picture of a complete society.

And it is the same in Wales. Welsh-speaking life in the anglicised areas is a very poor reflection of life in the heartland, even allowing for the erosion by English incomers. Even in a major centre like Cardiff, even the most ardent chapel-goer, Cymrodorion (literary society) member, Clwb Cinio (lunch club) dinner-eater, and Cymdeithas yr Iaith sign painter, all rolled into one, cannot live the life of Ceredigion or Arfon.

There are streets in the capital containing about 20 per cent. Welsh speakers : but these are English streets, and the language of even the youngest Welsh-speaking children is more English than that of their compatriots living in a wilderness of English. In the wilderness it is, strangely, easier for a family to keep its children apart.

With two Welsh-speaking families in a street, their children will play together, and it would be difficult to prevent English speakers

[2] ibid., pp. 99-100, for a fuller discussion.
[3] *Preliminary Report,* pp. 111-4.

joining in — and changing the language. It is this street play from an early age — usually from about when a child starts to speak — that is so destructive of Welshness in anglicised areas. After playing so much of his time in English, which is also, unavoidably, in very anglicised areas like Cardiff and the Valleys, the language of the school playground, it is no surprise that before long little Dafydd finds he is happier and more fluent in English, despite the attempts by his parents to keep the Welsh.

Thus is proved the adage that the community can be a more powerful influence on a child's language than the home. Fortunately, the Welsh secondary schools can do much to repair the damage, but never can it be said that Welsh is the undoubted first language of these youngsters. They may, in fact, be true bilinguals, but how long can that state last with Welsh in such an inferior position in the great wide world?

Apart from the favoured few, the language of work in the English areas is irrevocably English, with probably not another in the office or factory who can understand the language of the west. Ever tried asking for goods in a Cardiff shop in Welsh?

A Welsh speaker, when he enters an English area, must put on a different public identity. And English is so pervasive that it is inevitable that this public identity will affect his private one and he will become a poorer Welsh speaker : he will probably suffer linguistically and in vocabulary. But he will suffer in less tangible ways by becoming part of an English-speaking rather than a Welsh-speaking society.

No more can he be a full Welsh speaker, supposing such a person to exist. And to try and grab every bit of passing Welshness, such as by attending three chapel services every Sunday, is surely the way to ridicule, if not to insanity.

The situation would be healthier were ghettoes to exist, where the percentage of Welsh speakers was high enough to allow a large proportion of life to be lived through the old language, and where a proper society could develop. Without such a ghetto, strong individual willpower is necessary to maintain the language for more than a generation or two. Local minorities throughout the world are fated to be integrated : not that this is criminal, for that is precisely what is wished for immigrants into the heartland.

It is interesting to note the size of the ghettoes that kept alive Yiddish in Eastern Europe. Generally unemancipated, the Jews were forced to live together and they were not assimilated to the surrounding populations. In Warsaw before World War I, 50 per cent. of the population was Yiddish speaking, in Minsk 55 per cent., in Odessa 57 per cent., and in Berdishev 88 per cent. Many small towns were almost entirely Yiddish.[4]

A useful register of Welshness is provided by Clive James, based on very local fieldwork in Gwynedd.[5] To him, less than 25 per cent. Welsh speakers indicates " the extreme form of cultural penetration ", while between 25 and 49 per cent. " some form of community remains ". Once the percentages slump, little reliance can be placed on the census figures as an indicator of Welsh use, for many speakers will seldom meet another, or will not recognise them for what they are, or will prefer English because of the rustiness of their native tongue.

Some of these Welsh speakers in the diaspora do manage to create that community that is essential if a language is to grow, or even survive. But even in today's far more favourable climate, they can only consider their activities a success when measured against complete assimilation, their almost inevitable fate after a generation or two, a few mixed marriages, or a few sets of children who chose not to set language above so much else.

Measured against a real, vital Welsh society, their activities are a failure. The Cardiff Welsh may keep English out of their chapel services, but the invaders' tongue flows from their lips the instant they reach the door.

With the language in active decay, the only hope for the apologists lies in the creative outpourings of the literary few, the acid test of whether a local culture still incorporates the vitality which could give it a future. But when last did a bard from the anglicised districts win either crown or chair at the National Eisteddfod? If Elwyn Roberts (Llandudno) and Bryan Martin Davies (Rhiwabon) are excluded on the grounds that they live on the doorstep of the heartland, the answer is the Rev. Haydn Lewis, of Ton Pentre, at

---

[4] *A Panorama of Indo-European Languages,* p. 103.
[5] " The State of the Heartland ", *Planet* 23, p. 4.

Barry in 1968. Of the last 25 holders of the awards, 20 have come from truly Welsh areas. One of the few exceptions, which proves the rule, is Urien Wiliam, of Barry, one of the country's foremost dramatists.

It is to their heartlands that almost all cultures look for sustenance, not only in terms of immigrants but also of cultural backing. The maintenance of the Gaeltachtai as Irish-speaking areas is absolutely fundamental to the success or otherwise of that country's language policy. While many disagree with the present (1976) Irish government's policy towards the language, few deny statements by the Minister for the Gaeltacht, Mr. Tom O'Donnell, describing the Gaeltacht as the " source and fountain of the living language ". He adds : " No Gaeltacht, no language ".[6]

Mártín Ó Murchú points to the critical importance of the native speaker, the person who acquires his competence during his most formative years in a social environment (the " home-neighbourhood domains ") in which Irish-speaking forms part of a traditional way of life and is, therefore, conducive to linguistic self-confidence.[7]

He writes :

> The home-neighbourhood domains are certainly as funda-
> mental and crucial in the sociolinguistic pattern of our society
> as they are in others. The traditionally Irish-speaking areas
> are, accordingly, of the utmost importance for the development
> of a nationally-distinctive language pattern throughout the
> country, since they are characterised by the Irish language's
> being dominant in these critical domains and, as a consequence,
> are centres and symbols of the vitality of the language. As a
> result, they will continue for the foreseeable future to be the
> ultimate source of the bilingualism of other sectors of the
> population.[8]

Mr. Emyr Llywelyn put it more poetically at the Carmarthen National Eisteddfod :

> Trwy ei chymdeithasau y mae cenedl yn cyflwyno diwylliant
> i ddyn. Dyna pam mae cymdeithas glòs organaidd mor bwysig
> — yn wir, yn amhrisiadwy . . . Diogelu cenedl, amddiffyn

---

[6] Statement in the Dail, 31.10.1974.
[7] Máirtín Ó Murchú, *Language and Community* (Dublin, 1970), p. 30.
[8] ibid.

cenedl yw amddiffyn y cymdeithasau byw o'i mewn . . . Yr ychydig gymdeithasau Cymraeg sydd heb eto eu dinistrio — dyma gwpan ein diwylliant a ffynnon ein gwareiddiad. Eu cadw rhag eu dryllio, a datblygu yn llawn eu posibiliadau mewnol — dyma wir genedlaetholdeb.[9]

This sort of attitude hits directly at the " Glamorgan fixation " that has bedevilled so much thinking on the language. The fixation rests on its propagandists' numerate illiteracy in believing that total numbers are more important than percentages, that quantity out-ranks quality. The fixation demands that as much attention be given to the anglicised industrial counties as to the Welsh rural areas. Glamorgan's 141,000 Welsh speakers must gain the same concessions as Caernarfonshire's 73,000, never mind that in only one of these counties does a true Welsh-language society exist.

While one plank is visibly disappearing as the old native speakers die, another is being constructed out of the learners. Lord Heycock, one of the best monoglot English-speaking fighters for Welsh, did the language no good, however, when he spoke of a bilingual Glamorgan by AD 2000.

It raised hopes that Glamorgan's masses could come to the aid of the embattled west. In one small way they have, through the Welsh-medium primary schools. But success here hides a legion of failures. In English-medium schools, thousands of teaching hours have been poured down the drain each year during second-language lessons (probably more so in foreign languages than in Welsh, it must be admitted). And hardly anyone will ever learn Welsh solely at conventional night school.

And then there are the much-vaunted ulpanim — which are basically intensive three-hour-a-day courses giving 200 hours of instruction. When will the organisers cease extending their length? There have been successes, and spectacular failures such as Mrs. X

---

[9] E. Llywelyn, *Adfer Enaid y Cymro* (Llanbedr, 1974). " It is through its society that a nation introduces its culture to man. That is why a close organic society is so important — indeed, it is priceless . . . Safe-guarding a nation, defending a nation is to defend those living societies within it . . . The few Welsh societies which are as yet undestroyed, these are the cup of our culture and the well of our civilisation. To keep them from destruction and to develop fully their inner possibilities — this is true nationalism."

who has been on two courses and still can't use the language in public, or Mr. Y whose standard, when speaking to others, is that of an enthusiastic first former.

The big problem is the lack of a Welsh-speaking community where the language can be used naturally. For years I battled learning Welsh, but success has come only after having children, who act as unwitting guinea pigs. But how many other learners are fortunate enough to have created their own little community at the right time?

It is this problem which is so much exercising Bord na Gaeilge, the Irish Government's statutory body to push the language, and the committee on Irish Language Attitudes Research. They found that of those able to use Irish in most conversations, only 24.6 per cent. did so frequently outside the Gaeltacht. Only 59.7 per cent. of those with native-speaker ability used the language often in anglicised areas. The committee found no answer to this terrible waste of ability, which must be reflected in Wales, although the higher proportion of true natives should push up the usage levels.

It is nigh criminal that while enthusiasts have fiddled around with the learners' movement, the heartland that is their Rome has been burning. Certainly the learners have a place, but first we must absorb the lesson of Hebrew. That revival succeeded only because the learners were immediately immersed in a community. If our Welsh communities die or are much further weakened, no amount of ulpanim will restore the language : it will be dead, like Cornish and Manx, the plaything for the few with time on their hands, or for those with a great vision of the past.

It is argued by some that a language can survive without a region or country to call its own. It is, however, the paths of defeatism, taken by those without faith that the heartland can be saved. If Welsh is to survive, it must, they say, expand throughout the country.

But such a thin veneer of Welsh across a land speaking one of the world's most powerful languages will surely wear the pallor of death. The Irish talk in this way of creating " bilingual situa-

[10] Committee on Irish Language Attitudes Research, *Report* (Dublin, 1975), p. 183.

184

tions" throughout their fair isle, for instance, with Irish speakers resorting to Irish among friends in an otherwise English gathering. They hope people with a little Irish will make occasional use of it.

This is the very depth of defeatism. A sentence in Irish, or Welsh, at the beginning of a speech entirely in English isn't bilingualism. It is surrender to English. Ask any of those members of the Women's Institutes who have quit in disgust at "bilingualism" and joined Merched y Wawr.

Fortunately, a few in the Republic seem to have seen the light. Writing in the monthly journal of Conradh na Gaeilge (the Gaelic League), a correspondent said:[11]

> There is no point in distributing handy phrases, as it were, just as you might distribute leaflets or sweets. In that case you already admit that the language is dead and can be parcelled out in lumps.

Welsh, of course, could become like Latin, or Cornish, or Manx. A dead language, no one's mother tongue, but kept alive for special reasons. But let us have no illusions about Cornish, for instance. There is certainly a revised standard form of the language, examinations board, a magazine and newly-written books. There is even a Gorsedd and Cornish language church services.

But how many people will as much as pass the time of day in Cornish? None of those examinations board worthies: they hold their committee meetings in English. Of the thousands who say they speak the language, only four will initiate conversation in it, and one of these is a Devonian, and another lives in Aberystwyth and intermixes so much Welsh that scarce anyone can understand him.[12]

Perhaps Latin is the model? That language has certainly survived 15 centuries without a community, but where is the Welsh equivalent of the Catholic Church or the Roman Empire? The church adopted the language as its official medium. The church's tremendous prestige and power, and the undeveloped state of the vernaculars, for long meant the language held sway in diplomacy, government, the law and learning.

[11] Bearnard Mac Annraoi in *Rosc*, Vol. 24, No. 9 (1975).
[12] *Western Mail*, 23.9.1974.

But faced with the rise of languages understood by all in a given territory, Latin retreated until today it is the official language of only the Roman Catholic Church. But what does this mean? At the Catholic Seminary, Collegium Urbani in Rome, intending missionaries hear their lectures and undertake their formal discussions in Latin. But once outside the class, it is all Italian. The Vatican tried to insist on Latin being the language of the world synod of bishops. But even here, in 1974, almost half the speeches were in " foreign " tongues.[13]

Its life in Britain as a vernacular was short and probably restricted to the romanised South-East, in particular the towns, and from the middle of the fifth century it succumbed to the English invaders, and was kept in use only for the church, literature and education.[14]

Hebrew was similarly kept alive, in a fashion, by religious dictates. The form of Hebrew that was living, and not fossilised in a museum-synagogue, was Yiddish. Which is part of a very different story.

For any tongue to survive as a living language, it must dominate in as many domains of life as possible, as Eastern Yiddish did in the ghettoes. The persistence of Yiddish, spoken in 1939 by up to 12 million people, surely reveals the cardinal importance of local dominance.[15]

The recent revival of Hebrew has a few lessons for Welsh, but not as many as some argue. Firstly, throughout the Jewish community there is a greater dormant knowledge of the language (for religious reasons) than exists of Welsh in the non-Welsh-speaking areas. When Ben Yehuda, the father of the language revival, arrived in Palestine in 1881, he found it possible to speak Hebrew, for many people spoke it for limited purposes.[16]

Yet his demand that this occasional use of the language be turned into exclusive use of Hebrew was ridiculed, and 20 years later only ten families in Jerusalem spoke Hebrew at home. What turned the scales was immigration and the associated upheavals. A very

[13] *New York Times*, 18 and 20.10.1974.
[14] W. B. Lockwood, *Languages of the British Isles, Past and Present* (London, 1975), pp. 155-9.
[15] *A Panorama of Indo-European Languages*, p. 103.
[16] C. Rabin, *A Short History of the Hebrew Language* (Jerusalem, 1973), p. 70.

nationalistic group arrived from Russia intent on using only Hebrew in the colonies they set up.

As immigration increased, the use of Hebrew turned more into a necessity than a luxury as the babel of tongues worsened : the only common language was Hebrew, no matter how rusty the knowledge. Two factors crucial to the growth of the language's use were the schools — a thorough-going Hebrew-medium system was established from an early date — and the Ulpan intensive teaching system, since introduced into Wales in a shorter form.

The demands of the community ensured the success of the Hebrew revival in Israel. But in the Diaspora it is a different matter :

> Traditional Hebrew is languishing and has not been replaced by modern Hebrew, whether as a spoken language or as a vehicle for reading. Religion, culture, political thinking — all that concerns Jewry as a whole — go on through the medium of multiple translation . . . Every contact between the larger Jewish groups in the Diaspora necessitates translation.[17]

The writer further laments that English has become the accepted Jewish international language. The reason is simple : the ghettoes no longer exist and these Jews are really in dispersion. A language can flourish only in a community : if the Jews have no community, the language of the wider community within which they dwell prevails.

The success of any heartland policy depends more on the willingness of the people than on government leadership : indeed, in a revolutionary situation, the policies can succeed without the latter. While the revolution will not burst upon the Welsh countryside at once, there are several indications that people are according Welsh far greater importance.

Thus surveys around the Teifi valley reveal percentages approaching 100 wanting Welsh-medium secondary education. Cymdeithas yr Iaith find that in some areas, particularly in the north, activities such as holiday home occupations meet with active assistance from local people. This is happening increasingly as the connection between holiday homes, the community and the language is realised.

[17] ibid., p. 75.

187

Although Plaid Cymru denies it is the language which has gained them control (with the aid of sympathisers) of Gwynedd County Council and their three Parliamentary seats in Caernarfon, Meirionnydd and Carmarthen, the situation in the north-west is without doubt that of a new force having risen and taken control over quite a wide range of community life.

Plaid is part of a new feeling in Welsh politics which emphasises the community rather than the more usual English emphasis on the individual. And the language is seen by most people in Gwynedd as the most important symbol of that community. This is clearly seen by the county council, which regards its treatment of the language question as crucial to the future of Welsh, not only in the north-west but throughout Wales. Significantly, at the time of writing, the council was refusing to replace damaged road signs because they are demanding the Welsh Office allow Welsh above English.

This advance of Welsh in political esteem has happened throughout Wales. In the south-east this radicalisation of thought is evidenced most by the retreat of the anti-language lobby. Their somersaults are a sight to behold, as with each Government concession they are forced to take up a new defence line, which, by implication, concedes their acceptance of matters they had bitterly contested so recently.

Thus those men who only a few years ago were telling us how many bilingual road signs bought a kidney machine (since when were both in competition for the same funds?) are now falling over themselves to assure the world that they fully accept the principle, but they don't want to pay for the signs all at once.

The most significant change, though, has seen the halting and reversal of the drift of the abler youngsters from the Welsh-speaking towns and countryside. Even ten years ago, these were areas for those who couldn't " make it " elsewhere, and for those who wanted a quiet life. But now, belatedly, the Welsh-speakers have realised that if the heartland is to be saved, they had better roll up their sleeves and not moan for Government help.

The desire to get into the fray owes much to the leadership and sacrifices of young members of Cymdeithas yr Iaith. The true patriots are shown to be those who stay behind, at less pay than they could get in Cardiff or London. The exiles are at the same time being increasingly realised for what many of them are, money-grabbers whose concern for and knowledge of Wales is deep enough only to enable them to bathe in nostalgia at rugby matches and exiles' day at the National Eisteddfod.[18]

---

[18] See, for instance, comments by Mr. T. Elwyn Griffiths, secretary of Undeb y Cymry ar Wasgar (Wales International), *South Wales Echo*, 10.8.1973.

16

The Policies

THE SALVATION OF A LANGUAGE

A people can create even a new homeland, but never a language; when a language has died on the lips of a people, the people are also dead. But if a human heart shudders before the killing of a single transitory human being, what then should it feel, making an attempt upon the life of the age-old historic personality of a people, this greatest of all creations on earth?[1]

The idea of a heartland is superb in theory, but can it be defined? To the regret of those believing in the patchwork quilt theory of Welshness, there exists in Wales one continuous solid area of almost-pure Welshness which can be accurately delimited. It has its English inliers, but the frontier between the English East and the Welsh West is clear and the change is sudden.

If 70 per cent. Welsh-speaking is taken as the definition of a heartland parish, there is only one in the length of Wales which does not abutt many others. That is Llandeilo'r Fan in Breconshire : its westward neighbour, Llanfair-ar-y-Bryn, just fails to make the grade. (See map.)

And over the last 25 years this boundary has been amazingly stable. The map showing the distribution in 1950 of Welsh-speaking children in primary schools reveals almost exactly the same frontier. The only difference has been the growth, particularly on the coast, of English-speaking colonies. But such immigration does not even

[1] I. Dzyuba, *Internationalism or Russification?* (New York, 1974), p. 154.

190

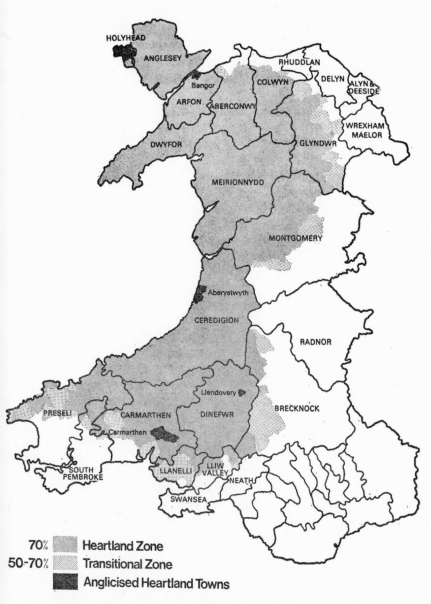

70%	Heartland Zone
50-70%	Transitional Zone
	Anglicised Heartland Towns

A linguistic division of Wales. Note the exclusion of Llanelli town from the transitional zone. (*Drawn by Roger Jones.*)

191

weaken the concept : the newcomers usually know their place, and are so anxious to fit in with the neighbours that they have even, as in Meirionnydd, been known to help Plaid Cymru election campaigns.

The only real problem concerns towns in the heartland that have for long been partly English-speaking. It is often said that those most strongly opposed to the language are those without it but closest to Welsh, such as the man who did not learn it from his parents. Although about one in two of the populations of these towns in a sea of Welshness speak *yr hen iaith,* concessions may have to be made to places such as Aberystwyth, Carmarthen, Llandovery, Bangor and Holyhead.

Similarly, there are rural areas along the eastern border where the language has been fading and it is now spoken by between 50 and 70 per cent. of the populace. Many of these parishes, of course, only just miss heartland status, in others a strong language border cuts through them, in yet others aged or pleasure-loving English immigrants hit the percentage but keep their distance from the locals.

The number of parishes where the language is actually falling out of use, where the percentage among natives approaches the critical 50 per cent. mark which presages a disastrous decline, seems to be small.

In any case, taking international comparisons, 50 per cent. is an absurdly high percentage at which to start a thorough-going language policy. Canada chose 10 per cent. after deciding that at 5 per cent. the minority group might not be able to provide the necessary staffing.[2]

Finland, again, takes 10 per cent., with communes changing sides after each decennial census. But existing bilingual areas are protested in that the minority must fall to 8 per cent. before a commune is declared unilingual.[3] In these bilingual areas, every public official must have written and spoken proficiency in both languages.[4]

[2] *Report of the Royal Commission on Bilingualism,* Book 1, p. 99.
[3] *The Language Act,* 1948-1922, Section 1. Translation provided by Finnish Embassy, London.
[4] *Act Concerning the Knowledge of Languages Required of Public Officials,* 149/1922.

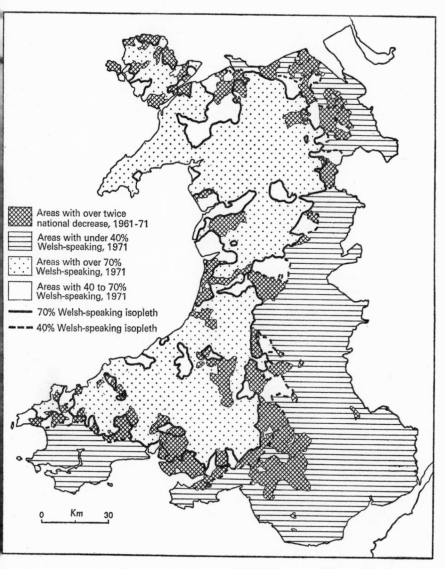

Areas with over twice
national decrease, 1961-71

Areas with under 40%
Welsh-speaking, 1971

Areas with over 70%
Welsh-speaking, 1971

Areas with 40 to 70%
Welsh-speaking, 1971

——— 70% Welsh-speaking isopleth

— — 40% Welsh-speaking isopleth

0 Km 30

The relation between Welsh-speaking areas 1971 and the decrease in Welsh speakers 1961-71. (From *Geographical Journal*, October 1974, p. 438.)

Ireland uses no percentage to define the Gaeltacht, merely an Order under a 1956 Act. Political jiggery-pokery has been alleged over the inclusion of certain areas, with consequent benefits to the local residents. But it is basic government policy that areas should be included to allow expansion of Irish: thus there is a Breac-Ghaeltacht, " areas in which English is the dominant language and some areas in which Irish is scarcely, if at all, used more than in some non-Gaeltacht areas ".[5]

In Wales, the census data is accurate enough to form the basis for a linguistic zoning based on parishes. Only in a few urban areas such as Llwchwr and the Llanelli rural area will existing publicly available figures have to be refined to enable a division.

Thus the *Heartland* (region A below) will be those areas west of the 70 per cent. Welsh-speaking isopleth. To account for recent immigration, Cwmrheidol (Ceredigion), inland parishes in Aberconwy District Council area, plus Beddgelert and Betws Garmon will also be included.

The towns of Holyhead, Bangor, Aberystwyth, Carmarthen and Llandovery are the only areas within the heartland with a native population which has lost its language. These *anglicised heartland towns* will justify a slightly different regime from the heartland itself. The aim will be the same as that with the Breac-Ghaeltacht in Ireland, to reintroduce the language by organic spread from the heartland. But the task in Wales will be much easier because the equivalent of the Breac-Ghaeltacht is smaller, is far more Welsh and is surrounded by heartland more Welsh than the Fior-Ghaeltacht is Irish.

Around the northern, eastern and southern edge of the heartland occurs the *Heartland Transition Zone* (region B), districts where between 50 and 70 per cent. of the population speak Welsh. In these limited areas the language is likely to be starting on the slippery slope, with Welsh increasingly being restricted to the older generations. Politics is the art of priorities: much good *could* be done here, but the activities would be more valuable in the Heartland itself and the Anglicised Heartland Towns.

[5] Gaeltarra Eireann/SFADCO, *An Action Programme for the Gaeltacht* (Na Forbacha, Gaillimh, 1971), p. 25.

Thus policies are watered down in step with reality — to force extensive bilingualism on an area like Rhymney Valley, where the remaining Welsh speakers are firmly wedded to official English, would be to create a backlash. But reality also is that although Welsh speakers in Cardiff amount to only 4.9 per cent., they add up to a lot of individuals (12,930), many of them keeping a close eye on their language rights. As the Finns legislated specially for their capital and made it bilingual,[6] so Cardiff should be boosted and given transitional status.

It is hard to treat areas with 50 per cent. Welsh speakers as part of *Anglo-Wales* (region C), but any language plan must be able to withstand the onslaughts of a couple of unfavourable censuses, and it is a demographic fact that in these areas the language is in the midst of a downwards plunge for which no remedy has yet been found.

In the Heartland, Welsh will be the official language, the primary language used by all organs of government both for public relations and internal work. English will be an also-ran, used only as much as it has to be.

The Heartland Transition Zone will be formally bilingual : everything the public sees will be bilingual, but the working language will be mainly English.

In Anglo-Wales, Welsh will be accorded National Language status. Essentially this means that everywhere its position will be upgraded to that accorded in the best Anglo-Welsh districts at present.

This does not mean these areas will be abandoned to their fate. The present learning boom here rests on two pillars : local people wanting to regain their birthright, and emigrants from the Heartland. The first group has by now gained considerable momentum; but the other half of the equation will not exist if the Heartland is not saved.

Let it be clearly understood that this is no informal division which is proposed. The time is long past for relying on " goodwill " alone for the pursuit of linguistic policies. Faced with the inertia of the civil and local government services (" There is no sphere

[6] *Welsh Nation,* February 7 and 14, 1975.

of activity where tradition can hold such a tight grip on practice "),[7] only clearly defined legal imperatives will suffice.

Any organisation which, after a short familiarisation period, fails to give Welsh its proper place should be held accountable at law to any ratepayer. The legal sting could vary : a specific action could be declared *ultra vires*; an authority could face a fine (but that would mean the ratepayers would pay), or the councillors and officers a surcharge. Perhaps most satisfactorily, an organisation could be barred by the court from receiving rates or government income.

That threat should suffice to dissolve each and every difficulty!

LOCAL GOVERNMENT, HEALTH, ETC.

Region A

Welsh will have primary official language status.

A basic point of policy for all authorities should be the maintenance of the health of the Welsh language : to this end, activities should be acceptable legally unless they can be proved illegal.[8] Planning applications to be refused if they harm the language.

All written material open to public inspection (such as posters, signs, forms, advertisements, documents, publications) to be Welsh only, or bilingual with Welsh first.

The language of work to be Welsh, although a few units working through English should be introduced to cater for present monoglot officers near retiring age as well as monoglots from the Anglicised Heartland Towns.

All written and oral communications from Heartland authorities to public service offices in Wales or to the central government must be in Welsh, thus ensuring primacy of Welsh. While central government and the Welsh Assembly must use Welsh in the reverse direction, other public organisations will have the choice of language.

[7] *Legal Status of the Welsh Language,* p. 35.
[8] At present, of course, local government is hampered by being unable to move unless specifically authorised by Act of Parliament or Government regulation.

All officers on counter duty dealing with the public must be Welsh speaking.

Road signs to be bilingual with Welsh first (in the Gaeltacht, they are supposed to be Irish only), including those saying the equivalent of Halt, Major Road Ahead, and Danger, Men at Work.

Except where an organisation already meets only in Welsh, simultaneous translation equipment to be compulsory in council chambers and committee rooms, with a legal right to use either language.

Region B

Welsh will have official language status.

The maintenance of Welsh remains a basic point of policy. All written material open to public inspection is to be bilingual with Welsh first.

The language of work will be English, but with the establishment of Welsh units. As with Heartland local authorities and to ensure that Welsh is effectively used, the units will communicate with other public bodies in Wales and with other sections of their own authority in Welsh, although communications in the reverse direction can be in either language. The exception, again, will be central government units.

To deal with the public in person, at least one Welsh-speaking official must always be on duty.

Road signs will be bilingual with Welsh first, and there should be a legal right to use Welsh in council and committee meetings. Provision of translation equipment would be optional.

Region C

Welsh will have national language status.

In these areas the present situation will be strengthened but not fundamentally changed. The majority of backsliding councils will be brought up to the level of the more enlightened.

Thus basic documents sent to or available to the public will be bilingual, although the size of the document may necessitate separate Welsh and English versions. Obviously, top of the list would be rate demand forms.

The public will have the right to deal in writing with these councils in Welsh, but the authorities themselves will be working entirely through English.

Road signs will, of course, be bilingual, but with English first (unless the Secretary of State decides otherwise in the cause of uniformity).

Boundaries

Are local authority areas drawn up for the benefit of Whitehall civil servants who want to see Englananwales neatly parcelled into similar-sized bundles by acreage, population and rateable value? Or are they meant to be based on the living communities of an area?

Some of the Welsh Office's present creations are real abortions : South Pembrokeshire, for instance, whose area sticks like a sore thumb into the centre of the Preseli Mountains, while Preseli D.C. includes the extremes of Welsh and English areas. Llandudno equally realises it is the odd man out in Gwynedd and Aberconwy.

Justice demands that an entire council area operate the policy of the most-Welsh district within its boundaries. The rush by councillors in some of the very anglicised areas thus encompassed to get out of the Heartland should provide an excellent opportunity to redraw the boundaries, taking linguistic facts more into account. The timing should just about coincide with the demise of the generally unloved county councils in the wake of the setting up of the Welsh Assembly. The idea of redrawing boundaries with an ear for language has already been mooted by Gwynedd County Council. In its *Community Councils Boundary Review* situation paper (1975), " cultural identity " is seen as one determinant of boundaries.

Pembrokeshire could be divided along the modern Landsker, Llandudno and the urbanised coastal strip of Clwyd could be split from the rural Welsh-speaking hinterland, and the Dyfi valley and tributaries could go into Meirionnydd. As Wales is a nation, despite its linguistic differences, I would be loathe to institutionalise the split with a separate Senate for the Welsh-speaking areas, even if it has only advisory powers, as has been accorded the Swedes in Finland.

198

Only if the present institutions prove incapable of correctly implementing the language policies — even if only part of their areas may be in the Heartland — can I see strong demands arising for a separate Heartland authority, a demand already conceded for the Gaeltacht. Interestingly, this follows the linguistic failure of the existing institutions and it was readily conceded only because peripheral districts of counties were concerned. Such a split would be strongly opposed in Wales because of the wide area which would be encompassed.

EDUCATION

The administration of education is very close to landing in the political melting pot. If, with devolution, the counties are abolished, the still-operative pressures for centralisation will probably result in the schools baby landing in the lap of the Welsh Assembly, despite the existence of district councils covering the same areas as some of the education authorities of just three years ago. Such treatment would strengthen the argument for a Heartland Education Authority.

Boundary problems should be few, as the principle of linguistic provision is already firmly entrenched in education administration, with some catchment areas redrawn to follow linguistic divides. Even if education does remain a fairly local responsibility, the argument for the provision of a new authority is strong, as it would be difficult under any boundary reorganisation for local council purposes, for example, to put all the Welsh-speaking areas of Montgomery into a linguistically homogeneous area.

Whatever administrative set-up is finally accepted, throughout Wales a basic legal right to Welsh-medium education would be enacted.

Region A

The basic education system will be Welsh-medium. Only in the Anglicised Heartland Towns will there be a legal right to English-medium primary education.

In the very Welsh areas, non-Welsh speakers can be integrated during the infants stage. For immigrants aged between 7 and 11,

199

special intensive language-teaching centres will be set up in the towns which possess secondary schools. Based on these towns because of the existence of secondary school transport and the possibility of finding spare accommodation, these second-language centres would give month-long courses.

All secondary schools will be designated Welsh-medium (i.e., Rhydfelen-style bilingual). Children incapable because of their linguistic background of using these schools would be transported to English-medium schools sited primarily in the Anglicised Heartland Towns. Distance may, however, force the establishment of such schools in towns like Cardigan.

A Welsh-medium higher education complex will also be founded, preferably at Aberystwyth, to utilise the major research facility of the National Library, although Bangor Normal College could be used as the basis. It would encompass all types of tertiary-level teaching, including technical, teacher training and university.

Region B and C

In view of the reluctance of some authorities to set up Welsh-medium schools, and the poor accommodation often allocated, it may be necessary to form a Welsh-medium Education Authority for these areas, similar to the Catholic authorities.

Schools will be basically English-medium, but with compulsory Welsh lessons (except in region C).

Primary school provision should match the linguistic variety of the populace :

(a) Totally Welsh (i.e., no English before age seven) schools to be provided for pupils with first-language Welsh wherever a demand comes from the parents of 12 or more children. If small schools can be provided in rural areas on social grounds, they can also be supplied in urban areas for language reasons.

(b) The provision of totally-Welsh schools for monoglot English speakers is to be compulsory in all towns of 5,000 people. These would be Canadian-style immersion schools and attendance would be voluntary. The core of these schools would be the present Welsh schools in the very anglicised areas which would have shed their native Welsh speakers to the (a) schools.

(c) The adoption of the Schools Council bilingual project (half the lessons are in Welsh) by district primary schools should be speeded up.

(d) English-medium primary schools.

For free transport, the nearest school should always be the nearest of the relevant linguistic type (as recommended by Gittins, par. 11.12.3).

To help the supply of suitably qualified teachers, training in Welsh should be available at all teacher-training centres.

CENTRAL GOVERNMENT AND AGENCIES

Throughout Wales there shall be a basic legal right to use Welsh and receive a reply in that language. Included under this head are organisations such as gas, electricity and railways.

Region A

A basic point of policy is to be the maintenance of the language.

All written material is to be Welsh-only or bilingual with Welsh first.

The language of work to be Welsh, with the existence of occasional English units. The main difficulties will appear in the nationalised industries, but even in technical fields such as electricity power transmission the change is feasible. Between 1963 and 1968, Hydro-Québec did just such a switch.[9] Crucial were pressures from lower echelons for a change allied to a linguistic switch at the top. Even in an industry swamped by Anglo-American technology, the men in charge succeeded in changing language habits by consistent example. At head office a staff of 10 translated manuals, while during the six years 731 employees took language courses at an average cost of $650 (£300) each.

All communications with organisations and individuals in Wales to be in Welsh unless specifically requested.

All officers on counter duty to be Welsh-speaking.

[9] *Report of the Royal Commission on Bilingualism,* Book 3, pp. 496-502.

For court proceedings, the use of Welsh is to be the norm, with simultaneous translation equipment provided in all court rooms.

Region B

All written material open to public inspection to be bilingual with Welsh first.

The language of work to be English with provision of Welsh units, especially in Cardiff. These Welsh units will be important to the running of a department.

For dealing direct with the public, at least one Welsh-speaking official must always be available.

Region C

Basic documents and signs will be bilingual.

It will obviously be sensible to reorganise districts according to this linguistic division.

Throughout Wales there will be a right to juries chosen on a linguistic basis. Arguments that this will lead to packed juries do not bear international comparison : such a right is often available, plus sometimes the right of defence or prosecution to quiz jurors on their views.

INDUSTRY AND COMMERCE

This is the most difficult area to deal with, and it is difficult to see a language policy working anywhere but in the Heartland. Within that region, the role of industry is crucial to the future of Welsh : on the one hand, unsympathetic introduction of factories with too many English key workers could gravely weaken Welsh; on the other, no factories means continued emigration and a slow decline for the language.

One of the few organisations which has really faced up to this problem is Gaeltarra Eireann, the Gaeltacht's own industrial development board :

Whether mobile industry is grouped on estates or developed on individual sites, it is likely that it will be staffed by managers and technicians (at least initially) who are English-speaking. There must, therefore, be serious concern about its effect on the use of Irish. Experience has shown that Irish can continue to be the internal working language of the factory provided that it is used by managers and supervisors.[10]

It is basic policy that

. . . development action must be specially concerned with preserving, enriching and increasing the use of Irish in the Gaeltacht.[11]

Indeed, Gaeltarra go as far as saying :

Development policies which, though otherwise successful, would diminish the use of Irish would, therefore, fail in (Gaeltarra's) basic objective.[12]

The powers of Gaeltarra (and its proposed Welsh equivalent) encompass also cultural, linguistic and cultural developments. To attract industries, higher grants are payable than in the rest of Ireland (66.6 per cent. against a legal maximum of 60 and a usual figure of 50), and, most important, Gaeltarra can take an equity holding (of 26 to 49 per cent.) or set up a joint enterprise, activities not permitted to the Irish Development Authority.

This not only gives a say over recruitment (immigrants are kept to a minimum), but may be the only way of attracting a socially-necessary project.

With Gaeltarra's headquarters now sited in the heart of the Gaeltacht, the little extras such as advice on finance, marketing and development, which are freely given, are considered important, as is the complete recruitment service which is offered. Gaeltarra are even taking university graduates, training them in their own organisation and then offering them as managers to incoming factories.

From 1980, Gaeltarra plan to pull Irish-speaking labour back from England. A register is being set up : after the locals refused

[10] *An Action Programme for the Gaeltacht,* p. 163.
[11] ibid., p. 23.
[12] ibid., p. 33.

to help (tax-avoidance reasons?) Gaeltarra sent out their own men to the Irish communities abroad.

Provision of service industries and entertainment facilities (to prevent people having to go to English-speaking towns) are an important part of Gaeltarra's overall strategy, and would be just as essential in Wales. It is essential that the Welsh organisation's powers range as much from the mundane to the sophisticated as do Gaeltarra's.

In Ireland, Gaeltarra cash has gone into village bakeries and a data centre with computer to provide sophisticated local jobs. The organisation is a partner in Aer Arann which runs nine-seat Britten-Norman Islanders on regular services from Dublin to Galway to the Aran Islands.

Individual Firms

In region A, major employers of labour (above 25 workers?) must launch a cymricisation programme to ensure that all its relationships with its staff are either in Welsh or bilingual. This would apply to such as working rules, notices and collective agreements.

The ideal would be to change the language of work to Welsh. But the close commercial links with anglicised areas and the difficulties about setting up Welsh-language units militate against legal initiatives in this field. Use of Welsh in business should result in more Welsh speakers joining the business world, just as has happened in Quebec now that French has a firm place.

Customers have an important place in determining language use. Thus the use of Welsh by central and local government can be expected to have a permeating effect on local businesses. It must be admitted that this field is probably the most difficult to extend the use of Welsh: thus the Welsh Language Commissioner proposed below must play an important part in recommending and advising.

It would be possible to legislate, however, that all external shop signs are Welsh only or bilingual. Such a move would do much to cymricise the streets.

A national Welsh-language daily newspaper should be established, publishing perhaps five times a week. It should aim for the popular end of the market. The advantages in converting *Y Cymro* could be outweighed by that paper's headquarters site in Oswestry : delivery costs and isolation from readers would militate against a daily operation at that site.

For delivery purposes, the best site would be Cardiff, with the new paper hooking into the *Western Mail's* nightly runs. If the operation is linked with suggestions for weekly papers, a superior site would be Aberystwyth where a new plant, capable of printing colour and utilising the very latest technical methods, could be established. As the operation would consist almost entirely of new papers, it should be possible to negotiate realistic manning levels with the unions.

To gain and hold circulation, the paper should aim at local reporting for the Heartland areas, allied, of course, with considerable Welsh Assembly coverage. Whereas one respects Mr. Elystan Morgan's fears about political bias in the news columns, a newspaper which does not have a view about the way of the world is gutless and hardly suited to a region that one is trying to revive.

Financial viability is the big worry. This can be alleviated by the paper being the vehicle for *all* local and central government advertisements having an effect in the Heartland. The printing establishment would be funded by the proposed Welsh Language Commission, which would also provide a subsidy for five years. Application of Scandinavian lessons, which ensure profitability for daily papers with circulations of 12,000, should ensure no need for commission cash after that period.

There is a grave need for an in-depth political weekly or fortnightly of *Hibernia* or *New Statesman* style, lying perhaps somewhere between *Y Faner* and *Barn. Y Faner* would like to fill this role and the paper already has a circulation base. *Hibernia,* published fortnightly in Dublin, shows what can be done with a full-time staff of just ten, four of them journalists. Printing 28 closely-packed tabloid pages, it makes a profit at 20p an issue on sales of 22,000 and between 60 and 70 per cent. of the income from advertising. Certainly, after the establishment of the Assembly there will be enough happening to keep such a journal very busy in Wales, in Welsh or English.

More important to the language is the role of the local weekly. While Caernarfon and Anglesey are already served by Welsh weeklies, county papers must be formed for Meirionnydd, Ceredigion and Carmarthen. With printing at the Aberystwyth press using colour, and publication at the beginning of the week with full sports reports, a profitable sale should be attained, with a five-year subsidy to help.

Encouragement of papurau bro, and the local initiative they embody, is also important. An index-linked annual grant of £200 should be provided for monthly publication, and £400 for fortnightly. A condition should be that they remain monoglot Welsh.

I shall pass over the radio and television plans: they are already afoot even if delayed by the London Disease of economic incompetence by successive governments.

The Welsh Assembly

There should be a basic legal right to use Welsh. Simultaneous translation should be provided at all meetings. All documents, including the equivalent of *Hansard,* Bills and Acts must be bilingual, with Welsh first; no action shall have legal force until the translation is completed and published.

It should be a basic point of policy to maintain and develop the language.

Region A

A continual Welsh counter-service must be available (this applies also to Cardiff).

The language of work to be Welsh, with provision of English units.

Communications with organisations and individuals to be in Welsh unless otherwise requested.

Regions B and C

Welsh counter-service available.

The language of work to be English, with Welsh units.

THE COMMISSIONER

Regulations are fine, but who is going to ensure they are kept, in spirit as well as letter? Recourse to the courts is costly and few are willing to use such a sledgehammer. But in a country where all Welsh speakers also know English, abuses will be legion, some purposeful, but others due to habit.

Only an official of considerable power and status would be sufficient for the task. Such has been appointed in Canada to cope with the passing of the Official Languages Act. An appointee of the Governor's, he has dual roles :

> He will be the active conscience — actually the protector — of the Canadian public where the official languages are concerned. His duty will be to examine particular cases in which the federal authorities have failed to respect the rights and the privileges of individuals or groups of Canadians.
>
> The Commissioner will in a sense play the role of a federal " linguistic ombudsman " by receiving and bringing to light the grievance of any residents concerning the official languages.
>
> The Commissioner will also offer criticism of the manner in which the federal Official Languages Act is implemented. He will have to scrutinise the linguistic aspects of the Acts of the federal government and its representatives in their relationships with the public in all parts of the country. Since he will have to report annually, the Commissioner will, in matters of language, function at the federal level as the Auditor General functions respecting government expenditures and property.
>
> He should have wide powers of inquiry, including the power to obtain copies of letters, reports, files and other documents deemed necessary to his scrutiny of the application of the federal Official Languages Act. He should also be able to question under oath any federal public servant. He should be able to receive and, if necessary, make public any complaint from citizens concerning the use of Canada's two official languages. It goes without saying that he should have a sizeable staff at his disposal.[13]

[13] *Report of the Royal Commission on Bilingualism*, Book 1, pp. 140-1.

Significantly, even the Act establishing the post refers to the need to ensure compliance " with the spirit and intent of the Act " [14]

In Wales, he would report to the Welsh Assembly, but his powers would be far wider. He would oversee the activities of all organisations and people affected by the Act. The Canadian Commissioner has, in fact, taken a very wide remit, upholding complaints, for instance, that a shoeshine machine at Ottawa Airport was violating the law because its instructions were in English only, and that a state-owned hotel in Montreal was likewise acting illegally in automatically supplying guests free each morning only an English-language newspaper. [15]

The Commissioner would also supervise delimitation and, later, alterations of the boundaries to Wales's four zones and areas. To ensure impartiality, he would be responsible for allocating language grants, such as to newspapers.

He would also be responsible for such linguistics research as is necessary to fit Welsh for its fuller role. Such work, which includes compilation of terminologies, comes under the remit of the Régie de la langue française, the Quebec equivalent of the federal Commissioner.

A major task will be upgrading the standard of spoken Welsh. The campaign of driving out English intruders in Welsh sentences will have to be light-hearted, but persistent. Ridicule could backfire. Weighty pronouncements, such as from the Academie Francaise, invite guffaws of laughter. Probably the best medium is television, the principal aim being to instil a pride in language.

GENERAL

When Welsh is used in a particular post, the ability to speak the language by the holder should be recognised for the extra qualification it is, and pay raised accordingly.

To aid the weak industrial base in the Heartland, local and central government organisation in that area should buy local goods when the price differential is not more than 10 per cent. Such a policy is worked by the State-owned Hydro-Quebec. [16]

[14] Official Languages Act, 1968-9 (Ottawa, 1970), c54 s25.
[15] *New York Times*, 5.5.74 and 5.6.74.
[16] *Report of the Royal Commission on Bilingualism*, Book 3, p. 496.

A very extensive programme of crash courses in Welsh must be provided throughout the country, run mainly by the education authorities for the Heartland and for Welsh-medium education in the anglicised areas. The primary aim will be to fulfil the Heartland's job requirements. No expense should be spared and employers must be obliged to release staff on full pay.

It is essential that suitably-qualified Welsh-speaking applicants apply for *every* post in the Heartland. Their present failure to do so is one of the major causes for the immigration which is destroying the language; another cause is the blind refusal by appointing bodies to realise that, even under the present system, knowledge of Welsh is nigh essential for many jobs, unless it is expected (which it is) that all Welsh speakers, many with inadequate English, should put themselves at a disadvantage when forced to deal with a recently-appointed monoglot English speaker.

Welsh speakers, even in 1976, are still being sacrificed on the great altar of "professional qualifications", Welsh, of course, never being a "qualification". Quite why even Welsh speakers, whom many would consider nationalists, should appoint to posts in the Heartland, involving considerable contact with aged Welsh speakers, men with not a word of the language, is almost beyond me.

Perhaps they are bedazzled by the continual pressures from English-based professional associations which regard successes in their examinations almost as a passport to messiah status. These organisations get very upset, but, of course, if the English have to put up with an Indian whose English is not quite up to scratch. But they care not a jot for a Welshman forced to deal with an Englishman who probably thinks "Prynhawn da" is the latest proprietary medicine from Russia.

Two examples came to light just as I was finishing this chapter. The first concerned the appointment of an Englishman to head a Gwynedd County Council social service office in Pwllheli. An uproar resulted immediately, headed by the entire staff of the office. The present head of that office, who had been appointed to "find her a post" in local government reorganisation, said bluntly that a non-Welsh speaker like herself was unable to do the job.[17]

---

[17] *Western Mail*, 18.9.1975 and 25.9.1975.

She had been able to occupy most of her time organising the office, but, even so, a number of jobs requiring knowledge of Welsh had had to be delegated to subordinates. And it was this side of her job which was now increasing. The county council said, naturally, that the man appointed was the best qualified.

He was so qualified, in fact, that he would scarcely know if most of his customers were speaking Welsh or gibberish. This case looks as if, once more, knowledge of Welsh has only been taken into account to choose between people otherwise equally " qualified ".

How often is it said in this sort of situation : " Everything else being equal, we will, of course, appoint a Welsh speaker ". How empty is this phrase can be realised if it is changed to : " Even if everything else is equal, we won't appoint a Welsh speaker ".

The second example concerned the appointment of a general practitioner for Y Felinheli (Port Dinorwic). The appointment would be made in London on the recommendation of the Gwynedd family practitioner committee, part of that stronghold of Welshness, Gwynedd Area Health Authority. The doctor's district is almost entirely over 80 per cent. Welsh-speaking.

Yet the advertisement, placed from Caernarfon, mentioned not a word about the language, but plenty about the proximity of Snowdonia and the Menai Straits.[18]

The excuse that Welsh speakers just are not applying for these jobs should be treated for what it is, just an excuse. Precisely the same was said about French speakers applying for jobs in the Canadian federal civil service. The tart reply, whose truth is only now being realised, was that if the service really wanted those French speakers, it would find them. Precisely the same applies in Wales.

With language qualifications played down to vanishing point, it is really no surprise that Welsh speakers do not respond as they could to jobs in the Heartland. If the call of " hiraeth " is heard, the returning exile feels it adequate to satisfy himself in Cardiff, rather than Caernarfon.

If the language battle is really joined, with an official zoning scheme, I have no doubt that many sons of the Heartland will

[18] *Western Mail*, 15.10.1975.

answer the call. How many will depend on the image borne by their old home districts : a community which is willing to use its own resources to fight to survive will attract; one which is happily dying on its feet will only repel.

One fight which has to be hard-fought will be against the professional associations and trade unions. Lack of Welsh independence in these fields will hinder the battle, particularly in that the overall British organisation may be fighting in ignorance of the real situation in Wales.

It is basic tenet of belief for most unions and associations that there should be freedom of movement of labour within the U.K. Their main fear is undoubtedly of a clique cornering a group of jobs for the boys, but the principle of freedom is used strongly against Welsh language qualifications.

There have been a number of noteworthy battles in the National Union of Journalists on this point : as far as I know, the outcome has always been pro-language. But the postal union dealing with sub-postmasters has taken the opposite view, and most vehemently, too. In view of the fate of so many sub-post offices, it looks very like industrial English branches trying to ensure nice Welsh country situations for their members nearing retirement.

Welsh-language cultural centres should be set up in major population or regional centres such as Cardiff, Swansea, Newtown and Wrexham. These would help to bring together the diverse elements which make up the Welsh-speaking populations in these anglicised areas. Their only centres now are the declining chapels, which are appealing increasingly only to the traditionally-minded old. A bar would bring life to these centres and fulfil a real need. Small auditoria and exhibition facilities should be provided : I don't like splitting art thus on a linguistic basis, but these areas are so overwhelmingly English that if Welsh gets a worthwhile look in, it is because of special circumstances, such as the presence of a Welsh speaker in an authoritative position. The day, however, is past that Welsh can rely on the goodwill of individuals, who perforce come and go. It is institutions that the language is crying out for.

Welsh speakers must form as many organisations as possible which work through Welsh only. The foundation of Urdd Gobaith Cymru and Merched y Wawr have been two of the greatest

211

linguistic events of the century. Groups like Cymdeithas Emrys ap Iwan (a group for linguists) and Cymdeithas Carafanwyr Cymru (Caravan Club of Wales) provide a valuable, but limited, service. It is time now that the members of the clybiau cinio (lunch clubs) slept off the effects of too much food and drink, took their courage in their hands and formed a Welsh-speaking and independent equivalent of Rotary. Eventually, such organisations will go some way to compensate for the decay of the chapels.

This decay is one of the more serious factors facing the Heartland, where the tradition of chapel-going has lingered longer than in the rest of Wales. But the decay is, bar a revival, irreversible. Perhaps it was only the example of the community (and risk of condemnation) that ever got most people to chapel. In which case, the weakening hold of all communities over their members, coupled with the influx of non-chapel-going English immigrants (the only English chapels are miles away in the towns), can only mean emptier pews.

Small, but valuable, assistance could be provided by the Government if translation equipment were available on loan with suitably wired halls available for hire throughout the country. Official bodies will need to undertake such work for their own purposes : the possibilities of other groups using the facilities should be actively borne in mind.

My policies are not particularly original : they are based on my knowledge of Wales and its workings, and on my very incomplete knowledge of the world outside. I am not interested in whether someone is (or can be) a better Welshman than another, merely in solving a problem in the context of the eight counties of present-day Wales.

Some people cannot stand the idea of a line being drawn through Wales : all I can say is that any boundary is to some extent arbitrary, but that if thorough-going policies are to be adopted in the Heartland there must obviously be a line at which they cease to take effect. To blur this line by establishing a series of Heartlands of various intensities (in line with the imagined language pattern) may be fine in theory, but will bring the whole idea into disrepute in practice.

212

If the English had a language problem, I trust this is the sort of solution they would adopt. I sometimes wonder if there is not a touch of the old inferiority complex among the opponents of the Heartland idea, a fear that Wales will fall if it is divided in any way.

Will these areas be cut off from the world? According to the English, they already are, because they speak Welsh. Within the Welsh context, I have taken care not to cut needlessly the links between areas.

No Heartland Authority, as the Irish are about to set up for the Gaeltacht in response to local demands, is proposed. The nearest approximation would be a Heartland Education Authority, but only if the existing education authorities (or their successors) proved unable to cope with the demands upon them.

The strongest criticism of the Heartland idea is that it will create a ghetto. But, unless I am mistaken, the old criticism of the ghetto was mainly because of the difficulty of leaving them for wider fields, and that's hardly any problem in Welsh-speaking Wales!

Inward-looking? The Welsh-speaking communities could have been accused of this ten years ago when they were debilitated by depopulation and the would-be leaders were on the first train east. But now there's a mood of confidence arising. Young people who could do well in Cardiff, or Birmingham, or London have stayed behind to put their community on its feet again, to restore its self-respect, an attribute as important to a community as to a person.

It indeed ill-behoves a monoglot English speaker to criticise, for which is the nation renowned throughout the world for its insularity, for its inability to speak others' languages, and for its refusal to believe an idea exists unless it has been printed in English?

The alternative to a full revival plan for Welsh is terrible to behold. It's not nice to see a man dying; it will be no nicer seeking the convulsions and death throes of a language. That way I see grave political dangers for Wales, and Britain. So far, apart from a few minor smashings of property, the language movement has been remarkably restrained, especially if viewed in a world-wide context.

But it is inadvisable to drive a man with a grudge into a corner.

213

Unless strong measures are taken before the arrival of the next census figures (presumably in 1983), I fear an escalation of protests which would not stop short of explosives, or even violence against official persons. The explosions which have so far rocked Wales have been all done basically on political rather than linguistic grounds.

But still waters run deep, and the numbers of those who have suffered financially and by serving time for the language vastly outnumber the straight political offenders in Wales. In the wings stands waiting John Jenkins, the bomber jailed for ten years, who, we are told, has been learning Welsh. He sees, quite correctly, that violence, or the threat of violence, has an important place in politics.

More sinisterly, also waiting just across the water is the IRA. Their men are fully occupied now in the Six Counties, but the protracted uban guerilla struggle over there means that there now exists within their ranks a tremendous amount of military knowledge. Should the army ever be stood down, there could remain a number of men itching for a bit of excitement.

Now, while it is incorrect to talk of any general pan-Celtic feeling, there are very strong links, both by sea and emotion, between Wales and Eire. The IRA played an active part in some of the first explosions in Wales, they supplied the generally comic Free Wales Army with a load of weapons, and I have little doubt they would again answer any call.

Politically, not much time remains. Linguistically, though, things are beginning to turn.

*   *   *   *

In 1962 Saunders Lewis, the guru of the language movement, commented on the radio that Welsh was the only political issue worth a Welshman's while to trouble himself about. He added that nothing less than a revolution would restore the language.

That fourteen years seems an age. How long ago was it that

214

Cymdeithas yr Iaith sat down on Trefechan Bridge in Aberystwyth and rocketed a movement to undreamed-of success?[19]

But the wheel has only begun to turn.

The closing paragraphs of that famous lecture were a call to action. But many people missed, perhaps on purpose, several crucial sentences. *Mr. Lewis was demanding Welsh in administration, and civil disobedience if it were not provided, in the Welsh-speaking areas, and only there.*

He said :

> This (demanding of forms) cannot be done reasonably except in those districts where Welsh speakers are a substantial pro-portion of the population.[20]

It is time now that our wheel was given a little further push towards its full revolution. My few ideas will take that wheel almost full circle, but not if the more ignorant idealists try to foist the full-blooded solution on Flintshire or the southern valleys.

In the Heartland the revolution, which is the only hope of seeing a living language in the 21st century, could be achieved. But the political dinosaurs who still control so much of Wales won't remove the chocks from under the wheels if others persist in trying to foist on the bulk of Wales a language that was willingly rejected. Of course, Welsh will continue to grow in these areas, but as a national and not a compulsory language.

I offer a quid pro quo solution, an answer to the problems rather than the myths that beset Wales, one that will get the backing of the vast majority of English speakers in anglicised areas. For, while Wales remains a democratic nation, no solution will be acted on without the consent of that majority.

Not that the result would be Ulster-style fratricidal conflict. It would be the London Government which got the blame, and the bombs. Although there are Welshmen strongly opposed to linguistic

---

[19] A not-untypical attitude was that of a senior student nationalist, later to edit *Welsh Nation,* who went to a cafe rather than to Trefecan Bridge, saying nothing would ever come of the protest! As a hint of things to come, the student newspaper, *Courier,* then edited by a citizen of Birmingham, refused to carry any mention of the events.

[20] S. Lewis, *Tynged yr Iaith* (Caerdydd, 1962), tt. 28-9. Translated in A. R. Jones and G. Thomas, *Presenting Saunders Lewis* (Cardiff, 1973), p. 140.

concessions, their numbers are few. As the language battle has intensified, their numbers seem to have declined. The point is that there is a tremendous fund of goodwill for the language, which has not decreased — and may have increased — with the pressures from Cymdeithas yr Iaith.

The Anglo-Welsh have seen plainly that their position in Wales is not threatened : they have recognised a plea for justice, and the great majority would not stand in the way of its achievement. Politically, not much time remains. Linguistically, however, things are beginning to turn.

And I believe Wales is not far from obtaining that consent. It is often said that anglicised Wales agreed to a Welsh language television channel because it cleared the language out of the hair of the non-speakers. Each group would be free to operate independently; the continual fear that incomprehensible Welsh programmes would take up a greater share of the air time vanished.

Similar negative reasons could be powerful in securing the idea of a Heartland and zoning. At present, the vast majority of non-Welsh speakers in Wales wish the language well and want it to continue. But their feelings are entirely passive. Fortunately for language campaigners, this group has not worked out what *real* bilingualism would mean. Make no mistake, if there were a reaction against every document being in Welsh, Welsh speakers at every public counter, simultaneous translation in every council chamber and committee room, and everything else which goes with a full-blooded policy, it would not occur at its greatest in Cardiff.

For in that city there are Welsh speakers sufficient in number, awareness and willingness to create a rumpus to ensure general acceptance of the policy. But it would be a different matter in many of the Valleys, in eastern Gwent, in much of Powys and on eastern Deeside. Here Welsh speakers are a small sub-stratum of the population. Welsh life is not highly developed. More significantly, these Welsh speakers accept that English is the language of their areas.

There are never many Trefor Beasleys around, and they are fewest in these very anglicised areas. Those who arrive from the West often hanker to return, and often do before long. Who is there to take up the standard? If the declining old are deleted from the equation, the few remaining would barely constitute a kamikaze squad. Why does Rhymney Valley District Council get so few letters in Welsh that it can blame each one on known local members of Cymdeithas yr Iaith?

No, these areas are English-speaking and they will never change their language in my lifetime. The Welsh language has an honoured place here, of course. It is the historic language of these areas : if justice is to be done, every child must have a realistic chance to education through the hereditary tongue. But if anyone imagines Welsh-medium education leads to a diminution of use of English, he should listen to the children playing in the school yard or waiting for a bus. The youngsters are indistinguishable from their compatriots in the standard English-medium schools.

If the plain truth of the situation were acknowledged — and certain nationalists threw out the outworn dogma that Wales must be treated as a unit for all purposes, including, presumably identical treatment for poor upland farms in Meirionnydd as for the lush pastures of the Vale of Glamorgan — it would be obvious that two sorts of language provision are needed.

First comes a really thorough-going policy to make Welsh the almost exclusive language of the Heartland. An outside expert whose volume appeared after I finished almost all this book sees such a policy as the only hope for the survival of Welsh, which could otherwise last only fifty years. He writes :[21]

> All the evidence shows that in this modern world a language is not likely to survive unless it is made official in an exclusive sense : it must have a monopoly in its own territory. This territory requires its own national administration and its own educational system operating through the national language. As a corollary, it will have its own mass media, that is to say, its own radio and television and a daily press using that language. Its speakers may learn as many foreign languages as they wish, but the national life is expressed solely in the national language. Only then can a language maintain itself and assimilate outsiders.

I believe that Wales would accept such a policy, but only for the areas for which it is intended, the Heartland. To try and expand

[21] W. B. Lockwood, *Languages of the British Isles, Past and Present* (London, 1975), p. 32.

217

its sphere of operation into the anglicised areas is to ask for trouble.

First, the chances of the policy's adoption is critically reduced — one may find only a few nationalists in favour. Granted, the world is changing and one day all of Wales may support such a revolution, but there is insufficient time for Welsh to wait.

Secondly, the difficulties in the way of implementing a blanket policy would be very considerable. Abuses would be legion. And in the absence of a boundary, who is to say at what point on the ground the abuses are to stop, who is going to preserve the Heartland from contamination?

If there is any question mark in my plan, it stands over the scheme for the anglicised areas. So much can be achieved here by local action. Some organisations will, in any case, prefer to operate a signs and documents policy on a Wales-wide basis, to the benefit of the anglicised districts. Once the ball starts rolling, the ignorance of the English can be turned to good account : one has already heard of the Wrexham store with bilingual signs and the Japanese factory managers who came to Bedwas and immediately set to learning Welsh.

The battle will still rage throughout the nation, but in the heartland it will have an altogether more crucial goal.

APPENDIX 1

AN IDEA STRUGGLING TO EMERGE

It is to an academic geographer that most probably must go the honour for pinpointing in recent years the existence of a viable Welsh-language heartland. That man was Professor E. G. Bowen, then head of the geography department at the University College of Wales, Aberystwyth. Geographers, of course, had always drawn maps showing the distribution of Welsh speakers, but these have all been on the basis of treating Wales as a unit.

Professor Bowen argues that while Wales is a political unit, it certainly has no geographical unity. In the *Transactions of the Institute of British Geographers,* 1959, he argued that a *pays* (region) was an area recognised by the inhabitants as having a certain physical or cultural unity. Within Wales, the *Pays de Galles* (the Welsh-speaking area) is the real *pays* from which the country as a whole took its name.

Using the 1951 census, he quickly spotted the paucity of areas where between 40 and 80 per cent. use the language. He then further refined the area by cutting out as insignificant districts with a very low population density. His core was thus the area with over 80 per cent. Welsh speakers, but with also over 50 people per square mile.

He proceeded to show that this division was not arbitrary : the linguistic division tied up with physical, settlement and economic facts : this was the area, generally, of dairying. The only major lack of correlation was South Carmarthenshire and West Glamorgan which, he says, remained Welsh-speaking because the broad valleys maintained a far larger agricultural substratum, which kept the language. Industrial development here was also post-1880, and thus drew labour from neighbouring counties, not from the entire U.K.

Indeed, perhaps this lack of correlation is the reason for the serious weakness of the language in this area, which I have demonstrated.

In 1961, Plaid Cymru put its toe in the water with a motion passed at its annual conference. A formal division of Wales was agreed, but only for education. Welsh districts would be those where over 60 per cent. of school pupils understand Welsh, mixed where the figure is between 10 and 60, and weak in Welsh with below 10 per cent.

The following year, Saunders Lewis delivered his lecture calling for civil disobedience in Welsh-speaking areas. His call was for Welsh as an official language " in local authority and state administration in the Welsh-speaking parts of our country ".

Cymdeithas yr Iaith, the child of that lecture, officially insists on ignoring that sentence.

In October that year the small flame promoting zoning as the only sensible policy flickered briefly with the publication in *Baner ac Amserau Cymru* of a five-year plan for the Welsh language. Its author was Dr. John Davies, now of the Welsh history department of UCW, Aberystwyth. He was blunt : " Our present task is to safeguard the language in the areas where it is now spoken ".

He divided Wales into three : " A " areas where more than two in three speak the language; districts with between a third and two-thirds Welsh speakers; and the rest. His fairly detailed policies for each area include one that until 1975 was forgotten : a register of businesses in the " A " area willing to conduct business through Welsh, and an organised boycott of the rest. In October 1975, at its annual general meeting, Cymdeithas yr Iaith started on that path with an approach to four chain stores demanding bilingualism, but they wanted it nationwide.

It was this article which formed the basis of Cymdeithas yr Iaith's evidence to the Welsh Office committee on the legal status of the language. Their proposals almost gave the chairman, Sir David Hughes Parry, apoplexy and he told them very tartly that he would never see Wales divided in his lifetime.

Another memorandum presented to the inquiry also proposed a division of Wales. But Cardiff and Barry District Committee of Plaid Cymru, having decided there would be blanket bilingualism across the country, were only dealing with qualifications for civil service jobs. In the " A " area (over 66 per cent. Welsh-speaking), appointments of non-Welsh speakers would be temporary and for two years only : this is similar to the Gaeltacht system where practice, however, is that few such appointees either learn the language or lose their jobs to Irish speakers.

In 1970, Chris Rees, then director of policy for Plaid Cymru, proposed a language policy which split Wales at the 10 and 60 per cent. lines for government purposes. The policy was largely accepted by the party's conference, but then dropped as unacceptable to certain senior officials who put more emphasis on the advantages they consider the Labour Party could gain from such a situation than on the needs of the language.

That same year also saw the publication by Cymdeithas yr Iaith of a small volume entitled *Areithiau,* a collection of speeches by Emyr Llywelyn. The most significant was the last, entitled simply Adfer, in which he emphasised the crucial importance to the continuation of the language of the maintenance of the strength of the Welsh-speaking areas : " Welsh will not be able to live except in communities where the language is the daily natural means of communication of the entire society. Welsh will not be able to live if its speakers are dispersed throughout the suburbia of anglicised cities ".

As if to emphasise his commitment to the Welsh-speaking areas, he added : " It is a witch's dream to speak of restoring Welsh in Glamorgan in a short period ". It was in this speech that he made his comment about building a fortress in the West, from which it would be possible to go out and restore the language in the anglicised areas.

In 1971, Ned Thomas cautiously tested the water in *The Welsh Extremist* (2nd ed., Talybont, p. 86), suggesting creation of Welsh districts, which could be regularly redefined, for the purpose of issuing forms.

In an article in the October 1972 issue of *Planet,* which he edits, he expands a bit on the same theme, even lumping Adfer and Cymdeithas yr Iaith together as organisations working, or seeming to be working, towards the idea of separate language policies for the various areas of Wales.

Mr. Llywelyn's ideas of first securing the Welsh-speaking areas before expanding into those which had lost the language were repeated by Emyr Hywel in another Cymdeithas yr Iaith publication, *Ateb yr Her* (Aberystwyth, 1974, p. 6). Neither author went into any practical detail.

None of these moves or suggestions became part of the general political consciousness. It took Emyr Llywelyn's rather extravagantly phrased speech at the Carmarthen National Eisteddfod in 1975 to jerk the idea to life. With his suggestion of a separate Senedd for Y Fro Gymraeg (Welsh-speaking areas), he went further than almost anyone else was prepared to.

But if his idea was to take an extreme line in the hope that a lot of people would stay at least half the course, he may have had some success.

About the same time, Mr. Cynog Davies, author of Cymdeithas yr Iaith's *Manifesto,* started to formulate his own thoughts in more detail. His ideas of strong, effective policies for the really Welsh-speaking communities were given at length in my series in the *Western Mail.*

In October 1975 he brought his ideas in the form of a motion on Yr Ardaloedd Cymraeg (the Welsh-speaking areas) to the annual general meeting of the society. The motion was passed overwhelmingly, but, unfortunately, it seemed to mean different things to different members. Yes, said some, it's an excellent policy, but we want it to work throughout Wales.

It will obviously take time for the society to work out whether they are going to ignore the motion in effect, or mould their policies to its terms.

In the meantime, the bitterest battle in the Welsh-speaking areas is that between the society and Adfer. Which only proves that people often prefer to attack those nearest to them in thought, rather than their real enemies just across the way.

APPENDIX 2

THE GAELS JUST DON'T WANT TO KNOW

" Within ten years, we won't have any children coming to school who can speak Gaelic, even from the remotest part of Lewis " — this statement in 1973 by the assistant director of education for Ross and Cromarty may be a scare, but one thing's certain, the Gaelic speakers of the few remaining fastnesses in the islands hardly care.

With the language expected to become moribund by 2025 and dead by 2075 (Lockwood, 1975), it seems the BBC's plan for a Gaelic language local radio station might be too late.

There is, however, a language revival in Scotland. It showed up in the 1971 census report with increases of around 50 per cent. in Gaelic speakers in almost all areas except the Gaidhealtachd. Enthusiasts were obviously at work, because of a sample of 35 "Gaelic-only" speakers in the anglicised areas in 1971, 30 of them only 10 years earlier recorded themselves as speaking not a word of the language.

The weak state of Gaeldom is revealed in the membership figures of the Scottish Language Society : of 450 members, only 50 are native Gaelic speakers, with less than 30, not one an activist, living in the Gaidhaeltachd. Advertisements in the *Stornoway Gazette,* the main local paper, for members have produced embarrassingly empty post boxes.

Not that the Gaidhealtachd is weak in percentages. The five parishes on Lewis and Harris, the most Gaelic area, show percentages of Gaelic speakers of 91.8, 90.5, 90.5, 86.3, 68.4 and 80.9. In this heartland there is, according to the census, very little evidence of decay among the young, of parents failing to pass on the language.

But these " safe " areas are so few, just the Outer Isles (with some nasty Armed Forces induced weaknesses in Benbecula), plus the parish of Kilmuir at the northernmost tip of Skye, and the electoral division of Duirinish West, on the island's extreme north-west. Elsewhere on Skye the language is fading rapidly. Even in Sleat, the south-eastern peninsula where a Gaelic college has been recently founded, the pattern of decline familiar in Wales is found.

The college, we are told, has brought new life to the Gaels in the area. Unfortunately, while 82 per cent. of the pensioners speak the old language, it is heard on the tongues of only one in two of the under-14s.

On the mainland, death has been savage and recent. The most Gaelic district is Applecross, where 50.5 per cent. speak Gaelic, a statistic which hides general knowledge among pensioners (76.8 per cent.), and a reasonable knowledge among those aged 10 and over in 1971 (30.8 per cent.); but among the primary school children the tongue is all but dead, spoken by only 14.3 per cent.

The only hope for a language in these straits, spoken by a mere 46,000 people in its heartland counties, is a determination among its speakers to fight and retreat no more. Perhaps the signs are beginning to appear. The newly-created Western Isles Council decided, after several hiccoughs, to go bilingual. Inverness, the council which previously covered Skye, had fought hard against such moves : they fought so hard and long against a local landowner's insistence on a bit of bilingualism on a road sign on land he was giving them that the cost of the road improvement for that land leapt by £25,000 to £126,000.

It is even said that the old cry from parents — " But what's the use of the language? " — is beginning to die away.

If Welsh survives, it will be due to such a changed attitude allied to the activities of language activists : their sufferings convince ordinary speakers that the speech they looked down on for so long is indeed a possession of value.

The Scottish Language Society (Comunn na Cànain Albannaich) was a brave effort to provide these martyrs. It was conceived in 1969 as a copy of Cymdeithas yr Iaith. Civil disobedience was an integral part of its programme, but the society never got off the ground in that way. It never attracted the people without responsibilities who could spare a month or two as guests of Her Majesty.

Perhaps more crucially it never attracted support from the Gaidhealtachd, from the people whose whole being was tied up with the language and who would thus be willing to suffer.

The group was formed as a result of disgust with the Highland Association (An Comunn Gaidhealach) and relationships between the two have usually been bad. The association get a Government grant (To shut them up, jibe the language society), and hold a Mod (where you would hardly ask for anything in Gaelic, adds *The Scotsman*). With the annual meeting in English and the Mod usually held in an English-speaking area (like Dundee or Ayr), it is hardly surprising that the few activists around regard it as a gathering for expatriates. The dislike seems reciprocal, with An Comunn acknowledging the crisis facing the language, but insisting that acts of salvation be entirely within the law.

In 1974 they produced a policy document on the language. It was noteworthy for zoning Scotland (but their Gaidhealtachd, not very realistically, included great chunks of the mainland), and for reprinting *in toto* Meirionnydd's education policy. But their main policy demands were vague, woolly and lacked thought.

The Scottish National Party is lauded as the only political party which cares for Gaelic. They have just issued some bilingual membership cards. One of the men behind them commented : " We had to be careful on this matter, because of the expense ".

For the second year, the 1975 annual conference of the party sported a bilingual banner across the stage : " That took six or seven years hard slog," commented the same person.

At that 1975 conference, there was just one motion on the agenda mentioning Gaelic, a rather weakly-phrased one on fundamental rights. The party's concern for the language was so great that the motion was never reached for debate. At the end of the session, the chairman called for the remaining motions to be passed by acclamation.

Most of the other motions were, but not Gaelic. There were from the floor several vociferous shouts of opposition to the motion and it fell. Apparently some people cannot forget raids on Lowland cattle by Catholic Gaelic-speaking Highlanders two hundred years ago.

While the language society has restricted itself to press statements, threats of a pirate radio station, the issue of leaflets, stamps and badges, plus a campaign of " irritation " against public authorities (which never seemed to have developed), one glimmer of real hope may have appeared.

Crann Tara, the language society newsletter, for April 1975 (which sometimes has to be produced entirely in English) announced the launching of a society for Gaelic-speaking students. Perhaps significantly Comhairle Oileanaich Ghaidhealach Alba has no English name. Headed by a native speaker, it stressed its non-violent and non-political nature, and immediately marched off to demonstrate against the BBC in Glasgow for its lack of Gaelic programmes.

The other hope lies in the Gaelic-speaking areas, and with such as Mr. Iain Noble, the gentleman who put Inverness County Council to such expense over a road sign. Based in Skye, he has a strong belief in the value of the community language and has founded five businesses, all with titles in Gaelic only, which use the language for work. In the same area, the Gaelic college is now flourishing, the only educational institute in the islands of higher than secondary school level.

Yes, Gaeldom is awakening, slowly. But there are few who believe it is not all too late.

APPENDIX 3

IRISH: SCARCE BETTER OFF THAN UNDER THE BRITISH

Only one factor prevents me beginning to fashion a coffin for the Irish language. This is the determination, or otherwise, of the 30,000 or so native speakers habitually using the language in the Gaeltacht.

For, despite all the bluster from the Government and the Dublin-based language groups, the battle in the rest of the Emerald Isle is all but lost. When the Coalition Government dropped compulsory Irish for school exams and civil and local government service entrance and promotion, they tore aside a thin veil under which had lain vast areas of the country which were more devoid of Irish than is eastern Gwent of Welsh.

On this great void they built a small superstructure of official Irish. Its foundation was Article 8 of the Constitution : " The Irish language, as the national language, is the first official language; the English language is recognised as a second official language ".

That prop has now been undermined, leaving the Irish speaker in a position "little better than that enjoyed by the Irish speaker under the British before 1920 " (*Éire,* Spring 1975, p. 112).

Despite the decision to set up Bord na Gaeilge, a state body with the independence of Aer Lingus, and with the aim of promoting Irish throughout the country, the writer in *Éire* comments : " Those who wish to bring about a language revolution in Ireland are more or less on their own ".

How on their own and how hopeless their cause is shown by the number of Irish-speaking families in Dublin. In a population of 566,000, only between 300 and 400 families are bringing up their children Irish-speaking : at the most that is 0.5 per cent. of the population.

No, if there is hope, it is in the Gaeltacht. Precisely where in the Gaeltacht, it is difficult to say. The boundaries of these so-called Irish-speaking areas have suffered a bit from political gerrymandering and favouritism : the concept was, indeed, wide open to such abuse as they were designed to include not only districts still Irish but also those where the language was fading (or, indeed, had vanished from recently). The rationale was that the language would, by including such areas in a Gaeltacht, creep back. Needless to say, the movement of the language frontier has all been the other way.

Of the eight Gaeltachtaí, most are all but dead, or so small that the slightest changes in the district around would swamp them. One of the largest in area, Mayo, has recently been decimated. Its deep poverty — which preserved the language for so long — remains, but most of the people have gone, and recently, and those who remain have all but given up Irish. In the 34 schools in this Gaeltacht, 18 have not a single Irish speaker on the roll. In only three are 65 per cent. or more of the pupils native speakers.

These figures, culled by Conradh na Gaeilge from official sources, are at such variance with the census (which says 73 per cent. of the local inhabitants spoke Irish) that it is no wonder the census is widely discounted.

The only areas where the language is still viable with any hopes of a long-term future are Donegal and Connemara. Gaeltarra Éireann obviously think so, too, because it is to these areas that almost all their energies are being directed. While Donegal has received the first industrial estate, Connemara has the radio station and the headquarters of both Gaeltarra and (soon) the government's Department of the Gaeltacht.

Both these areas in their heartland districts seem to be able to maintain their Irishness, a point confirmed by the recent Committee on Irish Language Attitudes Research *Report* (Dublin, 1975, p. 243). In Galway, 38 schools report over 70 per cent. of their pupils as Irish speakers, and the parishes of An Spidéal, Ros Muc, Carna, Leitir Móir, An Cheathrú Rua and Árainn report almost every school nearly solidly Irish-speaking, with some premises containing not a single English speaker, according to Conradh na Gaeilge.

The core of the Donegal Gaeltacht comes nearer to being split into several sections. Here 21 schools have over 70 per cent. of pupils Irish-speaking. The heartland parishes are Gort an Choirce and Gaoth Dobhair (Gweedore) in the north and part of Na Gleannta (Glenties) in the south.

Kerry Gaeltacht, which has for years been two separate entities, has 11 schools over the 70 per cent. mark, eight of them in the two northern parishes of Baile an Fheirthéaraigh (Ballyferriter) and An Daingean (Dingle), where they form a majority in each parish.

The Co. Cork Gaeltacht has two schools at over 70 per cent., but they are separated by 40 miles : one is at Cléire (Cape Clear) and the other near Baile Bhuirne (Ballyvourney). The Ring Gaeltacht in Co. Waterford contains only two schools : only one makes the heartland grade, while An Rinn (Ring) itself hovers at 66 per cent.

The tiny Co. Meath Gaeltacht supports only one school which is even half Irish, at Rath Cairn.

The remaining strongholds of the west do, indeed, have several advantages over their Welsh counterparts. While the absolute isolation which preserved them in the past has gone, they still remain largely out of commuting reach of towns. The distances are too great and the road too poor for even Galway to affect much of Connemara. The poverty of the land and the recentness of introduction of industry deters any rush from the east of families looking for a new life.

The church remains powerful and is now working through Irish, while, when religious observance falls away, as it is starting to, the pubs are already the heart of an Irish-speaking society. The Irish never suffered the narrowness of Nonconformity, which allowed the taverns of Wales to become the temples of the ungodly and the English.

The Irish language thus stands on a firm social base, aided by the pubs being almost entirely owned by local men, who are forced, by the existing customers, to employ Irish speakers.

But leave the church and zig-zag out of the pub and life becomes more English than in Wales. Throughout its recent history, Irish has been identified with poverty, and it is, indeed, only in the poorest farming areas that it has survived. The taint remains, though, and it will be hard to throw off while the Gaeltacht middle classes, almost to a man, are English-speaking only. The poverty of the countryside and the small villages would indeed repel the doctors and their ilk, who would prefer to work from the nearest town.

And these towns have always been English-speaking, partly due to past bans on Irish speakers within their walls.

One profession was, indeed, Irish-speaking, the ministry. In Wales its sons and daughters have rendered immense service; in Ireland the genealogical line ends with each priest. It may be because there has been no middle class chasing education that the Gaeltacht districts have little of the academic tradition that gives Welsh-speaking Wales such an immense depth to its society; the moan of the Gaeltacht is that the teachers they get are the worst, who never stay more than a year or two.

In this inflationary age, the Government grant of £10 a year to each Irish-speaking child would make not even a Catholic rich, although the grant of about £800 for a new house is acknowledged of more value — you can tell by the yells of protest from those who can't get it.

While the Government has talked a lot about helping the Gaeltacht, regarded as the fountainhead of the language they fought with arms to preserve, these areas have received very little

228

more than their fair share of public money. And the failure by both local and central government to provide fully-Irish services in all spheres has done much to undermine the language. By the Welsh standards of today, official Ireland has done so little that the founders of the Gaelic League must have turned in their graves many times.

Even the requirement that officials should speak the language has become almost a dead letter, as the deadline for attaining proficiency has been extended time and again. In some fields, the Gaeltacht sees English pushed when other areas have to put up with Irish. Thus CIÉ, the Government bus company, uses English destination boards on its Connemara vehicles, while in Wexford, where the language was dead by 1800, the blinds are Irish only.

While on the surface advances have been great, in practice " both the officials engaged in operating many (but not all) language regulations — such as those relating to certain appointments, to oral examinations in Irish for university students and those relating to the approval of secondary teachers — and the persons to whom they apply quietly conspire to set the regulations aside ".[1]

It is only from the recent work of Gaeltarra Éireann and the foundation of Radio na Gaeltachta that stems any hope that Leinster House really knows how to fight this battle.

Mention of the radio station brings me back to my first paragraph and whether the locals want to keep the lingo. For the radio was set up by RTÉ after the Government had been shamed into action by Gluaiseacht Chearta Síbhialta na Gaeltachta, the Gaeltacht civil rights movement, setting up a pirate station.

While mention of the language does not occur in the aims, the movement works to obtain proper services for the Gaeltacht in the language of the people. Founded in 1969, it has had a similar effect on the language situation to Cymdeithas yr Iaith's, awakening the speakers to its value and teaching them to fight.

The movement has since set up a monthly newspaper, selling 1,700 copies almost exclusively in the Gaeltacht (the local weeklies include scarcely any Irish, and the Irish-language weeklies sell few copies in the west). Recently it added signposts to the menu, obliterating the English names, which are larger than the Irish, with black paint.

Yet, again, direct action worked, for the Government told Galway County Council that signs should be in Irish only.

The civil rights movement is looked at a bit askance by most of the language organisations in Dublin. For one problem is that

[1] J. Macnamara, " Successes and Failures in the Movement for the Restoration of Irish ", in J. Rubin and B. H. Jernudd (eds.), *Can Language be Planned?* (Hawaii, 1971), p. 69.

Ireland is rift not only between Irish and non-Irish speakers, but also between the predominantly middle class speakers of Dublin and the east, who are often learners, and the speakers of the Gaeltacht who've got some mud on their boots.

With a State supposedly wedded to reviving the language, it was inevitable that existing groups would get official support and new organisations would arise to fill gaps espied by civil servants. The result is a group disparagingly referred to by the Language Freedom Movement (from compulsory Irish, etc.) as the Gaelgeoirs.

The contacts between the Gaelgeoirs, who are almost all Dublin based, and the Gaeltacht cannot be said to be very strong. Few of them are from the Gaeltachtai, and their opportunities for contacts with Gaeltacht emigrants is limited, as such people usually stop in Dublin only long enough to change trains for Holyhead.

While the importance of the Gaeltachtai is never discounted, the big aim has always been to Gaelicise all Ireland. The talk is of a situation "where one in every four people normally spoke some Irish to you ",[1a] and this means one in four in Dublin or Kildare.

The Gaelic League, the body which really got the language revival going in the 1890s, was indeed formed primarily of learners, as had been its predecessor, the Society for the Preservation of the Irish Language. Their aim, an all-Irish Ireland, demanded that the whole movement be based on the Gaeltacht, but that was not to be[2] and the league's biggest contribution to the language was its network of evening classes. But, massive though they were, attracting up to 75,000 students a year, they probably turned out in the 30 years to 1926 no more than 5,000 to 10,000 fluent Irish speakers, while the number of native speakers had dropped 120,000.[3]

By 1966, the number of native speakers had dropped to only 70,000, one-tenth of the 1891 total. Compulsory Irish at school enabled the 1961 census to return 700,000 people as Irish speakers, a quarter of the population. At most, 70,000 of these would be fluent, giving a total of 140,000, hardly enough for a revival.

Until 1901, the census returns can be taken as giving a good indication of the state of the language, with perhaps a little under-estimation. Under the British there was little incentive to claim oneself as Irish-speaking if one's knowledge did not extend far beyond a few sentences from a learners' manual. But with the arrival of the Free State, Irish was an asset and the learners rushed to

[1a] Seán Ó Tuama, " The Gaelic League in the Future ", The Gaelic League Idea, S. Ó Tuama (ed.) (Cork, 1972), p. 108.
[2] David Greene, " The Founding of the Gaelic League ", The Gaelic League Idea, p. 19.
[3] Breándan Mac Aadha, " Was this a Social Revolution? " The Gaelic League Idea, pp. 27-8.

classify themselves accordingly in the census. The falsity of modern figures dates in particular from the 1926 census : one area of Roscommon showed an increase in Irish speakers of 2,400 per cent. between the special enumeration of 1925 and the census the following year, and two other districts contained 228 and 114 " Irish speakers " respectively when the previous year neither had any.[4]

Even for those who have learnt the language to a high standard, the odds are very much that, the native speakers being so few, they learnt from a learner, an unsatisfactory situation in that although grammatical ability may be imparted, the essential conversational ease is less likely to be transferred.[5] Also in grave doubt is the standard of idiom learned.

More often does one, indeed, hear praised the high standard of grammar among the learners than their talkativeness. This, plus the fear of being very unfairly considered a Provo (IRA), there being so few native speakers around to set the record straight, undoubtedly goes a long way to explaining why so little Irish is heard on the streets of Dublin or any other eastern town.

Language enthusiasts do themselves often invite the charge of fanaticism. By rigidly segregating children from English speakers and trying to impose a hothouse regime of Irish, they give ammunition to the Language Freedom Movement and, by implication, reveal how false is the 1971 census figure of 25 per cent. Irish speakers in Dublin.

All around, the Gaelic structure built up with too little thought over the years is collapsing. Perhaps most significant is the decline, with hardly any associated protest, in the number of Irish-medium schools outside the Gaeltacht. The number of primary schools dropped from 623 in 1940 to 251 in 1970 (six per cent. of the total), and secondary schools from 104 in 1942 to 26 in 1972 (4.5 per cent.).[6]

Excuses centre around amalgamations being without regard to a school's language, the severe erosion in the value of special grants available to Irish-medium schools, the lack of text books (a scandal in truth), the lack of good teachers, and the system of management.

To try and close a Welsh school in Wales would be suicide for a politician. The lack of an Irish response casts grave doubt on the real depth of their revival.

But perhaps the real reasons are that Irish-medium teaching was introduced not by demand of parents but after pressure from the

---

[4] Brian Ó Cuív, *Irish Dialects and Irish-speaking Districts* (Dublin, 1951), p. 28.
[5] Paul Dwyer, " A Lesson from Ireland ", *Welsh Nation*, 10.11.72.
[6] Comhairle na Gaeilge, *Irish in Education* (Dublin, 1974), p. 17.

Department of Education. The department made it clear that not only was it teachers' duty to introduce Irish, but also that it was unimportant the stage or manner in which it was introduced.[7] Thus there was no continuity in use of Irish, not only from year to year for each pupil, but also from subject to subject. And a number of Irish-medium secondary schools took pupils exclusively from English-medium primaries.

To make amends for the general national mess, which includes disconnecting Gaeltacht telephones of subscribers who refuse to pay bills in English, the Government has now set up its board for the language, chaired, of course, by a learner.

The government argues that this move is against a background of greater public interest than ever in the future of the language. But it is debatable how much reliance to put on public opinion surveys of this sort. One feels sometimes that the less relevant the subject matter — as would be questions on Irish revival in most of Ireland — the more likely people are to give a favourable answer. Significantly, when the question probed attitudes to compulsory Irish (such as for civil service entrance and promotion), a clear majority of 66 per cent. was found opposed (Attitudes Survey, p. 63).

Perhaps significantly it was only the Gaelic organisations which kicked up a big stink when compulsory civil service Irish was dropped in November 1974 (the opposition Fianna Fail protests, which embodied comparisons with the near civil war state of the Six Counties, seem to bear the print of excessive politicking).[9]

Not that the compulsion was onerous : not one person had failed the Irish exam at the end of his probationary period since 1947. The entire government's attitude seems to include a good deal of hypocrisy. Dr. G. FitzGerald, Minister for Foreign Affairs, tells of all the northerners who would, but for the Irish qualification, join the Foreign Office. He omits to mention the cramming other civil servants offer unofficially for this oh-so-difficult exam; or the reputation the department has of being made up of Anglos who care not a bean, old boy, for the lingo.

It is difficult to believe the Minister for the Gaeltacht, Mr. Tom O'Donnell, is doing other than talking through his hat when he says that " by removing the element of hostility to Irish, both inside and outside the civil service, considerable increase in its use would be achieved ".[10]

---

[7] Department of Education circular 11/31, quoted in full in Department of Education, *Report of the Council of Education on the Function of the Primary School* (Dublin, 1954), pp. 330-4.
[9] *Irish Times*, November 7 to 9, 1974.
[10] *Irish Times*, 8.11.1974.

The situation seemed grave enough for the *Irish Times* to comment :[11]

> If it is the intention to phase Irish out, this should be stated publicly. The withdrawal of all incentives for learning the language seems a cheap way of eliminating it from our competitive society . . . There has been enough hypocrisy at national and local level.

In the anglicised areas one would expect it to take several years for government decisions to have any real effect on public attitudes. It was certainly premature to claim, however, as the government did, that the increased numbers going in the summer of 1974 to the Irish summer colleges in the Gaeltacht proved that the end of compulsion resulted immediately in a greater public willingness to learn the language. Early figures for 1975 showed a 30 per cent. drop, attributed by some to the lack of need to pass in Irish in school exams.[12]

It is legitimate to ask whether many of the country's politicians really believe in the language. Simultaneous translation equipment was recently installed in the Dáil, almost the only place it is found in Ireland. Although it seems a far larger proportion of T.D.s are fluent than among the population at large, for the great majority of the time the equipment lies idle. Although the translators are on permanent duty, only 1.6 per cent. of the speeches are in Irish.[13]

The main speeches in the ancestral language seem to be those dealing with the Department of the Gaeltacht. It is almost as if the T.D.s are keeping Irish in a little museum.

The museum charge is often brought against the very idea of the Gaeltacht, and it is true that the urban and anglicised attitude to these areas is that they are indeed little treasures, gems from the past that should be preserved for the future. The Gaeltacht is, without doubt, the essential fountainhead for Irish; but the area is so small that the natives must surely get the idea that they are specimens in a glass case to be pored over by tourists, Irish and foreign, and by the thousands of school children who descend on the Gaeltacht each summer with the supposed intention of bettering their Irish. (Some people reckon they go for a subsidised holiday.)

The summer colleges and the tourists are essential both to the economic well-being of the Gaeltacht and to the future, if any, of the language. But it is a bit much when everything has to be crammed into districts covering less than six per cent. of Ireland.

---

[11] *Irish Times,* 7.11.1974.
[12] *Éire-Ireland,* Fomhar, 1975, p. 133.
[13] Dáil Éireann, *Parliamentary Debates,* 5.3.1975, col. 1481.

233

In Connemara and Donegal, the old culture may still be strong enough to cope with the influx, but not so in some of the smaller Gaeltachtai.

A recent report painted a most gloomy picture of one of these areas — Co. Cork around Ballyvourney.[14] Perhaps only 1,200 Irish speakers remain, enough, however, with the good scenery, to provide a " perfect recipe " for tourism. But tourism is regarded as a major factor eroding the language.

Mr. Moss, the report's author, is very gloomy about the prospects for the future :

> The unavoidable conclusion is that the Gaeltacht is now a rapidly disappearing culture . . . But as long as the Gaeltacht remains, even in a molecular form, there is an emotional commitment by the Irish nation to do what it can, if not to preserve the Gaeltacht, at least to make its last days as comfortable as possible, whatever the cost.

If there is hope for Connemara, it rests on the self-help of the local people, on the civil rights movements and on the co-ops which have arisen recently and are doing so much for the people, factors generally absent in Ballyvourney.

Likewise, Cape Clear Island, with just 180 inhabitants and more than 50 miles from Ballyvourney, the next nearest Irish-speaking area, may just survive, again because of self-help. This is the community which formed a limited company with the aim of raising £50,000 to develop the island for the islanders, providing them with jobs in their home communities.[15]

The island has certainly become one of the most developed off the south coast, but the co-operative's chairman, Fr. Tomas O Murchu, sees no social or economic viability unless the population reaches 300. He may get this number, for a surprising number of the island's professional people are Irish speakers from anglicised areas, attracted presumably by the idealism, an idealism which is famed even in Llanaelhaearn in Llŷn. For it was on Cape Clear that Dr. Carl Iwan Clowes based Antur Aelhaiarn, the venture that is bringing new life and industry to that village.

While there are economic similarities between rural Wales and Ireland, linguistically the two countries are poles apart. The Gaeltacht policy has been to try and isolate the language from the harmful outside world, even to the extent of rerouting main roads.

[14] G. Moss, *The Gaeltacht, Planning for the Survival of Ireland's Traditional Culture* (Richmond, Surrey, 1974).
[15] *Cork Weekly Examiner*, 29.11.1973.

Everywhere the implicit assumption has been that Irish cannot stand up to competition.

Hence the excessive protectiveness so much feared in Wales. But then, what would be the reaction were Welsh restricted to an area as small and insignificant as the Irish Gaeltacht, if the language survived only in a group of villages around Llanaelhaearn, Bryncir and Nefyn; Trawsfynydd and Llan Ffestiniog; the Llandrillo, Frongoch, Bala and Llanuwchllyn area; Talybont and Tre Taliesin; Lledrod; Pumsaint, Caio and Llansawel; plus Eglwyswrw and Newport?

Almost the only similarity is that groups in both countries want a separate administration for their Celtic-speaking areas. In Wales this idea comes from Adfer; in Ireland it comes from the government, strongly supported by the Committee on Irish Language Attitudes Research, with plans for a Gaeltacht local authority — Udarás na Gaeltachta — taking over, apparently, not only all local authority powers in these districts, but many central government ones, too.

It is said that neither group has heard of the ideas of the other!

APPENDIX 4

DRAWING THE LINE

HEARTLAND

Based on community boundaries, the following areas will be within the *Heartland* :

Gwynedd: the entire county except Llandudno, Conwy, Penmaenmawr and Llanfairfechan.

Clwyd: all of Colwyn District Council except Colwyn Bay, Abergele, Abergele Rural, Cefn and Trefnant.

Glyndŵr D.C. : Nantglyn, Llanrhaeadr-yng-Nghinmerch, Llanynys Rural, Cyffylliog, Clocaenog, Derwen, Betws Gwerfil Goch, Gwyddelwern, Llanelidan, Bryneglwys, Llansantffraid Glyndyfrdwy, Corwen, Llandrillo, Llanarmon Dyffryn Ceiriog, Llangadwaladr, Llanrhaeadr-ym-Mochnant, Llanarmon Mynydd Mawr and Llandecwyn.

Powys: Montgomery D.C. : Llanrhaeadr-ym-Mochnant, Pennant, Hirnant, Llangynog, Llanwddyn, Llanfihangel, Llangadfan, Garthbeibio, Llanerfyl, Llanllugan, Carno, Llanbrynmair, Cemaes, Caereinion Fechan, Llanwrin, Darowen, Penegoes, Uwchygarreg, Isygarreg and Machynlleth.

Brecknock D.C. : Llanddewi Abergwesyn, Llanwrtyd Without, Llandeilo'r Fan, and Ystradgynlais Lower.

West Glamorgan: Lliw Valley D.C. : Llanguicke, Mawr, Talybont.

Dyfed: all of Ceredigion and Dinefwr D.C.s (except Aberystwyth district and Llandovery).

Carmarthen D.C. : the entire area except Carmarthen area, St. Ishmael, Llansteffan, Laugharne, Llanddowror, Pendine, Eglwyscummin, Whitland and Llanboidy.

South Pembrokeshire D.C. : Mynachlogddu, Llangolman, Llandillo, Maenclochog, Llys y Frân, Forlan, Llanycefn and Llandissilio West.

Preseli D.C. : St. Dogmael's Rural, Monington, Llantood, Bridell, Cilgerran, Manordeifi, Clydey, West Cilrhedyn, Llanfyrnach,

236

Penrhydd, Castellan, Capel Colman, Llanfihangel Penbedw, Llanfair-nant-gwyn, Eglwyswen, Eglwyswrw, Meline, Bayvil, Moylegrove, Nefern, Newport, Llanychlwydog, Llanllawer, Pontfaen, Llanychaer, Little Newcastle, Puncheston, Morvil, Castlebythe, and Henry's Moat. The detached portion includes Llanwnda, Granston, Mathry, Llanrian, Llanhowell, Llandeloy and Llanrheithan.

Llanelli D.C.: Llanedy, Llannon, Pontyberem and Kidwelly.

ANGLICISED HEARTLAND TOWNS

Holyhead and Holyhead Rural.
Bangor.
Aberystwyth, Llanbadarn Fawr and Llangorwen.
Carmarthen and Llangunnor.
Llandovery.

HEARTLAND TRANSITION ZONE

Gwynedd: Llanfairfechan.

Clwyd: Colwyn D.C.: Cefn.
Glyndŵr D.C.: Denbigh, Llangynhafal, Ruthin, Llanfwrog Rural, Efenechtyd, Llanfair Dyffryn Clwyd, Llandegla, Llansantffraid Glynceiriog and Llansilin.

Powys: Montgomery D.C.: Llangyniew, Llanfair Caereinion, and Trefeglwys.
Brecknock D.C.: Llanfihangel Abergwesyn, Traianmawr, Traianglas, Cray, Senny, Glyntawe and Ystradgynlais Higher.

West Glamorgan: Lliw Valley D.C.: Cilybebyll, Dulais (ward of Llwchwr).

Dyfed: Llanelli D.C.: Llangennech, Llanelli Rural, Pembrey, Burry Port.
Carmarthen D.C.: Llansteffan, Llanboidy and Whitland.
South Pembrokeshire: Llanddewi Velfrey, Llangan West, New Moat and Bletherston.
Preseli: Dinas, Fishguard South, Fishguard and Goodwick, Manorowen, St. Nicholas, Jordanston, Llanstinian, Llanfair-nant-y-gôf, Letterston, St. Dogwells, Ambleston, Hayescastle, St. Lawrence, St. Edrins, Whitchurch and St. David's.

Within the Heartland there are a number of parishes with between 50 and 70 per cent. Welsh speakers. These are:

Gwynedd: Ynys Môn: Llanbadrig, Amlwch, Penrhos, Lligwy, Llanallgo, Llaneugrad, Llanynghenedl, Rhoscolyn, Llanfaelog, Aberffraw, Llanddaniel Fab, Llanfairpwll and Menai Bridge.

237

Dwyfor D.C. : Llanbedrog, Beddgelert.
Arfon D.C. : Betws Garmon.
Aberconwy D.C. : Llansantffraid Glan Conwy, Henryd, Caerhun,
Llanbedr-y-Cennin, Dolgarrog, Trefriw, Llanrhychwyn, Llanrwst,
Betws-y-Coed.
Meirionnydd D.C. : Llandanwg, Llanaber, Barmouth, Brifdir
and Islaw'rdref, Llangelynnin, Tywyn.

Clwyd: Glyndŵr D.C. : Llansantffraid Glyndyfrdwy.

Powys: Montgomery D.C. : Llanwddyn, Machynlleth.
Brecknock D.C. : Llanddewi Abergwesyn.

Dyfed: Ceredigion D.C. : Ysgubor-y-Coed, Llangynfelyn,
Geneu'rglyn, Cwmrheidol, Upper Vaenor, Lower Llanbadarn y
Creuddyn, Llanychaiarn, Llanina, Llangybi, Llanfair Clydogau,
Lampeter, Penbryn, Aberporth.
Dinefwr D.C. : Llanfair-ar-y-Bryn, Llanddingat Without,
Llansadwrn, Llandeilo.
Preseli D.C. : Llantood, Bridell, Bayvil, Penrydd.

Also within the Heartland, but detached from the anglicised
Heartland towns, will be a few parishes where less than 50 per cent.
speak Welsh. These are :

Gwynedd: Ynys Môn : Llanfair-yn-Neubwll, Llanfair Mathafarn
Eithaf, Beaumaris, Llandegfan.
Aberconwy D.C. : Capel Curig.
Meirionnydd D.C. : Llanddwywe-is-y-Graig.

Dyfed: Ceredigion D.C. : Borth.
Preseli D.C. : Monington.

INDEX

The Appendices and Illustrations have not been indexed.

239

242

243